NURTURING QUEER YOUTH

A Norton Professional Book

NURTURING QUEER YOUTH

Family Therapy Transformed

LINDA STONE FISH AND REBECCA G. HARVEY

W·W·NORTON

NEW YORK · LONDON

Composition and book design by Viewtistic, Inc.
Manufacturing by Haddon Craftsman
Production Manager: Leeann Graham

Library of Congress Cataloging-in-Publication Data
Fish, Linda Stone.
   Nurturing queer youth: family therapy transformed/Linda Stone Fish and
Rebecca G. Harvey.
     p.   cm.
"A Norton professional book."
Includes bibliographical references and index.
ISBN 0-393-70455-6
   1. Gay youth—Counseling of. 2. Bisexual youth—Counseling of 3. Family
psychotherapy. 4. Family psychotherapy—Case studies. 5. Gay youth—
Family relationships—Case studies. I. Harvey, Rebecca G. II. Title.

HV1426.F57 2005
362.7—dc22   2004066409

W. W. Norton & Company, Inc., 500 Fifth Avenue, New York, NY 10110
www.wwnorton.com
W. W. Norton & Company, Ltd., Castle House, 75/76 Wells Street, London
W1T 3QT
1 2 3 4 5 6 7 8 9 0

LSF: To Ron, My Refuge

RGH: For Grace

CONTENTS

ACKNOWLEDGMENTS

This book would not have been written without the encouragement, guidance, diligence, and support of our editor, Michael McGandy. Thanks also go to Casey Ruble for her terrific copyediting. We would like to thank our colleagues affiliated with Syracuse University: Sheila Addison, Deb Coolehart, Janet Coria, Corey Fehlberg, Anne Gosling, Suzanne Haas-Cunningham, Kenneth V. Hardy, Roxanne Hill, Tracey Laszloffy, Barbara Levine, Eleanor Macklin, Mona Mittal, Jonathan Sandberg, and Maggie Waldron for their contributions to our model of family therapy. Special thanks must go to Ellie, a true force of nature, whose belief in the wonder and power of human relationships has profoundly changed us. She has instilled in us a belief that it is possible to create environments where many impossible things become possible. We want to acknowledge special appreciation to Sheila Addison who first forayed with us into queer theory and worked with us to design the first doctoral course in sexual identity and family therapy. Special appreciation also goes to Ken for naming "difficult dialogues" and for modeling their effectiveness.

We want to give a special thanks to Dr. Ritch Savin-Williams whose work has had a great impact on us. The day after my son came out I (LSF) called Dr. Savin-Williams for consultation about how to help navigate his adolescence. Though he had no idea who I was, Dr. Savin-Williams spent an hour on the phone with me, telling me what to expect and giving me useful suggestions about how to help create a nurturing environment for my son. Through his scholarly expertise but especially through the model of his princely compassion, Dr. Savin-Williams has helped my family, and without knowing it, contributes to the families I have helped, in more ways than I can recount.

We also want to give special thanks to the families we have worked with over the years who have taught us the importance of creating refuge from the cultural mandates that continue to brutalize their ideas about self and relationship. We hope this book pays tribute to their wounds and honors their strengths and courage.

LINDA STONE FISH

I could not have written this book without Rebecca's courage, knowledge, and passion. I have a deep and unyielding respect for her clinical acumen, her integrity, and her journey towards justice and peace.

I would like to thank the Stone Fish family (Ron, Isaac, Aarlo, Hugh, and Avery) more than words can acknowledge, for teaching me the importance of loving relationships in the development of agency. I would also like to thank them for giving me an appreciation of the myriad ways in which men can be powerful and gentle in their expressions of masculinity. They are men of integrity whose spirits know no bounds.

I want to thank Mary Jo Barrett for her steady love and true companionship. I value her like no other. I would also like to acknowledge how proud I am to be from the Hugh and Sandy Stone family, a family whose turbulent and traumatic beginnings drove us all to be wise and loving people of character who chose life partners equal to the task of creating refuge for our souls.

And lastly, this book would not have been written without the support of my life partner, Ron, whose wisdom I trust, whose love I need, and whose soul I cherish. He is my guide and my lake house.

REBECCA G. HARVEY

I would like to thank all the Donovan's and the Harvey's (my childhood family) with whom I learned to love fiercely, challenge lovingly, and laugh heartily. Thank you especially mom, Dorene, and dad. I would also like to thank the family I've created in my adulthood. I have been deeply blessed by many loved ones who sustain me, keep me honest and help me be brave enough to love myself. Thanks especially to Mel, Marq, Karen, Cory, Amy, Beth, and Beth. Thanks to Heather, Tom, and Mathijs, my home away from home. A very special thank you to Maggie for helping me get connected to my spirit and to Heather, my best friend (wow, who would have thought that when we were teens?) for always going courageously where few sisters dare to tread. Thank you Grace, for the refuge, support and especially the difficult dialogues. I would not be me without you.

I would also like to express the deepest gratitude and affection to Linda whose mentorship and love have quite simply changed my life.

NURTURING QUEER YOUTH

INTRODUCTION

A new generation of gay, lesbian, bisexual, and transgendered youth are coming of age in a society increasingly tolerant and yet still deeply divided about homosexuality and traditional notions of gender. On the one hand, there is more openness, media attention, and an older generation of openly gay and lesbian role models. On the other hand, there is a greater backlash in the form of religious fundamentalism, violence, and legal intervention designed to "protect" traditional marriages and families.

As our cultural values and mores shift, the coming out process evolves and changes. Original models of sexual minority identity development focused on the individual and were based on the coming out processes of adults, not youth, because youth did not have the developmental, social, and financial resources they needed to safely explore minority sexuality. Today, however, an increasing number of queer youth are coming out and at ages younger than ever before, making the process of identity development both an individual as well as a family process that has profound implications on current and future family relations.

Like all youth, sexual minority youth develop in a wide variety of family and community environments—in rural, urban, and suburban settings, in hostile family environments and more supportive ones, in conservative and progressive communities alike. Also like all young people, they are trying out their identities with the people they love, tentatively practicing to be the adults they will become. Unlike other youth, however, sexual minority youth must make difficult choices about when and how to come out, and to whom, always balancing their need for the basics (housing, food, protection, love) with the very real need to individuate, to be seen and validated for their whole selves. A 17-year-old woman wrestling with sexuality in a loving nuclear family within a conservative, religious community will have a far different experience than an 11-year-old coming out to himself in an urban environment within an extended family dominated by alcoholism. But they both will probably gauge their life situations, searching for ways to develop and explore while determining the risks and benefits of being out. Unfortunately, the implications for youth who misjudge the people around them can be devastating. As reported in the *New York Times* (Jacobs, 2004), national surveys suggest that almost half of homeless youth are queer. Carl Siciliano, who runs a shelter for gay youth in New York, believes that the number of homeless gay youth is growing, "inadvertently fueled by the identity-affirming pitch of gay rights advocates and the feel-good wit of television shows like 'Queer Eye for the Straight Guy' and 'Will and Grace' which encourage adolescents to declare their sexuality to parents on the opposite side of a yawning generation gap" (Jacob, 2004, p. 29).

The new media and cultural attention to queer sexualities also sometimes leads *parents* to start questioning their child's sexuality before the child even begins this process of self-examination. This can lead to anxious, worried parents who monitor and question their child or to family discussions in which the child quite simply is not ready to engage. Other times a child may share his or her sexual identity status with only one parent or a few close family members, creating alliances and subsystems that become part of the family landscape.

Because of the complexity of the coming out process and the implications for families, queer youth and their families are more frequently turning to family therapists for help. Unfortunately it is difficult to find family therapy interventions that address sexual minority youth or, more importantly, family therapists who have been adequately trained in the area of sexual identity. Despite decades of research indicating that being gay, lesbian, and bisex-

2

ual are normal variations on a continuum of sexual identity—no more or less pathological than left-handedness—the field of family therapy has not contributed a model that deals with substantive sexual identity issues for youth and how to work with them in a family context.

AIMS AND PURPOSES OF THIS BOOK

This book is intended to be a practical guide to help clinicians work with the burgeoning population of sexual minority youth and their families. We have combined sexual identity research, developmental and trauma theories, family therapy, and queer theory to produce a clinical model that works with sexual minority youth in a family context and *nurtures* queerness. The book introduces family therapists to queer youth and their families who have been directly and dramatically affected by cultural mandates around heterosexism, homophobia, oppression, and shame. Using queer theory, data drawn from research, and our own clinical work, we invite the reader into the lives of five families with sexual minority youth. All the parents in these families are heterosexual and, though they may have extended family members or friends who are queer, are experiencing the direct impact of sexual minority status for the very first time.

TERMINOLOGY

In our clinical work we are careful to begin with the language that makes sense to our clients. For this book, however, we use the terms *queer* and *youth* to capitalize on and expand our cultural use of language. We use the terms *queer* and *sexual minority youth* interchangeably as opposed to *gay*, *lesbian*, *bisexual*, and *transgendered* because the former terms are more inclusive than the latter ones. Given the controversial nature of the word *queer*, it is important for us to be clear about why we decided to so prominently employ this word in our title and throughout the book. We recognize that *queer* has been and continues to be used in a way that is deeply hurtful and violating to sexual minority individuals. Many of us cringe when we hear these words tossed around in academic theories for the sake of sounding chic. However, we find ourselves continually drawn to the word *queer* because it seems to help free people to explore, agree, disagree, and think. One of the reasons we use the word *queer* is because it has been used pejoratively to be hurtful to sexual minority individuals. We believe that words like *queer* lose much of their power to hurt when they are reclaimed and used in a positive way to refer to the very group of people they were intended to harm. Additionally, people make many assumptions when they hear labels like l*esbian, gay, bisexual,* or even *heterosexual* and jump to the conclusion that there is one way to be heterosexual, gay, or lesbian. It is exactly these assumptions and the prejudice and bias they fuel that we believe is so harmful to the full development of human potential. Of course, people also make assumptions when they hear the word *queer*. In our experience, however, they do not feel as confident in their understanding of this term. After all, why would anyone want to label himself or herself *queer*? To know more they must ask, which hopefully encourages more conversations and exploration of the queerness in all of us.

Our journeys through sexuality have taught us that being queer is not merely an issue of gender identity or sexual orientation. Being queer is also about recognizing the ways that one represents otherness, the unexplored, or the disallowed then, despite prejudice and injustice, insisting and insisting again that one belongs and that one is gifted, not in spite of these queer differences but because of them. It is this idea that we most hope to pass on to clinicians, as it would be a gift to the queer youth they serve.

Finally, we use the word *youth* as opposed to the word *adolescent* because the process of sexual identity development is longer than the period of adolescence. Sexual identity development begins before birth, but the ability to define oneself does not begin until childhood. The term *youth* encompasses late childhood and early, middle, and late adolescence. These categories of late childhood to late adolescence are not discreet stages from childhood to adulthood, and each child transitions in her or his own way. For our purposes, late childhood becomes early adolescence when the individual becomes pubescent. A child, then, is a prepubescent individual, and an adolescent is pubescent. Although some queer youth have knowledge of their queerness as children and many know they are not heterosexual in late childhood, the difference does not usually get sexualized until early adolescence. Adolescence ends, for our purposes here, with some financial independence from parents.

THE AUTHORS

We became interested in working with queer youth both individually and as a team. We met at Syracuse University and sparked each other's interest in this work while we were in supervision and in class. The process of the creation of this model of practice has been an integral part of our work with families. Although we have protected the identities of the families you will meet in this book, we have attempted to be as open and honest as we can about ourselves.

I (LSF) am a heterosexual woman who has been teaching and practicing family therapy with children and adolescents for over 25 years. After cocreating, the first doctoral course in sexual identity and family therapy in the country with Rebecca (RGH) and Sheila Addison, my clinical practice filled up with families in which sexual identity issues were prominent. When I had questions about the intricacies of the coming out process, Rebecca was my guide. Always reminding me that her experience was just one experience, she helped me create refuge for the families I saw by sharing her story with me. She also encouraged me to expand my simple definitions of heterosexuality and female gender identity. To witness her life experience fully, I had to bravely question the sacred tenets of heterosexuality that I held for many years.

I have been married for 26 years and my husband and I have four sons. In the spring of his eighth-grade year, our second son, Aarlo, came out as gay to the family. When Aarlo told his older brother, Isaac, then a junior in high school, Isaac hugged him, told him he loved him, and said he would be there for him. When he told Hugh, a sixth grader at the time, he sweetly asked Aarlo if it was still okay for him to take his shirt off in front of him. Avery, a first grader at the time, took it in stride. Now in fourth grade, Avery announced at dinner last week that he wasn't sure yet whether he was gay or straight but he would be sure to let us know when he decided. Aarlo's experience, and our family's response to his sexuality, taught me about the need for healing containers in the development of adolescent identity in ways I could never have appreciated without their love and guidance.

In 1984, I (RGH) was a nervous 14-year-old in the midst of coming out to herself. I was yearning for some positive information to combat the overwhelming negative image of homosexuals within my family and community. Sensing that I had reached the limit of what I could learn from "Donahue" shows and desperate to end my isolation, I mustered up the nerve to go to a bookstore to find a biography of Martina Navratilova, the only other queer woman of whom I had heard. There I was, book in hand, unable to muster up the courage to approach the checkout. The book was a hard cover and expensive. I thought I had just enough money to pay for it, but the thought of getting to the counter and having attention drawn to my purchase because I was short some change paralyzed me. I took the long way to the counter, trying to calculate tax as I went. Then a flash of green caught my eye. Sitting on top of a pile of books was a $20 bill! There was no one within 30

6

feet of me. I pretended to read nearby books and tried to wait to see if anyone came along to claim the money, but I quickly abandoned this effort, grabbed the money, and said to myself "I have been given a gift." Confidently, I made my purchase and left the store.

That experience was a turning point for me and I have never forgotten it. The idea that I was gifted was not a new one for me. I was raised in a wonderful family who nurtured me, protected me, and loved me well. But I believed I was loved and protected in spite of my queerness not because of it. The notion that queerness, was part of my gift, worth nurturing and protecting in its own right, began for me in that moment as a 14-year-old.

As a graduate student I was working with a family in which the eldest daughter was struggling to come out. Sexuality had become the main focus of the therapy and the family continued to make comments that made it clear they assumed I was heterosexual. I was unsure how to proceed. Not correcting their assumption was beginning to feel like an active lie. But outing myself felt frightening, even unprofessional. Could I be helpful as an out lesbian? I gingerly brought this up to Linda in supervision. Linda was very calm as she connected what I was feeling to her experience as a Jew. She explained that sometimes when people assumed she was Christian it felt innocuous. At times she corrected their assumption, other times she did not. But when she felt like she was holding a secret or participating in a lie that began to affect how she related to the family, she knew she had to tell them.

I took this as permission to use my gift—to value myself enough to speak the truth instead of expending energy keeping secrets in order to "protect" clients from my queerness. This spoke to the heart of my dilemma. Can an out lesbian be a family therapist? Could I be an effective family therapist not despite the fact that I was queer but because of it? I realized that Linda was inviting me into an environment, a dialogue, really, that would both nurture and challenge me to use all of my gifts to help families heal.

It is exceedingly rare to find environments that actually foster queer experience. As queer people we are so accustomed to this that we find ourselves conditioned to overlook continuous slights, we are grateful when we are not ignored and relieved when we are not overtly discriminated against, and then inexplicably angry in a discussion without knowing why. Family therapy is no different. We have helped families *deal* with the sexuality of their loved ones, not celebrate it. It is part of my challenge and my queer gift to nurture families as they create environments so that they nurture one another and celebrate all of the beautifully strange parts of themselves.

THE FAMILIES

Each family has a different story about how they handle the transition from simple definitions of "normal" sexuality to more complex views of their own children and their own lives. We follow the stories of five families throughout the book. To ensure confidentiality, we have changed identifying information about these cases and have created composite cases to further respect privacy. We hope we have been able to retain and illustrate the great gifts of courage, hard work, and tenderness exemplified by these families. The five families we highlight all struggled to change their visions of themselves so as to incorporate a queer child. Each family taught us something about the beauty and pain of that struggle.

THE PETERSONS. The Peterson family was a white, Anglo-Saxon Protestant nuclear family of four. Tom (56) and Lisa (49) had been married for 21 years and had two children, Matthew (20), a sophomore in college, and Joey (16), a junior in high school. Tom also had a daughter (25) from a previous marriage who lived on the other side of the country and was never involved in treatment.

Tom was vice president of a local engineering firm and Lisa was a real estate broker. The family first came to family therapy concerned that Joey was depressed. As you will see, the Petersons moved rather quickly from shock to acceptance upon hearing about their son's sexual identity. The course of therapy with LSF lasted about 9 months. With support from their extended community, they also became activists in the fight against homophobia.

THE NOLANS. The Nolans were a white nuclear family of three with no religious or ethnic affiliation. Julia (40) was a single parent raising her two sons, Craig (17) and Devin (15). Julia was unemployed and collecting disability insurance because she been injured 3 years earlier working in a factory. She was married to Devin and Craig's father when she was 21, divorced at 25, and was briefly remarried when the children were 12 and 10. Both Craig and Devin's father and stepfather were verbally and physically abusive to Julia and the boys. The Nolans lived two doors down from Julia's sister, Vera, who was raising two girls with her husband. Vera and Julia were very close, though Vera was a born-again Christian and judgmental of Julia's family. Craig and Vera were minimally involved in the therapy, which lasted about a year. Julia initially called RGH because she was concerned about Devin's sexual identity. Devin was running away and was involved with the police. He was being treated for depression and attention deficit/hyperactivity disorder (ADHD) but Julia did not think this was the problem. Julia described knowing that Devin was gay since he was 13, but it was not until they began family therapy that she discovered he was transgendered. She tried hard to support Devin but felt overwhelmed by the magnitude of his issues.

THE MARNIS. The Marni family included Jack (45), Carol (40), Michelle (16), Jana (15), and Kim (10). Carol was of Native American decent. Her parents had converted to Christianity before she was born, and she was raised in an evangelical Christian household. Jack, a nonpracticing Italian Catholic by birth, converted to Christianity and was baptized in Carol's family's church after his second arrest for driving while intoxicated. Carol was an administrative assistant at the local university; Jack was an electrician for the city school district and also worked part-time as a mechanic repairing school buses for the district. The family was referred to therapy because the school administration was concerned about Jana. She was overweight, dressed in counterculture clothing, recently had pierced her tongue, eyebrow, and belly button, and hung out with other kids on the margins. LSF saw the family in therapy on and off for about a year and a half. In the course of Jana's discovery of herself as a lesbian, she was able to garner some acceptance from her mother. At the time of termination of treatment, however, Jana was still closeted from her father, her entire extended family, and her church community.

THE EDWARDS. The Edwards were a biracial nuclear family of four. Chris (50), Rona (44), and Tanya (14) were the primary participants in family therapy. Chris and Rona's two other children, Robert (10) and Jennifer (8), were seen twice in family sessions but were not very involved in the clinical work. Tanya was Rona's daughter from a previous union. Rona was a nonpracticing Methodist caucasian. Tanya's father, Howard, who lived in Texas and had not seen Tanya since she was 2 years old, was an African American Baptist. Chris, also not religious, was an African American college professor and Rona was a social worker. Chris officially adopted Tanya when he and Rona were married. The family came to therapy because Tanya was getting into fights at school. Tanya's parents had her tested for ADHD, and the evaluator recommended family therapy because, the family explained, Tanya had an attachment problem. The course of family therapy with RGH lasted for about 5 months. When Tanya turned 17, RGH saw her again for four individual sessions. After the initial shock about Tanya's bisexual status, her parents were supportive and loving.

THE SMITHS. The Smiths, Rose (36), John (36), Michael (17), and Emily (14), were a white, nonreligiously identified nuclear family of four. Rose and John had met in high school and married the day after graduation. They had both been raised with some religious experiences but did not consider themselves religious and did not attend church. Rose was a secretary at a local insurance company and John managed the cafeteria at a local hospital. They had extended family in the area whom they saw on all the major holidays but to whom they did not feel particularly close. Michael initiated therapy with LSF, and the family was seen for 14 sessions spaced out over a year. Feeling lonely, overwhelmed, and frightened, Michael called LSF when his friend attempted suicide. The Smith family initially expressed some disappointment when they discovered Michael was gay, but they were relieved to be in relationship with him again through the course of therapy, and this connection became more important than his sexual identity status.

OVERVIEW

We have created a model of family therapy in which therapists work toward developing family environments that nurture queerness. This book details the key concepts of the model and uses case examples from the five families just introduced to illustrate the ideas. In the first chapter, we explore the basic concepts of queer theory and describe how incorporating those concepts has transformed our family therapy practices. In the second chapter, we provide an overview of the current status of queer youth in the United States, discuss specific identity tasks, and detail the processes that sexual minority youth go through as they come in to themselves and come out to others.

Chapter 3 explores the first key concept of the model—*creating refuge*. Creating refuge is the process of developing a therapeutic environment that challenges the cultural mandates of homophobia and heterosexism so that families can learn to know each other in more complex ways. In Chapter 4, we describe how *difficult dialogues,* the second key concept of the model, are used in family therapy to enhance intimacy between family members. Difficult dialogues are those in which members express themselves in ways that lead to conflict and highlight disagreement. Readers are introduced to ways to use these dialogues to help family members be more honest and open with themselves and each other.

Chapter 5 details the concept of *nurturing queerness,* which is the third key concept of our model. By helping families explore both the negative and positive aspects of sexual minority status, we help them create space in their lives for active and complex exploration of multiple ways to *perform* gender and sexual identities. This exploration is an *identity* exploration and should not be confused with sexual practice exploration, which is beyond the scope of this book. Family members who avail themselves of the opportunity to explore their youth's developing identity come to see queer youth as a gift. Rather than thinking of queerness as something to be tolerated, the integration of queerness becomes an enriching experience. The book ends with a chapter on encouraging transformation and details ways to help queer youth and their families outside the therapy office. We also describe how our family therapy practices have been transformed by our work with sexual minority youth—a transformation that goes beyond our work with this population.

We are worried about queer youth and rightly so. Much anecdotal and empirical evidence suggests that, for queer youth, the already bumpy road through adolescence is made particularly rough by stigma, oppression, and prejudice. And we are worried about their families. How will their relationships be affected?

How will they each handle their disappointment? How will they rise to the challenge to be loving and supportive? But we cannot only be worried. We must also see queer youth's beauty, gifts, and way of being and seeing the world as a blessing. We must be teachable and recruitable. We hope you will join us on the path of nurturing queerness. It is in the best interest of all the children and families who invite us into their lives.

CHAPTER 1

Family Therapy and Queer Theory

Integrating family therapy and queer theory is no small task. We live in a culture that has regarded homosexuality as threatening to families and children, equating it with immorality, mental illness, and sexual depravity. Unlike apologists for homosexuality who made gains in civil rights by convincing mainstream America that "we are just like you," queer theory asserts that although there may be similarities, differences certainly exist, and that these differences are no more or less valid than the heterosexual experience. So what are two marriage and family therapists doing espousing queer theory? It seems a contradiction a bit akin to being an atheist at a seminary. But it is perhaps because of the contradictions, where new ideas collide with staid theory, that our work transforms family therapy practice. In the same way feminism and multiculturalism powerfully inform family therapy practice, so too can queer theory make our work more robust.

FAMILY THERAPY PRINCIPLES

Although our work as family therapists has been transformed by queer theory, we are grounded first and foremost in systems theory. First, we work under the assumption that relationships are crucibles for individual growth and development. Relationships "grow people" (Satir, Banmen, Gerver, & Gomori, 1991, p. 3), they are vehicles for human growth, and relational dilemmas are to be expected as part of that growth. This principle is guided further by developmental theory and our knowledge about what makes environments more conducive for growth.

Second, our work is organized around the principle that relationship processes or dynamics are more important than content. In other words, *how* something happens is more important than *what* is happening. A father and son disagreeing about homosexuality can use sarcasm, violence, or cut-offs to punctuate their differing beliefs. Or they can disagree but utilize humor or respectful conversation in ways that keep their relationship vital.

Third, we believe that embracing complexity leads to individual and relational growth and development. Handling complexity is a survival skill in our increasingly complex world. Learning to embrace complexity, and to be informed and affected by it rather than overwhelmed, leads to individual and relational growth.

THE CRUCIBLE

> **crucible:** a vessel made of material that does not melt easily; used for high temperature chemical reactions (*WordNet® 2.0, ©2003 Princeton University*)

The term *crucible* was first introduced to the family therapy field as a metaphor for a relationship container by Napier and Whitaker (1978), and was later incorporated by Schnarch (1991). Napier and Whitaker used the term to illustrate the concept of a holding environment for a family in therapy. They wrote that a family comes to therapy with its own structure, rules, and pain, and that therapists needed to provide a container, a crucible, to hold the family so that they could trust the therapeutic relationship enough to change. Because family members are dependent upon one another, any change in family membership or change in one member affects the others in the system, causing relationships to "heat up." The crucible, then, must be able to contain the heat. Schnarch took the crucible metaphor a step further by suggesting that intimate relationships themselves are crucibles for individual growth and development. Therapists, then, are not merely providing a container but also fostering the development of a container that already exists so that it can withstand the powerful effects of growth.

Children develop into adults through their embeddedness in family relationships in which people take care of each other. At times children must care for and protect their parents, but there is a basic difference in responsibility between parents and children. Although no one is ever completely responsible for someone else, parents must be more responsible for the relationship than their children are. They are expected to be the creators of crucibles that can contain their children, protecting them as they grow while also being flexible enough to allow for development.

The relationship between parents and children guides the growth of the child in a complex way, which is articulated well in Kegan's (1982) developmental theory of environments conducive to growth. He suggested that youth develop in environments that *confirm* them, *contradict* the beliefs and behaviors that are no longer useful, and *continue* their support in the process. Family relationships, then, are the catalysts for children to develop. Embedded in relationships, children learn that they belong and are confirmed. They learn at the same time that they must move on—that they cannot be infants forever. At the same time they are learning that they must mature, they are embedded in relationships that continue to support them. We recognize this as an ideal and also know that families often need help along the way, in the form of family therapy, to contain the heat ignited by the stress of change.

As family therapists, we help families become, or get back on track to being, their own natural therapy environments. We *confirm* their ways of being when they present in therapy, recognizing that they are doing the best they can while also acknowledging with them that they want something different. We then help them be different by *contradicting* how they are and by exploring alternative ways of being. By recognizing how difficult change can be yet still being hopeful that change will occur, we *continue* our support as families struggle to be different. We create refuge in therapy by modeling a crucible that can contain the heat that is generated when members change.

RELATIONSHIP DYNAMICS

Family relationships tend to create a lot of heat because family members sense the interconnectedness of their lives. They are dependent upon one another and thus are greatly invested in each member's well-being. This investment makes it difficult for family members to perceive each other without also seeing how the behavior of that family member affects them. So, for example, when a daughter does something that makes her mother proud, her mother may feel like a worthy parent. When that same daughter does something of which her mother is ashamed, she feels like an unworthy parent. It is difficult for the mother to perceive her daughter's behavior as anything but a message about her and her parenting because the mother is the one responsible for the daughter's growth and development and, thereby, behavior. Meanwhile, the daughter's behavior is, of course, a message first and foremost about herself. However, it is also a message about the mother, and a message about their relationship as well. This is further complicated by other family relationships. It may be that the daughter's behavior is also a message about her relationship with her father, her siblings, her mother's relationship with her father, the mother's relationship with her extended family—the list goes on.

Relationship dynamics, then, organize family members' perceptions of behavior. It is practically impossible for family members to see behavior devoid of relational content. Parents have difficulty perceiving their children's behavior without a relational

18

lens, and children have the same difficulty. When a parent acts in an inadequate way, for example, children have a difficult time perceiving the inadequate behavior as a message about the parent. They are more likely to see the behavior as a message about their own inadequacies.

Because it is practically impossible for family members to perceive other members' behavior in a vacuum, it is also difficult to know how to respond to that behavior. When a little boy cries when he gets boxing gloves for his birthday instead of a Barbie doll, what's a father to do? When a 15-year-old girl who knows she is a lesbian is asked for the umpteenth time to daydream with her mother about her wedding day, what's a daughter to do? Both family members are confronted with another's behavior that is at once a message about self, a message about the other, and a message about the relationship. Because people do not take the time to talk about these relationship dynamics, they make assumptions about themselves, others, and their relationships based on inaccurate information. Sometimes this gets people into trouble. When families come into therapy, they are offered the space to slow this process down, talk about these dynamics, and discover one another.

These conversations are difficult because there is so much invested in family relationships. Difficult dialogues must take place in a family therapy environment in which all members of the family feel honored and supported. The art of family therapy is in knowing how to confirm and contradict family members as they talk about themselves in ways they may never have talked before. So, for example, when the dad recounts the birthday party in which his son cried for a Barbie and tells us how he felt outraged and sent his son to his room, we are called to honor and support his experience, as well as the experience of everyone else in the family. We would confirm the father's disappointment *and* challenge him to see his son's desire, in fact, to simply see, really see his son. We may ask the dad what was going on for him at the time and attempt to get him to articulate how his son's behavior affected a vulnerable place in himself, or we may ask the dad to talk with his son in therapy about the son's disappointment in his gift, or we may ask the mom about her thoughts. We have many choices in how to intervene to help create natural therapy environments in which individuals can develop in relationship to one another.

EMBRACING COMPLEXITY

Differences among family members are often at the heart of problematic interactions. Family members often believe that their relationships are too important to risk honoring these differences, so they rarely get discussed in fruitful ways. The father whose son prefers dolls, for example, might never discuss his son's gender identity with his wife because he is afraid they would argue, she would distance from him, and he would be lonely. He might believe that his relationship with his wife is too important for him to express his true beliefs, fears, and expectations. We believe, however, that it is in the difficult dialogue about those differences that relationships become more intimate.

Confronted by a diversity of experiences, beliefs, values, and opinions, relationships get tested and individuals develop. It is, paradoxically, in the discussion around differences that much growth and change occurs, increasing the stability of family relationships. In other words, family members who disagree with one another and nevertheless stay connected in relationship end up feeling closer. When family members see each other as people whom they love and completely disagree with, they must embrace a more complex view of themselves, their relationships, and the other members of their family. This increasingly complex view helps enhance members' curiosity about themselves and their loved ones, enhancing closeness and stability. The crucible gets stronger as it takes more heat.

Family therapists can help family members embrace complexity by encouraging dialogue about differences. Our curiosity about issues of gender and sexuality help clients define their dilemmas more clearly. These dilemmas are real and gut-wrenching, and often very politically incorrect. When the man whose son prefers dolls can share his views about masculinity with his wife, he also shares the constraints he feels as a man, his hopes and fears about his son, and how he understands his outrage. The father's reaction is complex. He does not like feeling out of control with rage, does not like that his son prefers dolls, and does not want to be like his own father, who bullied him into complying with gendered stereotypes of how men are supposed to behave. When family therapists create a place of refuge, a crucible that can contain the heat of this intense discussion, the man can share his complex views and his wife can listen. She, of course, will have her own complex views of her husband, their relationship, and herself in response to his disclosure. A difficult dialogue ensues.

Family members may not share all of themselves in their relationships with one another because what they have to share is threatening to themselves, the relationship, or both. Complex definitions of self are often easier to describe when family members are not sharing those definitions with the people with whom they are most intimate. In these cases it is valuable to see individual family members in therapy without other family members present. This is quite important when you work with adolescents. In our practice, when parents call about a youth, we see the parents first so that they can give us a detailed description of their concerns without the youth present (Wachtel, 1994). Then we see the adolescent individually for the same reason. We want to set, from the outset, an environment in which people are as honest with us as they are with themselves. Because of the toxic nature of adolescent material, it is often necessary to see individuals and dyads alone to pave the way for difficult dialogues to take place. We tell all members of the family that, when they are seen alone, the information they tell us is confidential and although we may encourage them to share information with each other, we will not share it ourselves unless someone is a danger to self or to other. Throughout the therapy process, depending on how the therapy is progressing, we see individuals, dyads, and differing family units along the way.

As we embrace complexity in our family therapy practices, we find that our simple definitions of gender and sexual identity no longer fit. We have now come to believe that the dichotomous thinking around gender and sexuality limit the relationships between family members in therapy. This is important for families in which all members are heterosexual and even more important for families in which some members are queer. Because, as a culture, we continue to encourage dichotomous thinking about gender and sexual identity, active exploration of more complex views is often met with resistance. For family therapists to embrace complexity, we would do well to encourage that exploration ourselves.

THE CURRENT STATE OF FAMILY THERAPY AND QUEER YOUTH

The mental health profession has gone from pathologizing *homosexuality* (a label developed by the psychiatric community and based on a disease model of minority sexual identity) to depathologizing it beginning in the 1970s (Herdt, 1989). Although homosexuality has been depathologized, discrimination of sexual minority individuals continues to exist in the helping professions. The American Psychological Association (APA) and the National Association of Social Workers (NASW) both take an activist stance against sexual orientation discrimination and have released statements depathologizing homosexuality. Further, the APA has released public statements that they do not advocate conversion therapies and cite evidence of their failure to work. In 2004, the APA released a public statement that it is unfair to deny same sex couples access to marriage and cited psychological research evidence of the ways in which discrimination is hurtful to sexual minority individuals.

THE CURRENT STATE OF THE MARRIAGE AND
FAMILY THERAPY PROFESSION

The American Association for Marriage and Family Therapy (AAMFT) created a task force to explore sexual minority issues among its constituents. At their 2004 national conference, AAMFT proposed a non-pathologizing stance and stated that the organization would not condone an amendment to the Constitution banning same sex marriage. The AAMFT seems to be trying to keep a variety of people at the table discussing their various deeply held beliefs about homosexuality. As systemic thinkers with a view toward conversation as a means of growth and change, we must ask ourselves some difficult questions. How do we balance our hope for respectful open conversation with the needs of oppressed people for justice and protection? How do we help these conversations not just be supportive of the status quo but also challenging to everyone at the table? And when should we draw hard lines that might cripple these discussions but also represent a stand against discrimination? How much injustice should be tolerated in the name of trying to keep everyone at the table?

THE CURRENT PRACTICE OF MARRIAGE AND FAMILY THERAPY

Ritter and Terndrup (2002) found that after 1988 there was a significant increase in articles about minority sexuality in a variety of mental health fields with the notable exception of marriage and family therapy. Clark and Serovich (1997) reviewed family therapy journals and discovered few articles pertaining to sexual minority issues, and Doherty and Simmons (1996) surveyed family therapists and found that only a little over half were comfortable treating gay men and lesbians. However, some family therapists are working with and writing about sexual minority populations in the traditional family therapy literature (e.g., Armesto, 2001; Beeler & Diprova, 1999; Bepko & Johnson, 2000; Elizur, & Ziv, 2001; Green, 1996, 2000; Green & Bobele, 1994; Green & Mitchell, 2002; Greenan & Tunnell, 2002; Krestan, 1988; Laird & Green, 1996; LaSala, 2000; Long & Serovich, 2003; Pearlman, 1992; Saltzburg, 1996; Sanders & Kroll, 2000) and family therapists writing in nontraditional literature (e.g., Hardy & Laszloffy, 2002; Johnson, 1998; Markowitz, 1999, 2001; Turek, 1998). These family therapists have given us substantial and positive information about therapy with queer individuals, yet they have focused almost exclusively on sexual minority adults.

THE CURRENT PRACTICE OF MARRIAGE AND FAMILY THERAPY WITH QUEER YOUTH

Studies suggest that the age at which queer youth self identify as members of a sexual minority has been decreasing, at least since the onset of the gay and lesbian rights movement (Coleman, 1982; Dank, 1971; Dube, 2000; Herdt, 1989; Newman & Muzzonigro, 1993; Remafedi, 1987; Troiden, 1989). Boxer, Cook, and Herdt (1991) theorized that because of increasing numbers of adults openly identifying as gay and lesbian, increasing media attention, cultural acceptance, and growing opportunities for socializing, more youth are coming out at younger ages. As this happens the coming out process changes as well. Older queer adults had no media images and no community in which to come out, whereas youth today are more likely to know gay and lesbian people, to have a sense of a queer community, and to see images of themselves in the media. Youth today are also more likely to identify first and then be sexual, although sex still comes before identification in many instances (Dube, 2000).

Although family relations are the second most common presenting problem among queer youth who seek therapy (Martin & Hetrick, 1988), the subject of youth coming out younger and matters of sexual identity thereby being involved in the family setting has not been addressed adequately yet in the family therapy literature. We know that adolescents are in family therapy offices, but family therapists are not writing about the lives of some of these adolescents. This is perhaps because parents are rarely the first person to know about a child's sexual minority status (Savin-Williams, 2001) and because if therapists are not open to the possibility that some of their troubled adolescents are struggling with sexual identity, it will not be addressed in family therapy. Although the family therapy literature is beginning to address family issues in the coming out process (e.g., Beeler & DiProva, 1999; Elizur & Ziv, 2001; Green, 2000; LaSala, 2000; Sanders & Kroll, 2000), few are writing about working with queer youth in family therapy offices and even fewer are writing specifically about transgendered youth.

It may be that queer youth are not adequately addressed in family therapy practice because we have a tendency to confuse sexual identity with sexual practice. Communicating about sexual practice is awkward in the best of circumstances and most awkward when adults are attempting to discuss it with youth. Sexuality, then, is not a comfortable topic of conversation in family therapy sessions. If sexual minority status is discussed or suggested, individuals have a tendency to immediately think about sexual practice and the discussion is muted. Heterosexual youth have the privilege of maintaining a distance between themselves and their sexual exploration (which may or may not include sexual practice), whereas sexual minority youth, when they came out, expose themselves in ways that may interfere with their developmental trajectory. Because sexual identity and sexual practice are falsely merged, identity is rarely explored in family therapy practice.

25

The literature, however, has recommended family therapy to help with the coming out process (Beeler & Diprova, 1999; LaSala, 2000; Saltzburg, 1996; Sanders & Kroll, 2000). Saltzburg suggested that family meetings can provide parents with the education, modeling, and support they need to hang in there with their children, regardless of how little they may know about what its like to be a sexual minority. LaSala recommended separate sessions with the queer individual and the family to allow everyone to express thoughts and feelings they may not want to express in front of other family members.

Family therapists are in the eye of the storm. Although as a professional culture we may have begun to move away from blatant pathologizing of homosexuality, the family therapy field seems to be in an uneasy truce, especially when it comes to the treatment of children in family contexts. The field's stance appears to be one of managing homosexuality or coping with it. The focus is on the negative impact of queer sexualities and on minimizing this impact. We may be able to sit with a family and help them grieve about lost dreams or share their anxieties for their queer children, but we are not equally able to challenge these families to embrace the gifts that queerness has to offer. It is one thing to hold liberal views of sexuality or even to be accepting of sexual minorities, but it is quite another to intentionally and purposefully help our children grow up gay, as the queer theorist Sedgwick (1993) suggested. For clinicians, the lack of supportive theory, knowledge, and clinical skills makes adopting such a stance even more difficult.

Homophobia and heterosexism continue to define the family therapy field's professional identity. As members of professional organizations and as practitioners, we must examine the decisions we make every day about where we stand in both our personal and professional lives. We have come to recognize that the current state of family therapy lacks the theoretical base it needs in order to help sexual minority youth still living at home garner the love and support they deserve from their families and to help families support and nurture their queer members.

Heterosexism and Homophobia

Homophobia and heterosexism are two of the staples of our culture, regardless of our own sexual identity or our exposure to queer people. *Homophobia*, put simply, is a fear of homosexual people, thoughts, feelings, and actions. *Heterosexism* is the taken-for-granted assumption that all people are heterosexual. The language of homosexuality itself is steeped in pathological thinking. It was developed to refer to the pathological identities of those who desired or had intimate relations with same sex partners (Herdt, 1989). The terms *gay* and *lesbian* were developed, and then embraced by those to which they referred, during the social movements of the late 1960s and 1970s. The power to name oneself was claimed by gay men and lesbians in order to depathologize the labeling that occurred by established communities. Subsequently the term *queer* usurped *gay* and *lesbian* to some extent. Once derogatory, it is now claimed as an all-inclusive label for anyone who violates the basic assumption of heterosexuality. To call oneself *queer* embraces one's difference and rejects the notion that the norm of heterosexuality is one to which we all aspire.

It is practically impossible to be raised in a heterosexist, homophobic culture like our own and not be influenced by some of the negative messages about queer people. Even the atypical parent is tempted to hope for a typical child. We want our children's lives to be easy and those who live on the margins know how difficult it is when the rulebook was not written with you in mind. Those of us who have been the targets of violence and hatred may desire to protect our children even more than the privileged parent who believes people get what they deserve. Even parents who embrace sexual minority status often have some reservations!

27

Queer parents especially feel pressure to produce heterosexual children. In 2001, an episode of the news show *20/20* featured Barbara Walters interviewing gay and lesbian parents and their adolescents. The goal of the show was to show that lesbian and gay parents can raise happy and healthy children. The parents and adolescents triumphantly proclaimed that the youth were heterosexual. For an oppressed minority barraged with questions about their fitness for parenthood, it was a chance to show how well they had done.

Family therapists are also raised in this culture and when these attitudes remain unexamined, it is difficult to leave them out of the therapy room. If our adult clients do not self-identify, most of us assume they are heterosexual. When we see children and adolescents in family therapy, most of us assume, as do their parents, that they are burgeoning heterosexuals, unless they give us some blatant reason to suspect they are not. In therapy rooms across the country, when queer youth are finally acknowledged, they are accepted with caution.

Nurturing queer youth in family therapy requires a model of practice that respects the relational process of development and youths' understanding of their own identity. Shifting this understanding away from simple definitions of youth's sexuality to complex views of differing identities takes a model of practice informed by compassion, new theory, research, clinical experience, and a real openness toward learning. Nurturing this more complex view of sexuality is fostered by the incorporation of queer theory into extant family therapy practice.

QUEER THEORY

Traditionally, if you are born with male genitalia you are considered male, you become a man, you act masculine, and you desire women. Likewise, if you are born with female genitalia you are considered female, you become a woman, you act feminine, and you desire men. Queer theory proposes a way to conceive of sexuality that challenges these dichotomous categories and offers a more complex view. Sexuality and gender are considered infinitely unique, complex and evolving. After extensive research into gender and sexuality, Fausto-Sterling wrote, "labeling someone a man or a woman is a social decision. We may use scientific knowledge to help us make the decision, but only our beliefs about gender—not science—can define our sex" (2000, p. 3).

I (RGH) was a stereotypical tomboy who enjoyed playing sports of all kinds. In elementary school, Sister Eileen, my teacher, had very poor vision and did not realize until well into the second half of the school year that I, a girl, had been playing football with the boys every day at recess. Sister Eileen spotted me one day and pulled me out of the game to lecture me about how I had no business playing with the boys. I would certainly get hurt and my development would be stunted. I should be where I belonged, socializing with the girls. I tried to reason with her by innocently explaining that I was not afraid for my own safety. The only people that needed to be afraid were the guys who tried to keep me from the end zone. This was all to no avail. I was banished to jump rope with the rest of the girls.

When I realized that Sister Eileen was serious, I brought in the big guns, namely, my mother, who informed the teacher that indeed I had her permission to play, that I was physically able, and that to keep me from playing was patently unfair. Sister Eileen solicited input from the school nurse and the principal. They beseeched us to listen to reason. My mother was unrelenting. She fought for me until the bitter end. I was allowed to play football again, but the victory was bittersweet. No one looked at me the same after that. The boys I had played with were openly contemptuous for the first time. Before, my ability and desire were assets that got me picked first for teams. Now they became liabilities, as no one wanted to admit they wanted a "freak" on their team. I became subtly ashamed of my abilities and desires because I knew it marked me as different. I started to understand that I threatened my peers and authority figures alike. I lost the innocent joy I got out of playing sports with friends. I continued to participate, but the act had lost much of its naturalness. Instead, it had suddenly become a political act.

The teachers and staff at my school implicitly knew what queer theorists (Butler, 1993; Sedgwick, 1993; Spargo, 1999) later pointed out: Destabilizing ideas about gender, even among fifth graders at play, reveal and threaten the questionable rules upon which current social order depends. Based on a deficit model of queerness, their worry makes sense. They believed there was a *natural*, *right*, and *essential* way to be a girl, and if I failed to learn it, the rest of my development would suffer. What other ideas would I get into my head? What other rules would I seek to bend? What was I learning about being a woman? Where would it end? They were trying to avoid nurturing my *queerness* partly because they believed it was immoral and bad for me and partly because my existence threatened their worldview.

Queer theory disputes this essentialist view of sexuality and gender, and it rejects the notion that queerness is pathological. Instead, it posits that sexualities are *constructed* within social contexts. Labels like *heterosexuality*, *homosexuality*, and even *queerness* itself do not exist separate from the cultures and societies in which they are created. They are cultural reference points, representations of organizing principles for what is or has been allowed and disallowed. Consider how important it is in our culture to know if someone is male or female. It is the first question we ask about newborn children. It is on virtually all forms we fill out, all records we keep. These labels are cultural shorthand and help us organize our thoughts, interactions, and expectations of ourselves and others. At the same time they limit other possibilities. By naming *female* and *male* as sexual categories we eliminate from our worldview the existence of other potential sexual categories. Furthermore these organizing principles oversimplify and

dichotomize. Consider how little we actually know about someone after labeling a person male or female. Similarly, to label oneself *homosexual* actually says very little about who one is as a
person, what one desires, or how one experiences relationships.
To label oneself *heterosexual* arguably says even less, because so
much is assumed and so little examined under the heterosexual
moniker.

Queer people, on the other hand, have in common the experience of trying to survive in a social context that overtly disquali-
fies and oversimplifies our lives. This oppression creates
recognizable life patterns, challenges, and experiences. Although
all queer people are not the same, growing up in the margins of
our culture we tend to be quite aware of the ways in which our
lives are invalidated. Heterosexuals who live front and center tend
to be less aware of the disallowed and oversimplified aspects of
their own sexuality. Perhaps it is precisely the marginal existence
of queer people that makes this experience instructive and valuable: Only in the harsh borderlands of the margins can critiques
of the status quo flourish. Only under the intense pressure of
oppression can we be enlightened about the parts of each of us
that have been left undeveloped because they have been contextu-
ally disallowed. By exploring what is disallowed, a more complex,
richer reality develops for all of us. Queer theorists recognize the
power and value in the borderlands, where what has been elsewhere disallowed is explored and what before has been unimag-
ined becomes possible. When we move past the dichotomies of
male–female, masculine–feminine, and gay–straight, we start to
understand that all sexualities are unique and complex. It is in
these borderlands that new possibilities for love, commitment,
and family structure emerge.

Marital and family relations in particular have been enor-
mously limited by over simplified ideas and prejudices about gender and sexuality. We are encouraged through social constructs to
assume much about who and what we are as well as how we

should or should not live and love. We learn to label ourselves and to stop asking basic questions. We are continually encouraged to stop exploring the borderlands. By focusing on the mismatches or the contradictions inherent in the dichotomization of gender and sexual orientation, queer theory provides a crucial hand-hold on questioning what we know about maleness, femaleness, and family relationships. This questioning has obvious and far-reaching implications for the structure and function of marriages and families. Queer theory encourages the active exploration of deconstructing gender and sexuality rather than assuming discrete categories of male and female, heterosexual and homosexual.

Queer theory suggests that there is not just one way to be heterosexual or homosexual, but rather many evolving ways to be a fully sexual being (Spargo, 1999). Gender and sexuality are evolving identities, yet the culture in which we live makes it difficult to explore these possibilities. The very act of exploration is threatening to the status quo. We expect masculine men to be heterosexual, for example, and are often more surprised by a football player's declaration of homosexuality than we are by a dancer's declaration. Similarly, if a man comes out as homosexual, and then says that he wants to marry a woman, we doubt his acknowledgement of self. Transgendered individuals completely challenge the status quo because we assume, sometimes incorrectly, that a man who has an internal sense of himself as a woman, must be attracted to other men. When we explore all the possibilities surrounding gender and sexual identity, we begin to question all the information we have used to structure our worldviews. Queer people have an added advantage in this exploration because they have the experience of not fitting the status quo.

When you are queer you find a home on the borderlands where the ground may be eternally shifting. As Butler (1993) discussed, *queerness* itself is constantly defined and redefined. For queer people, who have had to question the status quo in order to know themselves, sexuality is both more freeing and more complicatcd. It is more freeing because, once you acknowledge that gendcr and sexual identity are more complex than we are taught, you are able to explore multiple ways to think, feel, and act. You can have female genitalia, for example, and be male-identified in some areas and female identified in others. You are less constrained, then, by the cultural mandates that come with gender. Yet, without those constraints, life is more complicated. The multiplicity of choices is coupled with little institutional support.

Developing any sexual identity, and especially a minority one, involves weaving one's essential biological and innate characteristics with social constructs of sexuality. Thus, for example, two men may engage in the same sexual practices but identify themselves differently—the first as a gay man and the second as a heterosexual man who has sex with men. "People achieve their sexual identities in idiosyncratic ways based on how they reconcile their personal scripts and meanings with socially constructed roles and functions. The process of blending *essential* characteristics of the self with *social constructs* of the community to form a sexual minority identity is often lifelong and evolving" (Ritter & Terndrup, 2002, p. 89).

Language intersects with identity because we often conflate identity with how one is labeled or how one labels oneself. For example, the term *homosexuality* continues to reflect the pathologizing stance taken by the mental health profession (Herdt, 1989). The terms *gay* and *lesbian* have been usurped by the *GLBT* (gay, lesbian, bisexual, transgender) label, which encompasses multiple identities. Dube (2000) has further defined the coming out process of gay and bisexual men by referring to men who have sex and then label themselves based on their actual sexual practice as *sex-centered* and those who label themselves first as *identity-centered*. The broader term *queer* reflects the emerging pride in sexual minority labeling. Because *queer* continues to be used as a derogative term, referring to those who violate the most basic assumption of "rightness," it has become a way for people to embrace their differences. Given that language is so important, we have attempted to define some terms that have often been merged together in the literature.

SEXUAL MINORITY. This is an umbrella term used to refer to those who transgress social expectations of sexuality or gender.

SEXUAL ORIENTATION. Sexual orientation has been most often conceived of as an internal sense of one's attractions to partners of a specific biological sex. For example, Savin-Williams defined sexual orientation as a "preponderance of sexual or erotic feelings, thoughts, and fantasies one has for members of one sex, or the other, both or neither" (2001, p. 14). The accent is on biological sex. However, from a queer theory perspective, sexual orientation is more than an assessment of one's attraction to specific genitalia. The term denotes the existence of discernable patterns of who and what attracts you not only physically but also emotionally; it also includes what type of person (despite biological sex) one is attracted to (e.g., gregarious, introverted, intelligent, challenging), as well as what types of relationships are desired. Klein (1990) created a grid expanding the definition of sexual orientation to include attraction, behavior, fantasies, emotional and social preference, lifestyle, and identification.

Attractions and desires are both biological and relational. As relational therapists we must recognize that it is not only our gay, lesbian, bisexual, or transgendered clients who have sexual orientations—all of our clients have unique, complicated orientations to specific relational dynamics, to specific parts of the anatomy, to specific gender roles, and to specific sexual acts. From a queer theory position there are not merely two options for sexual orientation but multiple heterosexualities and homosexualities, each of which deserves exploration.

Complicating this further, queer theory makes room for sexuality evolving over a lifetime. Although some research suggests that our sexual orientations are internal, stable, and consistent from early childhood (Newman & Muzzonigro, 1993; Ritter & Terndrup, 2002), we know from our own experience and from the lives of our clients that what we prefer, whom we are attracted to, and what kinds of relationships we are drawn to can ebb and flow. In studying young women, for example, Diamond (1998) found much variability in how they come to their own understanding of the development of a sexual minority identity.

SEXUAL IDENTITY. Sexual identity is a broader term used to describe one's internal sense of a whole sexual self, which may include one's gender identity, gender role, and sexual orientation. A variety of cultural, relational, biological, and sexual experiences informs one's identity. There is an important difference between *identity* and *orientation*. One can experience same sex desire (orientation) but label oneself heterosexual and live as a heterosexual forever (identity). Others might never have genital sex with someone of the same-sex and still label themselves bisexual or queer. One's sexual identity is claimed socially, whereas sexual orientation is an internal experience which can be claimed socially or not. Youth with same sex attractions may claim any number of identities—hetero, bi, gay, lesbian, trans, or queer. Each would have different meanings to the youth and the community around them, and these meanings would need to be explored and nurtured.

Freud's original theory of sexual identity development separated people into either heterosexual (and healthy) or homosexual (and unhealthy). Homosexual desires that persisted beyond puberty were thought to be caused by unsuccessful resolution of the Oedipal complex (Ritter & Terndrup, 2002). Alfred Kinsey, on the other hand, theorized that sexuality existed on a continuum where the guiding force was sexual *behavior*. Kinsey's work did not conceive of the existence of homosexual or heterosexual *identities*, merely of people whose behavior could be classified. According to Kinsey, people's sexuality could theoretically be reclassified if their sexual partners changed from one gender to

35

another. Kinsey's work emphasized the diversity that exists in human sexuality despite cultural mandates for heterosexuality. Kinsey's work has been critiqued, however, for conceiving of homosexual and heterosexual behavior as opposites (the more heterosexual you are the less homosexual you are) and for focusing on behavior as the only measure of sexuality (Ritter & Terndrup). Other theorists (Coleman, 1982; Klein, 1990) have expanded on Kinsey's work to conceive sexual identity across a variety of variables in addition to behavior. Klein's work, for example, considers sexual identity to be best measured by a combination of sexual behavior, sexual attraction, fantasies, emotional and social preferences, self-identification, and lifestyle over time.

GENDER. Cultural ideas about how biological sex shapes personalities constitute gender. These ideas (or *constructs*) are deeply ingrained in our society and maintain that there are two genders (male and female) and that there are *right* (or at least *more right*) ways for men and women to think, behave, dress, act, and desire. We cannot *not* perform gender.

GENDER IDENTITY. Gender identity is one's internal sense of self as male or female, masculine or feminine. Gender identity is a vital and powerful combination of the internalization of the social construct of gender and the discernment of where one fits or feels most at home. Although we all have masculine and feminine parts, for most of us, our biological sex matches our sense of gender or what we think and how we feel, desire, and behave.

Often gender identity is misunderstood as being the same as or akin to sexual identity or sexual orientation. This misunderstanding is helped along by the tendency among many transgendered individuals to identify first as gay or lesbian. These concepts, however, are discreet. Gender identity does not address whom one is attracted to. It is a self-reference point, a matter of how one understands one's own gender category.

36

GENDER VARIANT. Gender variant is a broad term used to describe a *pattern* of cross-gender behavior. Gender variant people stick out because they consistently transgress the social boundaries of what is expected from males or females. Some gender variant youth identify as gay, lesbian, or bisexual. Other gender variant youth identify as heterosexual and/or transgendered.

TRANSGENDERED. Transgendered individuals "have a deep, developed, and valid sense of their own sex that does not always correspond to the cursory decision made by a delivery-room obstetrician" (Feinberg, 1998, p. 8). Transgendered youth transgress similar gender and sexuality boundaries as gay and lesbian youth, and therefore face many of the same developmental and family dilemmas gay and lesbian youth face. In this book, we have included trans youth in the *queer* category. However, although they share similarities with other queer youth, there are important differences.

The main difference is that many of these youth will be beginning (or intent on beginning) a *transition* away from living as their biological sex and toward living as the opposite sex. Istar-Lev (2004) defined this transition as:

> . . . the process that transgender people move through in accepting their gender identity, particularly the physical, legal, and psychological experience of moving from one gender identity to another or allowing others to see their authentic identity. Transition is similar to a rebirthing experience, in which the person reemerges with the social identity that is the best expression of their internal core gender identity. Part of this process involves cross living as the other gender or going through the real life experience or real life test to experience what living as the other gender is like before being referred for sex reassignment surgery. Transition often implies hormonal and surgical

37

treatments and the physical changes that accompany
them. (p. 399)

This means that some youth will desire to alter their appearance
and bodies through cosmetic, medical, and perhaps surgical intervention. It is important to remember that not all transgendered
people elect to go through full surgical interventions. Like all of
us, trans people are trying to express their sense of themselves as
gendered people. Some women feel more comfortable in dresses,
many other do not. Some men enjoy primping and some wear
make-up while others would never dream to. Similarly, all trans
people make individual decisions about how they are comfortable
expressing their sense of self. For some this means merely being
able to cross-dress, for others hormones are enough to help them
match the internal with the external, and for still others surgery is
the best option.

Transgendered youth have an internal sense of themselves as
different from their gendered biological characteristics.
Unfortunately, our culture does not articulate the differences
between sexual and gender identity in ways that make it possible
for youth to have a clear sense, when they come out, exactly how
they experience themselves. Some youth who have always experienced themselves as gender variant go through a period of time
when they label themselves as gay or lesbian; others go through a
period of time when they label themselves as transgendered. In
any case, these youth are not following the simple definitions of
heterosexuality and are stretching the boundaries of once discrete
categories like *male, female, gay,* and *straight.* We categorize all
who do not fit into traditional models of heterosexuality as *queer.*

Queer Theory for Everyone

Thinking about one's sexual orientation, sexual identity, and
gender identity is not just for those who live on the margins. When

you read about queer theory and are thoughtful about the ways in which you have categorized yourself and been categorized, new awareness emerges. I (LSF) have learned a great deal about my heterosexuality, for example, by incorporating queer theory into my practice. I take note not only of the ways in which I organize my thinking about my clients' lives in terms of dichotomous gender categories but also about how this thinking has encouraged views of my own life. For a long time I felt like a terrible mother because I did not enjoy traditional female activities. I felt inferior to my female friends and family members who liked to cook, enjoyed entertaining, and knew how to make their houses look inviting. I could not reconcile the belief of the good mother as a beacon of heterosexual femininity with my lack of ability in the household and domestic sphere. Queer theory has helped me to embrace my masculinity and still acknowledge all the ways in which I am completely maternal. I can be a good mother while being an incompetent typical female. It has also helped me to acknowledge and admire the femininity and masculinity I see in others without feeling threatened because of my own incompetence.

Queer theory is the conscious recognition of the powerful potential in the unexplored and the disallowed in all of us. Because we assume and privilege heterosexuality, those who live outside of it are continually and actively disallowed, unexplored, and silenced. Queer theory posits that all of us can learn a great deal about ourselves if we explore our sexual identities in greater detail. Queer people often are expected to make an accounting of their sexuality. We are expected to explore, explain, and defend our desires. This process is rich and powerful, especially when it is not done under threat or coercion. This is a gift that queer people have to offer their straight counterparts. The offer, however, has not been taken and we continue to think about heterosexuality and homosexuality as discreet and different categories.

The families we work with have taught us to move beyond managing homosexuality, to allow for increasingly complex views

39

of gender and sexuality, and most importantly, to trust in their unique developmental process by learning to assist it rather than try to control it. Surrounding ourselves with research and theoretical literature, and learning from our clients, friends, family members, colleagues, students, and our own journey, we have incorporated queer theory to create a model that calls for a transformation of family therapy practices.

When sexual minority youth first begin to come out, many parents, and even the youth themselves, struggle to understand why they are gay and if they did something to cause it. An important part of creating space for families to wrestle with this question is to *queer* the process—perhaps by exploring with a family what they think causes heterosexuality, or to propose the existence of heterosexualities and homosexualities as an infinite number of unique ways to be a fully developed sexual being.

Most heterosexual parents assume their children will be heterosexual. When dreaming about the lives their children will lead, a same-sex partner is generally not part of the picture. Entertaining the idea creates fear and anxiety. Parents are afraid for a range of reasons. They are worried about how life will be more difficult for their child who exists outside of the mainstream. They may feel alienated from their child, who might now seem like a stranger and anxious about how this difference between them will affect their relationship. And some parents believe that homosexuality is a sin which will compromise their child's spiritual life. The belief that we have control over our children's sexual identity also organizes parents, who may think if they discourage atypical gender behavior, their child will turn out straight. If their child isn't straight perhaps it is their parenting skills that are at fault. The typical heterosexual parent is afraid to entertain the possibility that their child may be a homosexual because once you relinquish control over something so basic as gender and sexual orientation; any control over your children may seem tenuous at best.

Many therapists, even the most progressive, routinely assume that the teenagers they work with are heterosexual. Minority sexuality rarely comes up unless it is brought up in a crisis or the youth discloses the information. When youth's sexuality does come up, it and they often become the "problem" of the therapy. In recent years, family therapists have gotten better at helping families manage the discomfort, grief, and fear that sexual minority's status may bring. Now we must learn to not only help families cope with their gay children, but also to actually nurture their queerness and help children grow up gay (Sedgwick, 1993). We have to shift our thinking about gender identity and homosexuality from damage control to nurturing queerness. More than a decade has passed since Sedgwick pushed this envelope. Today we are encouraging a serious conversation about this idea. To create refuge for all of our youth—those who do not fit in as well as those who go through adolescence unscarred—we must shift our dichotomous thinking and learn to nurture the queerness in everyone who enters our therapy room. Sedgwick (1993, p. 76) wrote, "The number of persons or institutions by whom the existence of gay people is treated as a previous desideratum, a needed condition of life, is small . . . The scope of institutions whose programmatic undertaking is to prevent the development of gay people is unimaginably large." We propose the radical idea that queerness is a valuable, even necessary goal that has important lessons to teach all of us.

FAMILY THERAPY TRANSFORMED

Although the culture in the United States is becoming more accepting of alternative lifestyles, our youth are still growing up in communities that largely pathologize their lives. Heterosexuality is still completely assumed; sexual minorities are routinely viewed as immoral and unnatural. Youth who recognize that they are different are told in countless overt and covert ways that there is something wrong with them. They may also experience invalidation by others simply because of their age. They may be told that they are too young to know themselves in this way, that everyone passes through these phases and it will go away, or that they are too impressionable. Though some are able now to see media images of themselves, youth continue to be surrounded by societal institutions and intimate others that deny or denigrate them.

Jana Marni's experience is a good example. She lived in a small, conservative Christian community. Her childhood interest in cars, ham radios, steam engines, and knives was tolerated in her family because these were her father's interests and they were a way to be connected to him. No one outside the family knew of these interests and she learned, very early on, to disparage them and feel shame about having them outside her family. In church groups, when the boys and girls split up to do traditionally gendered activities, she always wanted to be doing what the boys did. She was not allowed to wear pants to church although she badly wanted to. She was keenly aware that many of the ways she behaved upset her mother but she felt like she couldn't help behaving as she did. Because her heterosexuality was just assumed, Jana had no language to talk about alternative ways of living and being. Instead, she would hear continuously about how no man would want her given her interests. On many occasions her gender identity, or the way she "performed" gender, confused the people around her, who also had no language or concepts for a life lived outside of masculinity and femininity. They would ask Jana "What are you?" In this way, Jana learned first that she was not feminine and second that whatever she was it was "wrong," and Jana was fairly certain she was going to hell.

Although Jana had only the vaguest, fragile notion of her sexual feelings toward women, she was abundantly aware that her father took every opportunity he could find to make disparaging comments about the queers, fags, and butches on television. When a lesbian couple moved into the apartment complex in which his sister lived, Jana's father encouraged his sister to move out as soon as possible. "You don't want your kids to be influenced by that kind of behavior," he said to his sister, "and I certainly don't want mine to either."

The increased visibility of queer lifestyles may well be a blessing for the youth of today. Yet there is a darker side to mainstream acknowledgment of queer lives. As visibility increases so does the level of discomfort and even hatred. In some communities, this means being even more vigilant about ensuring that children know that homosexual behavior is sinful. In more liberal communities it may appear that sexual minority status is an accepted lifestyle choice. Although there are acceptance coalitions in an increasing number of urban and suburban high schools, the very existence of these groups produces backlash against the members. As a result, many queer youth stay in the closet. One of our clients, a vital member of his high school acceptance coalition, recently reported that another student pushed him against his locker and said, "If I stick a broom up your ass, will it be considered a hate crime?" Queer teachers who might assist in the complicated process of coming out—dealing with the consequences, handling prejudice, and creating some sense of respite from the stress—are rarely out themselves and are hesitant to talk to youth because of the threat of job discrimination and harassment. The mythical fear that gay adults will seduce youth is still alive and contributes to an environment where youth must attempt to develop without local in-school adult mentoring.

Sexual minority youth and their families are seeking family therapy services. Our therapeutic task is neither to minimize the way queer sexualities affect development and relationships nor to overstate it. Instead we must ask questions which seek to understand youth's experiences. What might it be like to be Jana struggling to understand her life in the midst of her father's homophobia? What impact might that have on her development? What affect does being threatened sexually with a broomstick have on a young, newly out, and proud gay man—as if that were part and parcel of his sexuality? Our therapeutic task is to create a crucible that can validate the special pressures faced by queer youth, lessen isolation by promoting identification of self with like others, and also promote a sense of one's uniqueness while improving the family context so that it can hold all of its members. The therapeutic imperative, in short, is to nurture queerness.

Creating Refuge

To nurture queerness we must create a crucible of refuge. We were first introduced to this idea by the work of psychiatrist Sandra Bloom (1997). She wrote about creating sanctuary away from the toxic world in which we live so as to promote healing. Bloom's sanctuary takes the form of an inpatient psychiatric facility for patients surviving trauma: "A 'sanctuary' is a place of refuge and protection. For our purposes the word connotes a place of temporary respite, where some of the rules of our present everyday society are suspended to allow for a different kind of social experience" (Bloom, 1997, p. 10). For us, *sanctuary* or *refuge* is an attitude that nurtures complex ideas about gender and sexual identity. To nurture queerness we must suspend the rules of culture. In everyday life we are constrained by what we have been taught is normal. Therapy becomes a haven in which we can challenge cultural norms and come to recognize what we know about self and other.

In therapy we honor and nurture each individual's own knowledge of what is normal. All thoughts and feelings are acceptable. All action is acceptable if it is not harmful to self or other. The therapist has an attitude of respect for alterity or otherness (Compton, 1998). We can never know the full extent of another. In thinking we can know someone else, we foreclose the multitude of possibilities of who they are and can be. This respect for the inability to ever really know others leads us towards witnessing as action. Weingarten wrote about witnessing trauma as a therapeutic stance: "It is the moment when we know we are struggling to descend into the abyss, to see it, to render it, to share this with

44

another equally dedicated soul, and to emerge in some relation to the effort more sad, more sober, and, yes, more free" (2000, p. 394). To help families nurture queerness, we must create refuges from the outside world so that clients are free to know each other without the constraints of debilitating social messages that restrict that knowledge. We do this through responsiveness, an attitude of critical consciousness, and the act of witnessing.

Difficult Dialogues

Once you have created a crucible of refuge—an attitude in which you have relayed the message that you can tolerate all that comes your way and that you can be helpful—therapy moves toward creating a space for difficult dialogues to occur. Because relational dynamics in families speak louder than actions and words, families are often constrained in their dialogue with one another. It is difficult to spontaneously open up and share their most intimate thoughts while fearing abandonment. Making it more difficult is the youth's stage of development. Although difficult dialogues occur in all stages of development, adolescence is a particular challenge in family therapy. Compounding the intensity is the subject of sexuality.

Difficult dialogues are conversations that change the dynamics in a relationship and the people in them. This change occurs, usually, through microtransitions in interaction—that is, in small steps (Breunlin, 1988). The threat of abandonment may not completely disappear, but conversations move in the direction of more intimacy, albeit in fits and starts. Contained in a crucible of refuge by a therapist who is able to hold individuals in their awkward learnings about each other, family members tiptoe into uncharted territory. Therapists encourage honesty. Always respecting the hierarchy embedded in parent-child relationships as well as the developmental trajectory of adolescence, the therapist guides conversation so that it is different from how it was but not so different that it is intolerable. The therapist carefully increases intensity so that intimate thoughts can be shared in ways they have not been shared before.

This stage of therapy is particularly challenging in environments that pathologize queer people. Although all of us have internalized the dominant messages about homosexuality and heterosexuality, there is rich variation in cultures, religions, neighborhoods, and families when it comes to our ideals about human behavior. When important people in a queer youth's life invalidate her or his very being, a therapist's job is quite challenging. There are situations in which it is unsafe for a child to attempt a difficult dialogue with certain family members or her or his whole family, and we do not advocate this unsafe practice. Sometimes we must work with youth to find alternative families to help nurture their growth and development. Once we have created a safe refuge, we test the waters.

Nurturing Queerness

To help sexual minority youth continue to be supported by their families, therapists must help families move beyond tolerating and accepting their youth and work toward nurturing their development. The concept of *relational ethics* (Boszormenyi-Nagy & Spark, 1973) helps support a family's appreciation of their sexual minority member by involving families in the practice of giving to each other. Giving is the act of helping someone. When a family member is able to give to other family members, it enhances the giver's self-esteem. When queer youth are able to expose other family members to different ways of being in the world, and that difference is appreciated, all involved benefit. This challenges many simplistic notions of giving, parent-child hierarchy, and how children should grow and develop.

There are any number of ways to nurture queerness; the possibilities are limited only by our imagination. In therapy, we encourage youth to actively explore the formation of their identity individually and with family members. This process begins the expansion away from traditional heterosexuality as a norm to more complex views of gender and sexual identity for everyone in the family. We help families nurture their youth's burgeoning queerness and integrate their youth's identity into an expanded vision of their own family. This can be likened to queering the family. Nurturing queerness is about broadening the family's center and involving them in a community larger than the one they had before.

Encouraging Transformation

What if the field of family therapy embraced queer theory the way it embraced postmodern ideology—not just for queer youth and their families, but for all families? What if we began looking to sexual minorities for new ways of forming and being in relationships? Family therapists have been open to the possibility that there are multiple ways to understand an event, to view the world, or to have a perspective. We are open to a multicultural perspective, recognizing that our views of childrearing are based on a white, middle class perspective. Yet we continue to hold dear the notion that family environments must nurture heterosexuality. If family therapy embraced queer theory and all family therapists entered into relationships with their clients open to nurturing queerness, we might have a quiet revolution on our hands. The current and ongoing revolution is being fought in the courts, in the schools, and on the playgrounds all over the country. As family therapists, we must also get in the game.

SPECIAL ISSUES IN TREATMENT: WHEN TO REFER

Queer youth can frighten us because their journey through identity development poses difficult questions that challenge all we think we know about gender, sexuality, and identity. Not every therapist can work with queer youth in a family context. Therapists who do not embrace the relational perspective of family therapy, in which relationships are used for growth and development, would do well to refer to family therapists for the family work. Family therapists may also want to refer to other family therapists who are more successful in creating environments that nurture queerness.

For some family therapists, strong religious or political beliefs about homosexuality may get in the way of creating a refuge for sexual minority youth. You should refer a family if you believe that same sex sexual activity is sinful and youth should be converted away from homosexuality. You should also refer if your agenda is to push a youth out of the closet regardless of the consequences. A strong political agenda to out all queer people may have dire consequences for youth who may suffer the loss of support, safety, and security of home.

If a family wants conversion therapy, it may pose an ethical dilemma for the therapist. Is it ethical for a therapist to refer to another therapist who provides conversion therapy if the referring therapist believes that conversion therapy is unethical? We prefer, first and foremost, a conversation. When family members ask us about conversion therapy, we explore the curiosity behind their questions. Family members may ask about conversion therapy because they want the youth to try to convert to heterosexuality before they accept the youth's sexual minority status. Others ask about it because they do not understand the complexities inherent in sexual identity. They know that a youth's life will be more complicated and they want to know if there are options. Exploration of these issues, then, become a part of therapy. If family members find queer youth completely unacceptable and do not want to explore any option other than conversion therapy, we encourage continued dialogue on the issue because we believe we can be helpful even while holding different beliefs. If families refuse treatment, we carefully explain our stance and suggest that they may be better served elsewhere.

Straight and queer therapists alike may have difficulty working toward creating environments that nurture queer youth. Straight therapists who have had the luxury and the misfortune of not having to examine their own sexual identity, heterosexism, and homophobia may have difficulty providing a crucible for difficult dialogues. Queer therapists who have not had these environments modeled for them may also find the work difficult. Queer therapists who work in environments in which it is unsafe to be out may find it difficult to create safe environments in their therapy offices.

Clearly not everyone is meant for this work. We believe, however, that if you are open to helping families nurture queerness, this book will help guide you toward it. We do not believe that a therapist's sexual identity privileges her or him in this work. Queer and straight therapists have different gifts to bring to family therapy. Queer therapists know the journey and can help youth with their depth of understanding. They can also be role models for developing youth. Straight therapists can let youth teach them about the process, which can then be validated as a true gift. Youth can know that straight people will accept them, a validating experience of its own.

CONCLUSION

As youth come out at ages younger than ever before, family therapists are called upon to help work with families through the transition from a family of heterosexuals to multiple sexual identities in the same household. Traditional family therapy principles form a solid basis for helping families through this process. The metaphoric crucible that contains both a family and the family therapy environment as well as the sophisticated understanding we have about relational dynamics help therapists support and challenge family members. Embracing complexity as a principle helps therapists hold families as they struggle with divergent views and try to stay in relationship with one another.

To nurture queer youth, not just manage homosexuality, queer theory adds to foundational family therapy principles, suggesting that there are many evolving ways to be human. As Butler (1993) discussed, queerness itself is constantly defined and redefined, so when queerness is embraced in a family setting, it frees all of the members to explore different parts of themselves. In a family therapy environment in which therapists have created a crucible of refuge, family members are supported in their positions and are challenged to be different in relationship with one another. Difficult dialogues take place and allow family members to explore different parts of themselves in relation to one another. Queer youth in those environments, then, are more likely to be nurtured and appreciated for the gifts they have to offer their families.

To help families nurture their queer youth, it is important that we know something about how they are both different from and the same as other youth who seek therapy. Most of the literature that does exist about queer youth in a family context is not coming out of the family therapy field. (If you are a family therapist reading only family therapy literature, you will know little about queer youth.) This book helps to fill that gap by addressing the relevant literature about queer youth and their families.

CHAPTER 2

Queer Youth

Queer youth are simultaneously similar and different from heterosexual youth. Like all youth they are moving from childhood to adulthood on the same developmental trajectory. They are different because their trajectory includes the discovery of sexual minority status. The timing of this discovery varies from youth to youth. Some recognize a marked sense of "differentness" in early or late childhood. Often this sense of otherness is connected to gender atypical behavior, where boys act more effeminately and girls more masculine than their mainstream counterparts. Studies have suggested that many gay, lesbian, and bisexual adults report gender atypical behavior as children (Hammersmith, 1987; Rottnek, 1999). (Heterosexual adults are rarely studied for whether they recall gender atypical behavior.) This brings up questions about memory and how it is affected by identity. For instance, it seems plausible that self-identified gay or lesbian adults may have more permission and support to remember the gender atypical pieces of themselves than do heterosexual or even bisexual people who go on to lead more traditional lives. In fact, queer people are encouraged in overt and covert ways to justify their *differentness* and explore their lives for the "causes" of their queerness. It is common to hear youth do just this by connecting their love of creative arts or sports, dolls or cars to their sexual orientation or gender identity as they struggle to understand who they are and the stigma they face.

The transition from late childhood to early adolescence is marked by puberty and the sexualization of the body. It is during this time that most youth begin to identify as sexual beings. We distinguish here between sexual identity and sexual practice. Most youth identify as sexual beings without having sexual relations with others. Identity is an internal state of knowledge that affects and is affected by others, yet it is not the act of sexual relations. Our culture has so merged the two that youth often find it quite difficult to discuss their burgeoning feelings of identity.

Some youth know they are queer in early or late childhood, with puberty merely underscoring their understanding of themselves. For these youth sexual identity unfolds slowly and steadily. For others, puberty is wake-up call. They are suddenly faced with sexuality in a more overt and intense way. As one of our clients explained, the word *fag* had been constantly thrown around in his school for years. He accepted it as a constant background noise to which he paid little attention. But then one day in school, he heard the word *faggot* and it seemed to fly down the hallway like a brick and hit him hard in the head. *He* was a faggot. And he suddenly felt exposed, vulnerable, and ashamed whenever he heard the word.

Gay, lesbian, and bisexual youth who are gender typical may not get harassed, ostracized, or criticized because they fit in to gendered expectations. This may create great pressure to continue to hide and pretend, as these youth have much to lose and little to gain by connecting with other queer youth or dealing more overtly with sexuality. These youth often go undetected by teachers, counselors, and helping professionals. At the other end of the spectrum are transgendered youth, who, though they may still be relatively rare, are being referred to us in increasing numbers. There is scant research on transgendered children and youth, and we are still only beginning to understand how to best help these young people. Our own clinical work is teaching us that puberty is often a time of crisis for trans youth, as the sexualization of their bodies often brings to a head the conflict between how they feel on the inside versus how their body looks on the outside. One young person we worked with explained that he had so firmly believed that he was female that he assumed that eventually his body would catch up and figure it out. When puberty began and his body masculinized, he became terrified, finally realizing that his body was going to continue to feel more and more foreign to him. Regardless of when youth know that they are not heterosexual or that they are transgendered, they all must incorporate this knowledge into their identity.

IDENTITY DEVELOPMENT

Queer theory identifies the multiple possibilities inherent within the human spirit. Those who study individual development, on the other hand, ground us with the knowledge that, although much is possible, human beings evolve in stable, patterned stages (Kegan, 1982). As youth develop, maturation requires them to walk a fine line between developing an individual self and integrating that self into family, peer, and community systems. One of the goals of development from childhood to adulthood is to form a consistent and stable identity (Erikson, 1963) that incorporates a congruence between how you view yourself and how others view you.

Kegan (1982) articulated the process of youth development starting from the childhood stage of the impulsive self to the adolescent stage of the imperial self:

> In differentiating from his impulse confusion within the family, the child grows out of an undifferentiated adhesion to these older people with whom he lives, and into the role of the "child" in relation to "parents." This process of identity development, although embedded within the family and the peer group, is one in which the child takes over the controls and authority which were formerly exercised by the parents. (p. 162)

So, although the youth is always in relationship with others, she or he is also learning about the self in relationship to his or her own identity. The child can begin to see him- or herself from the perspective of the various contexts in which she or he is embedded. What queer children see about themselves from the perspective of their parents, families, and communities often is contradictory and confusing. On the one hand they may feel loved and valued, but on the other hand ashamed and judged. When parents, families, and communities ignore or denigrate sexual minorities, it leaves their queer children with the task of seeing and integrating this undesirable, unwanted part of themselves. Children must either learn to reject the view that queerness is pathological or reject pieces of their own existence.

COMING IN TO SELF

Although all youth development occurs in the context of family and peers, for the sake of exploring queer youth, we have divided the process of identity into *coming into oneself* and *coming out to others*. For queer youth a dual individuation process occurs. First is the development of a unique autonomous self and second is learning to negotiate the feelings of being different from a majority of peers, family, and community and yet remain connected to them. Although for some youth this happens simultaneously, current research suggests that on average, youth are about 10 years old when they first realize they are not heterosexual, 14 when they self-label, 16 when they disclose to a friend, and 18 when they tell their parents (D'Augelli, Hershberger, & Pilkington, 1989). Newman and Muzzonigro (1993) studied ethnically and racially varied male youths and found that they reported first awareness of their "gayness" between the ages of 8 and 16, with the average age being 12.5 years. The average age of a first crush was 12.7 years. They wrote, "The age ranges reveal that a number of the respondents must have realized that they were gay even before they had a crush on another boy. This supports the view that sexual orientation is a more integral part of identity than sexual behavior alone" (Newman & Muzzonigro, p. 223).

Theorists have tried to capture the developmental processes using stage models that identify developmental milestones that queer youth move through as they develop mature minority sexual identities (Cass, 1979; Coleman, 1982; Troiden, 1979, 1989). These models propose that youth deal with dilemmas like sensitization, confusion, experimentation, exploration, and then eventually acceptance, identification, pride, and integration. Stage models are invaluable reading for therapists who work with queer youth, as these models highlight possible dilemmas and pathways for queer youth. We must remember, however, that these models are based on information about the sexual minority youth of past decades. Those who developed the stage model theories relied almost entirely on the recollections of adult, usually, white, European American men. These models also tend to create the impression that there is one healthy, linear, and universal pathway through queer adolescence. As Savin-Williams suggested, these models have one major downfall: "Most profoundly, they are not true—at least in a universal sense. Although a linear progression is intuitively appealing, extant research suggests it seldom characterizes the lives of real sexual minority youths" (2001, p. 16).

Current researchers like Dube (2000), Diamond (1998), and Savin-Williams (1998) interviewed youth (rather than adults) in various stages of development and found that young people desire, behave, and develop in various ways. Dube critiqued the stage theories of coming out for suggesting that young men experience attractions to other men, then have sex, and then label themselves gay. Dube found that a greater number of youths identify themselves as sexual minorities before having sex. Youth studied prior to 1990 were more likely to have sex first. Youth after 1990 were more likely to use other forms of experimentation like dating and Internet chatting before they had sex. Diamond also critiqued the stage theories of coming out after interviewing young women who either labeled themselves as a sexual minority or declined to label themselves at all. She found that a majority of those interviewed did not experience awareness of same sex attractions, consistency in same sex attractions, or feeling different or gender atypical as a child. The signs that are typically thought to indicate a sexual minority youth in development are absent for some youth who develop into adults who self-define as a sexual minority.

Only 2% of the male youths Savin-Williams (2001) interviewed followed an approximation of a stage model. Especially telling, none of the female youths he interviewed followed a model at all. Eliason (1996) argued for the usefulness of coming out models yet was quick to point out the inherent constraints of these ideas. As queer theory reminds us, gender and sexual identities are complicated and it is too easy to fall victim to our urge to organize, quantify, and understand what is often quite incomprehensible. Eliason further critiqued the coming out models for not considering race, religion, class, and gender and how these intersect to make unique avenues through which to come out.

We understand the process of queer identity development, or coming into oneself, from Savin-Williams's (2001) perspective of *differential developmental trajectories*. Rather than trying to fit a young person's experience into predetermined stages, Savin-Williams proposed grasping how queer youth develop similarly to heterosexual youth, differently from heterosexual youth, similarly to other queer youth, and also differently from other queer youth because of unique life circumstances and personalities. Although queer youth each develops in his or her own way, there are specific developmental tasks that await on his or her trajectory toward adulthood.

SPECIFIC IDENTITY DEVELOPMENT TASKS

Once young people come into themselves and recognize that they are sexual minority individuals, there are a number of tasks with which to be dealt. Youth have to attend to the social stigma associated with a nontraditional lifestyle and learn how to deal with a toxic environment. They must also work on self-acceptance and, if they come out to others during their youth, they must struggle with the reaction of others. Although coming out is a lifelong process, like anything else, it is often the beginning part of the process that proves to be the most difficult.

Dealing with Social Stigma

The major difference between sexual minority youth and heterosexual youth is the social stigma and cultural assumptions that create contexts in which heterosexuality is assumed, protected, and promoted. Not being heterosexual in a climate that so overwhelmingly assumes heterosexuality creates unique developmental challenges that coexist with the rest of the developmental challenges that youth face. Researchers suggested that there is about a 2-year period for most youth when they self-identify as nonheterosexual but keep this information to themselves (D'Augelli et al., 1989; Newman & Muzzonigro, 1993; Savin-Williams, 2001). To develop a positive identity, queer youth have to wade through a quagmire of heterosexism and homophobia. The assumption that heterosexuality is superior often makes it difficult for youth to explore and embrace their sexual minority status (Strommen, 1989; Troiden, 1989). Rejection of the negative view taken of homosexuality and a creation of a positive, integrated sense of self (Strommen), as well as a validated and positive view of ones' intimate and sexual self (Radkowsky & Siegel, 1997), is a specific identity developmental task of sexual minority youth. Because of the stigma associated with homosexuality, youth find it difficult to positively integrate their sexual identity into a sense of self and may think it has more meaning than it actually does (Hammersmith, 1987; Radkowsky & Siegel). In other words, when anything goes wrong, which happens quite a bit in adolescence, youth wonder whether it is because they are queer.

Although youth are driven by an internal sense of identity development that is universal to some extent, they are also unique individuals living in unique circumstances. Research done in the 1990s, when most youth were coming out later than they are today, suggests that there were major risks associated with self-labeling at an early age (Deisher, 1991; Remafedi, Farrow, & Deisher, 1991). Deisher discovered that for every year a sexual minority youth waited to self-identify, the odds of attempted suicide went down by 80%. Deisher found that adults are better able to cope with the stigma of minority status than were young people who self-identified in their adolescence.

Hardy and Laszloffy (2002) wrote of four aggravating factors that queer youth must wrestle with—devaluation, disruption/erosion of community, dehumanization of loss, and suppressed rage. The first three feed the buildup of suppressed rage, which for some youth is the catalyst for violence directed either at the self or at others. During the coming in process youth learn to handle these factors. As youth first realize their nonheterosexuality, they are confronted with various forms of devaluation, from constant assumptions about their heterosexuality to constant silence about any possibilities other than heterosexuality, to outright contempt and disgust for anyone who experiences same sex desire. "Initially, [this ranging recognition] generates extreme confusion in young children who never receive any acknowledgment that same sex relationships are even a possibility, let alone that they are a valid, normal possibility. Then these kids start to internalize the devaluation they encounter. This leads to a deep sense of shame because most conclude early on that their feelings must be wrong and unnatural, and so therefore there must be something wrong with them" (Hardy & Laszloffy, p.10).

Dealing with a Toxic Environment

"Gay male, lesbian and bisexual youths experience unique stressors in their lives that are directly related to their sexual behavior and identity" (Savin-Williams, 1994, p. 261). For youth who haven't come out, these stressors can include isolation, self-doubt, loneliness, self-esteem problems, and the fear of being found out, harassed, and kicked out of home. Youth in the process of coming out may have to deal with other's reactions, fears of being kicked out, being financially cut off, and being ostracized.

The research on the difficulties queer youth experience was mainly conducted in the early 1990s. We believe that for some queer youth today, these experiences are still very present whereas for others they are not. The majority of queer youth studied in the early 1990s reported verbal or physical threats of violence by their peers because of their sexual identity status (D'Augelli, 1995; Hetrick & Martin, 1987; Rosario, Rotheram-Borus, & Reid, 1996). Fifty percent of ethnic minority youth reported being ridiculed because of their homosexuality, 46% reported violent physical attacks, and the top stressors for these youth were coming out to their families or being found out and harassed by others (Rosario, Rotheram-Borus, & Reid). Those who were least likely to fit gender role stereotypes were most likely to be abused (Hetrick & Martin). Most of the youth expected to be abused again, hid from or avoided situations that might arouse suspicions about their sexuality, and did not report any of the abuse to authorities (D'Augelli).

There is certainly sufficient evidence to suggest that queer youth, even today, fear or are the targets of physical and verbal abuse, to the extent that they hide their true identities in many contexts. The stress of a toxic environment results in a variety of consequences. Research data consistently point to the rate of suicide attempts (20–40%) among gay, lesbian, bisexual, and transgendered youth, who are at a considerably elevated risk compared to heterosexual youth (Remafedi, 1987; Remafedi et al., 1991; Roesler & Deisher, 1972; Rotheram-Borus, Hunter, & Rosario, 1994). It needs to be made clear, however, that not all gay youth attempt suicide; if 20–40% do attempt suicide, it means that 60–80% do not.

Researchers have discovered that suicide attempts were linked with sexual milestones like self-identifying as gay, lesbian, bisexual, or transgendered (Deisher, 1991, Remafedi et al., 1991). They also found that multiple factors influence suicide, not solely the process of discovery of sexual minority status. Physical or sexual abuse, family dysfunction, young ages coming out, acting out, and drug use all increased the likelihood of suicide. The reason most often cited for attempted suicide was "family problems" (Remafedi et al.). Differences in race, religion, depression, and feelings of hopelessness were not correlated with attempts at suicide, nor were internalized homophobic thoughts or experiences with homophobia (Deisher, 1991).

Radkowsky and Siegel (1997) suggested that, because of the stigma and pervasive belief that heterosexuality is superior and the one and only outcome for healthy human beings, queer kids must develop coping techniques. They suggested that many youth go through denial and repression, try to repair themselves by becoming straight, and tell themselves that they are just going through a phase. Some deny their queer identity by getting pregnant or having numerous sexual partners of the opposite gender. Some become flamboyant and hyperidentify as queer, flout traditionalism, and encourage rejection. Still others may cope by attempting to be perfect overachievers.

Self-Acceptance

Numerous studies suggest that sexual minority youth are at increased risk for depression, anxiety, suicide, and substance abuse. Studies on queer adults, however, suggest that as youth they experienced difficult adolescent periods but responded to them by increasing their psychological adjustment and turning their lives around as adults (Elizur & Ziv, 2001). Self-acceptance, then, is an essential task of adolescent development for queer individuals. Affirmative sexual minority identity is associated with mental hcalth. This conclusion is based on empirical studies that demonstrate a positive association between gay male identity formation and feelings of self-worth (Helminiak, 1989; Savin-Williams, 1990), well-being (Carlson & Steuer, 1985), psychological adjustment (Hammersmith & Weinberg, 1973), and adult attachment security (Elizur & Mintzer, 2001).

These findings suggest that adolescent transitions are especially difficult for queer youth but that once an adult identity is formed with adult resources and coping tools, no difference in psychological function exists between heterosexual and homosexual adults (Elizur & Ziv, 2001). It is imperative that we understand that unique stressors exist for queer youth. On the other hand, we must be cautious about drawing conclusions regarding how these stressors affect queer youth. As Savin-Williams (1990, 1994, 2001) pointed out, the vast majority of queer youth deal with these stressors successfully on a daily basis without becoming suicidal, drug, or alcohol addicted, depressed, or prone to acting out. And they go on to become vibrant, contributing members of their communities. The youth we read about most frequently, and see in our offices are often already in trouble.

Many queer youth remain hidden, which makes validation of self by others difficult. For a period of time (which varies from youth to youth) it is painfully difficult to reconcile the person they feel developing inside them with the person they are assumed and asked to be by everyone else (Owens, 1998). There are no dating rituals, rites of passage, or ways to explore their burgeoning identities (Radkowsky & Siegel, 1997). As comedian Ellen Degeneres famously said, no one throws you a coming out party and says, "Yeah! You are gay and out." This makes it challenging to develop an integrated, positive sense of self. This is especially true for adolescents who are managing hormones, self-identity, and knowledge about self, all under the microscope of family, peers, and culture. How do you accept yourself when a big part of you is pathologized, ignored, and disallowed?

To deal with the social stigma and toxic environment in which they are raised, queer youth must face the task of developing a sexual minority identity (Owens, 1998). This process has become colloquially known as "coming out" (Newman & Muzzonigro, 1993). Because we all assume that we will be heterosexual, queer youth are often surprised and confused when they first realize that their feelings are atypical and "come out" to themselves (Cass, 1979; D'Augelli & Hershberger, 1993; Herdt, 1989; Newman & Muzzonigro; Savin-Williams, 2001) A task, then, for individuals who are queer—above and beyond what their heterosexual counterparts must do—is to acknowledge that they are different and then learn to relate to themselves and others as members of an oppressed group (Saltzburg, 1996). They must learn to value themselves in a culture that devalues their very being. This is the lifelong process of self-acceptance, which begins when youth first identify.

We do not want to create a stereotyped picture of queer youth as troubled, abused, depressed, and victimized. Nor do we want to give ammunition to those who paint dire pictures of queer youth as "more troubled" because they are morally bankrupt, victims of sexual abuse by adult homosexuals, or subject to a culture that torments them in severe ways. We also do not want to minimize the extent of the stressors that queer youth face. Yet research suggests that heterosexual and nonheterosexual youth vary little in self-esteem and self-concept (Savin-Williams, 2001). We are hoping to understand the way these stressors may affect the lives of youth and to develop ways to spark the unique resiliency in the youth and families with which we work. There are many ways to achieve a positive sense of self. A main one is a supportive family (D'Augelli & Hershberger, 1993).

COMING OUT TO OTHERS

Youth today are more likely to know adult gay and lesbian people, to have a sense of a queer community, and to see positive (or at least not totally negative) images of themselves in the media. Boxer and colleagues (1991) theorized that this cultural shift toward increased openness and acceptance probably accounts for the decreasing age at which youth self-identify as sexual minorities. Indeed studies suggest that the age at which sexual minority youth self-identify has been decreasing at least since the onset of the gay and lesbian rights movement (Boxer et al. 1991; Coleman, 1982; Dank, 1971; Henderson, 1998; Herdt, 1989; Remafedi, 1987, Sanders & Kroll, 2000; Troiden, 1989).

Past generations of queer youth had no media images, no role models, and no community in which to come out. Given the intense stigma and the total lack of support, being young and queer would have been overwhelmingly unsafe. As Henderson (1998) noted, the well-known group PFLAG (Parents, Families, and Friends of Lesbians and Gays) commonly assisted families with queer children over 20, but queer youth under the age of 15 were simply unheard of 10 to 15 years ago. Many people waited to deal openly with their sexual identities until well into their twenties when they had the emotional, physical, and financial resources of adults.

Youth today are also more likely to be drawn to and feel a part of the gay, lesbian, bisexual, and transgendered community even before they experiment in romantic and sexual relationships (Dube, 2000). This was impossible for earlier generations when no such community existed. Individuals and couples were left to explore sexuality in isolation. Now the ways out of the closet are more numerous and complex. For youth who are *identity-centered* rather than sex-centered, the sexual minority label is not strictly about sexual behavior. It is an identity—i.e., a community of people where they feel a sense of familiarity and belonging.

Most research suggests that youth are more likely to come out to peers before they come out to their families (Boxer et al., 1991; D'Augelli et al., 1989; Savin-Williams, 2001). Youth are more likely to come out to a same-age peer, and this experience of disclosure is likely be a catalyst for further disclosures to family and other friends (Boxer et al.). Peers are important to all adolescents as they begin development of their adult identity and individuate from their families. Peers may be especially important to queer youth, who often feel isolated from parents and friends whom they are afraid will not understand or will reject them once they know about their sexual identity. Savin-Williams (1990) interviewed 14- to 23-year-old queer youth and found that 57% of them said that the most important person in their life was a gay or lesbian friend.

COMING OUT TO FAMILY

The process of coming out to one's family creates pivotal moments of interaction in a queer youth's life trajectory. Regardless of whether the youth chooses to come out, is found *out* in an accidental way, or is not out, the negotiation itself is memorable. Development is determined to a large degree by what has previously transpired in an individual's life, including genetic predispositions, environmental events, and their interaction. Yet, within any life history, turning points or critical incidents occur that set particular developmental processes or transitions in motion. For many sexual minority youths, one of these is their parent's discovery of the youth's sexuality (Savin-Williams, 2001, p. 9).

Coming out to one's family is a developmental milestone that may or may not occur in a queer person's life. LaSala (2000) suggested that a gay man or lesbian who never comes out to family may never achieve full emotional maturity. Green (2000), on the other hand, stated that the research is inconclusive about whether coming out to family is always in an individual's best interest in terms of his or her psychological maturity. There are many queer people living full and satisfying lives, embedded in rich and supportive communities, who are not out to their families.

When youth come out to their families, they risk a great deal. Adolescents who live at home are dependent on their families for physical and emotional support. If they misjudge their parents, they have a great deal to lose. This suggests the intensity of the conflict—to be a fraud who has a home, food, and safety, or to risk being more individuated but lose safety. There are risks and consequences either way (D'Augelli et al., 1989; Henderson, 1993). Comfort from these sources of support and validation is crucial for adolescents, especially queer adolescents who need this to protect themselves from the overwhelming social and cultural stigma. However, isolation from this comfort and protection is what youth risk when they come out. Unlike members of ethnic, religious, or racial minorities, queer youth cannot and do not expect their families to accept or tolerate their identity, much less help them nurture it.

Research suggests that children often withdraw from families rather than risk outing themselves and disappointing their parents or being rejected, abandoned, or abused (D'Augelli et al., 1989; Savin-Williams, 1994). Some research suggests that youth who have close relationships with parents tend to come out younger to their families (Beaty, 1999). Other research suggests that some children who are close with their parents may avoid and withdraw more than youth who are not close because losing their parents' support would be more devastating to a youth who was used to relying on it in times of stress (Waldner & Magruder, 1999). This leaves them isolated and without the support they are craving but protects them from outright rejection. Parents do reject their children; evidence shows they may be kicked out of the home (Boxer et al., 1991), ridiculed (Saltzburg, 1996; D'Augelli, 1995), or cut off (Strommen, 1989). This is what youth weigh when they are deciding to come out to their families.

When they do decide to risk exposure, queer youth are more likely to come out to their mothers than to their fathers, reporting better relations with their mothers and fearing retribution from their fathers (Ben-Ari, 1995; Boxer et al., 1991; D'Augelli et al., 1989; Savin-Williams, 1990, 2001). When queer youth come out to their parents, their motivations and timing are usually multidetermined. Reasons include the desire to be honest and reduce the strain of deception, increased confidence and self-esteem resulting from self-acceptance, and anger (Boxer et al., 1991). There is also evidence that coming out to parents can be a source of self-esteem for some queer youth (Savin-Williams, 1989a, 1989b, 2001), although other research suggests that there is a higher incidence of suicide attempts by youth who disclose to families (D'Augelli et al.).

Although hiding oneself from family members is stressful, for some youth coming out to parents can cause greater conflict and distress (Savin-Williams, 1990; Troiden, 1989). Minority youth seem to bear a special burden, as there is some evidence to suggest that when they come out to parents, family ties to ethnic, racial, or religious communities make it difficult for the parents to accept their youth's experience of him- or herself. This leads to angst, with some youth feeling alienation or pressure to choose between being a sexual or ethnic minority. Other youth choose to alienate themselves from ethnic ties, hoping to avoid and protect their families from shame (Tremble, Schneider, & Appathurai, 1989; Dube & Savin-Williams, 1999).

The implications of coming out go far beyond one's individual sexual identity (Weston, 1991). Coming out to relatives does introduce sexual behavior as a topic, but mostly it demands the negotiation or renegotiation of family connections. The naming of relationships, who calls whom what, and who is part of the family and who is not define how we are all connected. How an individual comes out in his or her family can also set the stage for how the family will later incorporate a partner (Laird, 1993).

PARENT REACTIONS TO COMING OUT

Queer individuals usually wait a number of years after they know they are a sexual minority to tell a family member. Once they disclose, however, youth often forget that their own adjustment period took some time, and expect their parents to adjust quickly and take it in stride. Queer youth often have unrealistic expectations of their families, failing to take into account the time needed after disclosure for the family to acquire information, assess this new reality, and reexamine the internal assumptions they have lived with for years. Youth further overestimate their parents' awareness and knowledge of sexual minority issues, probably because their own senses are so heightened and honed to pick up this information (Henderson, 1993).

When parents do learn about their child's sexual minority status, a process that some have compared to that of grief occurs (Radowsky & Siegel, 1997). Some parents struggle with initial feelings of grief over losing the life hopes they had for their child, and some report feeling guilty and wonder what they did to cause their child's sexual minority status (Robinson, Walters, & Skeen, 1989). Ben-Ari found that parents who perceived that their child's motivation for disclosing was to be more honest were significantly more accepting. He also found that not having experience with homosexuality was the most consistent predictor of difficulty for families after the initial disclosure from their children. Ben-Ari (1995) also found that when youth disclose and then describe positive feelings about their identity it is easier for their parents to adjust.

Stage theories of coming out as a sexual minority predict that disclosing to family members is a crucial developmental task (Cass, 1979; Troiden, 1989) that can have powerful consequences for the entire family. LaSala (2000) likened the coming out process to a family crisis. Beeler and DiProva (1999) explored what happens for families in the long term following disclosure of a sexual minority youth. They found that families face a two-fold dilemma: First, they must deal with their own heterosexist thoughts, beliefs, and values; second, they must deal with the heterosexism of their extended families, communities, religious groups, and cultures. Beeler and Diprova found that the metaphor of grieving can be helpful to families, yet their research suggests that grieving is only one of many themes they found present for families. By focusing on grieving as a universal theme for families (Collins & Zimmerman, 1983; Devine, 1984; Mattison & McWhirter, 1995), clinicians may be trying to fit a square peg in a round hole and may be missing more helpful entry points into the family dialogue.

Many researchers and theorists have suggested that a coming out process exists for family members after they discover their youth's sexual minority status (Boxer et al., 1991; Devine, 1984; LaSala, 2000; Robinson et al., 1989; Savin-Williams, 2001; Switzer & Switzer, 1980). After the initial shock, which may be filled with disappointment and worry, parents report learning from their children about what it means to be queer. They become socialized by their children, who introduce them to a gay and lesbian community that presents opportunities to see and hear normalizing messages, as well as the possibility to experience gay and lesbian life firsthand. This socialization may in turn facilitate parents' coming to know or know anew the child they may have felt alienated from. Parents may begin to restructure their hopes, dreams, and expectations, changing from those that assumed heterosexuality to those that do not (Boxer, Cook, & Herolt, 1989; LaSala, 2000; Strommen, 1989).

HOW SEXUAL MINORITY YOUTH MAY PRESENT IN FAMILY THERAPY

The process of youths' coming out to their families while still living at home is so new to the family therapy field that we are just beginning to explore the ways in which they present in family therapy. We do know, however, that often there are different presenting concerns, based on the youth's stage of development. Although there is tremendous variation in how children develop into adults, late childhood to late adolescence is a time of great cognitive, emotional, moral, physical, and sexual development for queer as well as heterosexual youth. Some refer to the development from childhood to adulthood as the "adolescent tunnel." But the tunnel is porous: Information gets in and out, and parents, therapists, and other adults still have a great deal of impact. At late childhood, children enter the tunnel. This usually coincides with the beginning of adolescence, some hormonal or physical changes, and, for some queer youth, a pronounced sense that they are different from the heterosexual mainstream. Early adolescence, then, is the time when many youth come into themselves.

As they move deeper into the tunnel, adolescents become preoccupied with their peer group, with fitting in, with not being so involved with their families, and, for some, with the knowledge that they really don't fit in at all. Middle adolescence, smack dab in the center of the tunnel, is the time when many secondary sexual characteristics emerge and queer youth acknowledge on some level that they have attractions that are out of the ordinary. Most youth who, in middle adolescence, acknowledge their sexual attraction have known for a while that they are different. With the advent of intellectual skill development in adolescence, secondary sexual characteristics, and access to information, they are able to find a label for what they have already known. Late adolescence is usually marked by coming out of the tunnel, becoming hormonally more balanced, and attaining a understanding how they fit in their environments. Although sexual identity is never stable, by late adolescence, youth most likely have done a great deal of internal exploration, and have formed a grounded sense of their own identity.

Late Childhood and Early Adolescence

First person narratives (e.g., Feinberg, 1993; Heron, 1994; Owens, 1998) suggest that youth who show signs of minority gender and/or sexual identity status to their families in late childhood and early adolescence are often referred for individual therapy. The research and our own clinical experience suggest that youth who come out to supportive families during late childhood and early adolescence (approximately ages 10–13) are an exception and often not seen in family therapists' offices except for consultation purposes. Youth who are comfortable enough with their own status to talk with their parents about it at this stage are already immersed in environments that nurture them. Conversations about sexual identity have been commonplace in their homes. Usually they are closely involved with queer people, it is an accepted lifestyle, their religious community is progressive, their culture manages (as opposed to pathologizes) sexual minority status, and their families have nurtured their youth to be true to themselves. Although these families may not need help from therapists, they may seek support and consultation. Some members may mourn the loss of a typical youth and work through that loss with a therapist. But these families rarely make it into therapists' offices for difficult dialogues.

In some families, parents believe they know about their children's sexual minority status before the youth is aware that homosexuality is even a possibility. Gender variant children often indicate homosexuality to these parents. Some research suggests that atypical gender behavior in children sometimes leads to homosexuality, but there is by no means a 100% correlation (Savin-Williams, 1998). Parents may seek therapy to discover if their youngsters are gay. We do not recommend asking early adolescents about their sexual preference before they have some knowledge of their own preference. The discovery of one's sexual identity is a unique process for each individual. Because there is such a profound stigma associated with being different in our culture (particularly at this stage of development) and there is such shame attached to the process, openly acknowledging the possibility of being queer at this stage of development is a tender position.

Some parents may show great concern about the possibility that their child is not gender typical and present in therapy at this stage to change the child. Usually parents are not completely honest, even to themselves, about why they are concerned, and deny that it has anything at all to do with fear of their youth's sexual identity. Their child is atypical, the parents have tried to get him or her to conform, they believe there is something essentially deviant about the child, and they feel helpless in their attempts to have an impact. The youth knows that she or he is a disappointment and is troubled. The youth may show signs of depression, have difficulty in school, or act out in disruptive ways.

Middle Adolescence

Regardless of their sexual and gender identity, by the time youth have reached middle adolescence (approximately 14–16), they have learned that it is not cool to be different. *Queer* and *fag* are names that most kids use to describe kids who are different. Most boys in middle school get called *fag* at least once, no matter how progressive adults believe the environment to be. With many queer boys, the label sticks. Girls are less likely to be called names; instead, they are shunned from peer groups. No matter how hard they try to hide, the scent of difference smells strongest in middle school. Middle school usually coincides with youth being in the middle of the tunnel. This is the time when it is most important to fit in and kids are least likely to share what went on during the day with their families. Instead, they act out. Although most adolescents in environments that are not conducive to coming out hide their true selves, some youth *crash out*. Crashing out is the process of loudly identifying as different and difficult, regardless of whether that is really true. These youth are usually part of the controversial peer group in middle and high school. They are brought into therapy not because of anything having to do with sexual orientation but rather because they are troubled.

Queer youth most often come from families who are dissimilar to them. Unlike other oppressed minorities in our culture, most queer kids have no family role models to show them the ropes. Heterosexual parents who are supportive are still at a disadvantage, because unlike ethnic, racial, and religious minorities they do not know firsthand what it is like to be queer. It can be confusing even for parents who do want to be responsive to know how to inoculate their children against the onslaught of oppression. These youth need help to prepare, and they expect their parents to be role models of how to deal with oppression and how to survive (Saltzburg, 1996). Unfortunately, many queer youth grow up in enemy territory. And when they become conscious of the fact that the playground is a war zone, they are more than likely to keep this to themselves. To fit in, the only goal of middle adolescence, they must hide. To hide, they numb themselves from pain, knowledge of self, and their friends and families. The adolescent task of self-discovery goes unattended to, as queer youth must subjugate knowledge of self, particularly in families that pathologize homosexuality. This subjugation can lead to difficulty in other areas of functioning, which brings the youth into therapy (Owens, 1998). Sexual minority youth who present in family therapy at middle adolescence, usually, present with other concerns, such as school problems, harassment by peers, depression, anger, and withdrawal.

Parents who bring youth at this age into therapy are often terrified about their child's behavior, although the fear may present itself as anger or helplessness. They are afraid for their child's physical and psychological safety, and they are often afraid that any intervention on their part will exacerbate the situation. A youth's sexual identity status may be the presenting problem, may be one of the presenting problems, or may not come up at all. If parents are strongly homophobic and have some inkling that their youth is not heterosexual, they may seek conversion therapy. Some may ask specifically for conversion therapy whereas others may want a therapist to fix their deviant child, believing that their youth's sexual identity is one of a myriad of mental illnesses afflicting him or her.

Late Adolescence

Many queer youth have not yet come into themselves at this age. Some are out to a few of their peers and come to therapy with families who have no idea about their adolescent's sexual minority status. Others have come into themselves and present as sexual minorities when seen individually in therapy but have not told their families. Youth may or may not present in therapy as sexual minority individuals in late adolescence (approximately 17–19). Although cultural mandates are organized around family, ethnic, religious, and cultural environments, coming out is greatly affected by peer group affiliation. As a matter of fact, when interviewed, most queer youth say that a sexual minority peer is the most important person in their life (Savin-Williams, 1990). A queer youth's choice of peer group is influenced by all sorts of variables other than sexual orientation, but openness about a minority sexual orientation in adolescence may have something to do with group status in addition to family environment.

By late adolescence, youth have developed a different relationship with their families. Most have independent thoughts and feelings, while still living at home and financially dependent. This independence has more to do with coming out of the tunnel of self-discovery than with independence from relationships with family. Late adolescents may seek therapy on their own and may or may not want help with family issues. Others are urged into therapy by their parents, who are concerned about the "stranger" living in their house who used to be their child. Queer youth may want help navigating the coming out process and they will seek a therapist who can support them and nurture their growth.

COMING OUT IN THERAPY

The ways out of the closet now are more numerous and more complex. Although youth may seek individual therapy to help with the coming out process (Owens, 1998), they may also be attending family therapy sessions without being acknowledged as sexual minority. Many times minority sexuality never comes up unless youth themselves bring it into the therapy room, usually in times of crisis. When queer youth are finally acknowledged, their sexual identity often becomes the problem in therapy. They may be questioned by parents and therapists alike about what caused their queerness, how they know they are queer, and whether it is just a passing phase. In an effort to be helpful, therapists may attempt to convince youth of their open-mindedness rather than simply being open-minded. Or we tell queer youth that being gay is acceptable, not realizing that we have just made it unsafe for them to tell us about their own feelings of disgust. Other times we may attempt to get youth to label themselves in ways that help us make sense of their lives. We recently worked with a 19-year-old who, at 14, knew she felt different and was taken by her mother to a therapist who labeled her as *transgendered* because of her masculine appearance. At 19, she knew she was sexually attracted to women and not men, but she had been boxed into the *transgendered* label. It took months in therapy for her to admit that she questioned whether in fact she was transgendered.

Youth may come out to parents while living at home or parents may discover a youth's minority status accidentally. Either mode of disclosure may force a family into therapy, because the parents want help supporting their child or because the parents do not accept the youth's disclosure and want help changing the youth or themselves. Some families come to therapy for other reasons and discover a youth's sexuality in the course of therapy because an environment in which they can be honest with each other has been created. For some families this produces a crisis;

for others it does not. Like Savin-Williams (2001), who suggested that youth do not fit into predetermined stages of identity development, we find that families process their youth's sexual identity in unique ways that depend on the family's character and particular life circumstances.

OUR FIVE CASE STUDY EXAMPLES

Like all queer kids, each of the youth we present in this book had her or his own trajectory of identity development related to peers, family, and the process of family therapy.

JOEY PETERSON (16) was quiet and had a few close male friends in early and middle adolescence but was not nearly as social as his older brother, Matthew. By late adolescence, when Joey began to come into himself, he stopped being comfortable around other boys and became more of a loner, preferring to practice piano rather than be with people. Because his older brother was so popular and Joey was friendly enough at school, he was not picked on and was left alone. He figured out he was gay by surfing the Web for information about why he felt so different. He also knew he had a gay uncle, who was talked about openly at home, though his nuclear family had no contact with him. He became close to a few girls in his Spanish class and told one of them about his sexual identity long before he told anyone else. She came out as a lesbian a few years later. He came out to his parents during the course of therapy and gradually told a few other female friends in high school before he graduated.

DEVIN NOLAN (15) had a negative relationship with almost everyone in his public school career. He was marginalized by most of the children and pathologized by most of the school staff and faculty. His family moved frequently during his younger years, and by high school he had a few other marginalized acquaintances who did not know him very well. Devin could not remember a time when he didn't know he was different. When he wasn't being ignored, he was made fun of and called names. Kids made fun of his sexual and gender identity as well as his social awkwardness. He always felt like he was from another planet, but, because of the chaos in his family, he was unable to figure out what part of feeling different was attributable to his gender and sexual identity and what was attributable to his unstable environment. His mother brought him to therapy because she felt he was self-destructing and she did not know how to help.

JANA MARNI (15) was a controversial figure in her high school. Being overweight, artistic, and male identified, Jana did not fit in with any girl group and spent most of her time with a few boys who did not fit in either. They dressed in Goth fashion, dyed their hair, and tattooed and pierced their bodies. Jana was filled with hatred about her sexual orientation and had a hard time adjusting to knowledge about herself that had been obvious to her for a long time. She did not come into herself until she had a sexual experience with a girl. Once she came in, she was openly affectionate with her girlfriend at school. Because most of the kids in high school already thought Jana bizarre, coming out as a lesbian in school was for her just another statement about her counterculture views.

TANYA EDWARDS (14) was in the theater crowd in middle and high school and, because she physically matured earlier than most of her elementary school friends, was friends with older kids. While she was still in middle school, her friends were in high school and openly discussing gay, lesbian, and bisexual topics. She had always been attracted to both boys and girls and did not hide those feelings. By eighth grade, everyone at school who knew

Tanya also knew that she was a bisexual, and proud of it. She seemed to come in to herself and out to others at the same time.

MICHAEL SMITH (17) thought of himself as a nerd. He was picked on throughout his childhood, was raped, and retreated into depression by the time he was in high school. He played computer games and surfed the Web when he wasn't sleeping. He was not close to his family, who left him alone because they thought that was what you were supposed to do with adolescent boys. Because he did not have a peer group with great influence over him, he felt he had more freedom to make decisions about his identity at an earlier age. He told no one about his status but did not hide either.

LABELING AND GENDER IDENTITY DISORDER

Unfortunately, the diagnostic labeling of sexual minority individuals is still quite common. As noted earlier, in the first edition of the *DSM*, published in 1952, homosexuality was listed as a psychiatric disorder. By 1968, it was classified in the revised edition as a sexual deviation. After much debate and intense lobbying from gay and lesbian activists in the early 1970s, homosexuality was replaced by *sexual orientation disturbance,* a term describing those who were distressed by their same sex attractions and desires. In *DSM-III*, sexual orientation disturbance was replaced by *ego-dystonic homosexuality,* and in the *DSM-IV*, the term *homosexuality* does not appear at all. A remnant of these earlier diagnoses remains in *DSM-IV* under the category of psychiatric illness known as "gender identity disorder" (GID) in children, and may still imply that homosexuality is a deviance in children who show signs of nonconformist gender identity. GID is used to diagnose both sexual minority youth and transgendered youth because, although these are discrete identities, they both do not conform to social ideals.

The criteria for GID are problematic because they are based on the assumption that there are two discrete genders and that there is a clear distinction between what boys do and what girls do in terms of how they dress, act, play, and choose playmates. In this framework it can easily be considered pathological for a girl to act like a boy or vice versa. The guidelines suggest that in order to be labeled with GID there must also be intense discomfort and distress. The distress that many young people diagnosed with GID report is with the surrounding environments that are continually reactive and hostile to them.

Furthermore, GID is a deceptively broad diagnosis that can include youth who believe they are the other biological sex, those who want to be the other sex, and those who are more comfortable acting out their gender identities in ways that are atypical for their biological sex. In fact, young people diagnosed with GID often grow up to identify as homosexual rather than transsexual, "meaning that it might not be 'gender' identity dysphoria that is being identified but early manifestations of sexual orientation diversity. This raises a red flag about the treatment of potentially prehomosexual children in a psychiatric system that supposedly does not identify homosexuality as a disorder" (Istar-Lev, 2004, p. 176).

SPECIAL ISSUES IN TREATMENT:
TRANSGENDERED YOUTH AND THEIR FAMILIES

Transgendered (trans) youth transgress similar gender and sexuality boundaries, and therefore face many of the same developmental and family dilemmas as gay/lesbian/bisexual youth. Youth in both groups are assumed to be things they are not: Gay, lesbian, and bisexual youths are assumed to be heterosexual; trans youth are assumed to have an internal sense of themselves that matches their external male or female body.

Gender identity and sexual orientation are closely linked yet distinct. Queer youth themselves do not know how they will end up identifying. Some queer youth begin by identifying themselves as gay or lesbian, process this, and end up identifying as trans. This can also happen in reverse. The process of identifying oneself is ongoing and can shift many times. Queer youth, whether they self-define as gay or as transgendered, share the experience of having to come to terms with pieces of their identity that are despised in the culture around them.

Although it is difficult to discuss differences between trans and other sexual minority youth without categorizing, dichotomizing, or labeling, there are some differences worth mentioning. Before discussing those differences, we must reiterate that gender and sexual identity are not the same thing. Although trans people may first present as gay or lesbian, it is often because they have been acculturated with the stereotypes of effeminate gay men and masculine lesbians. Whom you are attracted to sexually and whom you feel yourself to be gender-wise are certainly connected but definitely not the same. It is one thing to be a man attracted to other men. It is quite another to be a biological man attracted to other men as a woman. This can be complicated and hard to grasp and yet, for individuals experiencing this, nothing is more basic. It is quite simply a difference between one's own internal knowledge about self (gender identity) and one's internal knowledge about who one is attracted to (sexual identity).

Trans people currently seem to be more threatening to the general public than gay, lesbian, and bisexual people. When someone has a penis and says that she is a female, it is hard to know how to respond. It chips away at very fundamental ways in which we organize the world. We expect men to act masculine and attract women. When a man acts effeminate we expect him to be gay, not insist he is a she. We might call these people deluded, but most are not. They are not suggesting they are physically not their biological gender, merely that in their heart, deep within their soul, they are the opposite of what their biological sex suggests. How can this be argued? How can one know what lies in the soul of another being? Who gets to decide what it means to be or feel feminine/female or masculine/male? These are questions that surface when trans people challenge the ways people make sense of the world. Bornstein articulated the dilemma that transgendered people experience: "It was a strange kind of lie. It was a lie by action—I was always acting out something that everyone assumed I was. I wonder what it would have been like if someone had come along and in a quite friendly manner had asked, Well young one, what do you think you are: a boy or a girl? What would it have been like not to have been afraid of getting hit because of some wrong answer?" (1994, p. 9).

Transgendered people may have histories of gender variant childhoods. Gender variant children may begin to express their variance at very young ages even beginning as early as age 2 or 3 and they frequently are clear and very matter of fact about their identity (Istar-Lev, 2004). In our experience, transgendered individuals report having had a surprisingly consistent belief as young children that they *were* the opposite sex and being forthcoming about their desire to behave, be seen, and be validated as this sex. However, this desire often goes underground for a period of time because the social sanction against it is so strong. Unlike gay youth who can stay closeted, trans youth have a more difficult time hiding. As they begin to explore their identities many begin to dress, act, and live as the opposite gender. Initially the crossdressing may be laughed off as a joke but as this transition persists or intensifies it becomes embarrassing and finally viewed as outright disturbing by many families.

A relatively new treatment population for family therapists, trans youth are more complex to treat than are transgendered adults. The difficulty is in deciding how far a youth can or should pursue the gender transition while below the age of consent. Some youth merely want a safe refuge to discuss their feelings of being transgendered. It can be quite intimidating to be surrounded by people who are so clear about being males or females when you yourself are not clear. Other youth come in because they are being harassed and are experiencing the anxiety and depression that often accompany a stigmatized existence. These youth may be forthcoming about why they are being targeted ("I am a girl in a boy's body") or they may not feel ready or able to discuss this more clearly ("I don't fit in, they call me names, I don't like doing what they do"). Still other youth may be coming to therapy to get help in beginning their transition process.

Because treatment of transgendered, or gender variant individuals (diagnostically labeled GID) is complex, experts advocate the Harry Benjamin Standards (Benjamin, 1998) as a minimum of care. They are as follows:

The Adult Specialist

The education of the mental health professional who specializes in adult gender identity disorders rests upon basic general clinical competence in diagnosis and treatment of mental or emotional disorders. Clinical training may occur within any formally credentialing discipline—e.g., psychology, psychiatry, social work, counseling, or nursing. The following are the recommended minimal credentials for special competence with the gender identity disorders:

1. A master's degree or its equivalent in a clinical behavioral science field. This or a more advanced degree should be granted by an institution accredited by a recognized national or regional accrediting board. The mental health professional should have documented credentials from a proper training facility and a licensing board.
2. Specialized training and competence in the assessment of the *DSM-IV/ICD-10* sexual disorders (not simply gender identity disorders).

81

3. Documented supervised training and competence in psychotherapy.

4. Continuing education in the treatment of gender identity disorders, which may include attendance at professional meetings, workshops, or seminars or participating in research related to gender identity issues.

The Child Specialist

The professional who evaluates and offers therapy for a child or early adolescent with GID should have been trained in childhood and adolescent developmental psychopathology. The professional should be competent in diagnosing and treating the ordinary problems of children and adolescents. These requirements are in addition to the adult specialist requirement.

Intervention

There are currently three lines of thinking around clinical intervention for children diagnosed with GID (Swann & Herbert, 1999). The first and still most prevalent is intervention designed to "fix" children so that they begin to act, dress, and live as the appropriate sex. These interventions tend to be very behaviorally focused, where desired behaviors are rewarded and unwanted responses are suppressed. It is important to note that this continues to be the standard approach for youth diagnosed with GID despite the fact that there is little evidence to suggest that it actually succeeds in obtaining the intended outcome (Istar-Lev, 2004).

The second theory of intervention is to support the child and family as they deal with the day-to-day issues of gender variation. The third line of thinking, beyond the scope of this book, is physical intervention in consultation with a mental health specialist. It is in the second line of thinking that the majority of family therapists can be and ought to be helpful.

Clinicians must be able first to identify who is in the most distress about the child's gender variance—the child, the family, or the school or community? Usually there is some measure of tolerance for cross-gender behavior, so it is important to know not only who is in distress but what specific issue or behavior is causing the distress. By helping family members air their concerns, a thoughtful therapist can assist them in a course of action that will be supportive and protective of the child and the family. For example, in one case a school was uncomfortable with a young boy wanting to exchange clothes with girls in his class so that he could wear their dresses. During therapy family members were able to work out a plan where the child could dress how he pleased at home but would agree to not dress in skirts at school.

Trans youth may present for therapy with a supportive parent looking for help or an unsupportive parent who wants the child fixed. In both situations, we are curious about the experiences of all family members and work within the same guidelines we use when treating queer youth. Particular issues are often more pronounced with trans youth than with other sexual minority youth. Because trans youth are often more provocative, we frequently find ourselves problem solving and advocating more actively than in other family therapy situations. We help define what family members are most worried about. If the safety of their youth is at issue, we help the family establish some rules they can all live with about ways to act, dress, and behave at home and in public. Most of the time young people are very clear about who is upset the most and what the consequences are of transgressing gender expectations. Because of this, youth can be brought in to a discussion of how to balance their needs with the needs of the people around them.

A growing number of young trans people are on their own—kicked out from their homes or ostracized until they leave. In these situations, it is often necessary to use crisis management techniques to find supportive environments and safe housing. We can then begin to create a crucible of refuge as they explore their development. Our hope is that at some point, youth can reconnect to family, if this is done safely.

Trans youth often need even more help than other sexual minority youth in advocating for their needs. Schools are beginning to have acceptance coalitions for gay and lesbian students, but coalitions that include trans young people are still a long way off. Dealing with hostile environments is usually the most difficult problem for trans youth. Parents are often embarrassed and confused by their youth, and peers are threatening and violent. School officials are ill-equipped to handle issues like what bathroom trans youth can use and what pronouns to use when referring to them.

We recommend that family therapists become advocates for trans youth. It can be immensely helpful to set up meetings with schools, teachers, and community organizations to help grease the wheels of communication between family and community, as well as to help inform, inspire, and challenge when it is needed. We have met with school personnel on behalf of our transgendered clients and have been pleasantly surprised with their openness toward attempting to find solutions to problems that affect these students. Important questions to pose when meeting with school and community members are: Who are the rules/policies protecting? and What are the unintended affects on the environment? More directly, school and community members must address: Is a gender variant youth going to disrupt other children? Could the child simply live as the opposite sex despite what school records show? What bathrooms should they use? What should be done about gym class? What about harassment?

In the name of "protecting" children we may avoid discussing difficult topics with them—missing out on the opportunity to teach them about our values and include them on problem-solving and community building. We should not miss this opportunity.

I (RGH) worked with a biological female youth, who was passing as a male. "She" desired to be treated as such in school but felt this was impossible because her school records listed her as female. Every time a new student confused her as a boy, a teacher was ready to correct the student ("no, she is a girl") out of empathy for my client, not realizing that she really wanted to be referred to as a boy. My client, for her part, believed that because her school records reflected that she was a girl, standing up for herself would make her stand out as a "freak." She had been shuffled from school to school, had experienced many negative social interactions, and was afraid that standing out as a freak would mean not being able to finish high school. Therefore she felt unable to say, "No, I'm a boy." When I talked with the school and proposed the idea that school officials and teachers begin to treat my client fully as a male, they were worried about how she would feel but otherwise open to the idea.

We have learned from our work with trans people that there are as many genders as there are people who have them. We all have a gender identity that develops throughout our lives. Adolescence is a time when development around sexuality and gender happens in great leaps and bounds. Gender variant people go through this crucial developmental period struggling with the dissonance between what the culture tells them they are and whom they feel themselves to be internally. If you are a woman, imagine how you would feel if you were told forcefully and repeatedly that you are a man. If you are a man, imagine being told again and again that you are a woman. You can begin to understand the conflict this would create—the hiding, the shame, and the turmoil. Should you act how you feel or act how you know they want you to be? The trans youth and trans adults we have worked with have reported that the intensity of the differentness they felt began very young. Gay and lesbian youth tend to feel different even as young children but hit real trouble during adolescence, when their latent sexual desires underscore the way they are different. Young trans people, however, begin to transgress gender boundaries at a very young age. Picked on, humiliated, and abused, they learn the hard way that this is how we keep people in line about gender beliefs. Family therapists with a systemic understanding of relational dynamics and knowledge of queer theory can help.

CONCLUSION

Queer youth are growing up in families, towns, and cultures quite dissimilar from one another. Regardless of these differing environments, all youth move along a developmental tunnel from childhood to adulthood. Although each youth's passage is unique, all of them enter the tunnel with toxic messages about gender and sexual minority identity. Some have heard these messages directly from family members, their peers, or religious study. Others have heard these messages indirectly, via the presupposition that they were heterosexual. While youth are learning about themselves, they are learning that parts of who they are may be unacceptable.

Regardless of how youth and their families present in therapy, our task is the same: We have to be open to the possibility, at all times, that there are people in the room who have knowledge about themselves that they believe is too toxic to share. We also have to believe that this knowledge, when explored, actually helps individuals and families. For families to nurture each other, we must create space for them to share knowledge and beliefs that may be different from their expectations. We must create a refuge, a therapeutic context, in which new knowledge is tolerated.

CHAPTER 3

Creating Refuge

Creating refuge is the process of organizing therapeutic environments so that families are able to be more honest with each other in a way that facilitates intimacy and nurtures queerness. To create such environments, therapists become conduits of the intimate interaction. It is through our facilitation of these environments that families learn how to become therapeutic presences for each other. This is the beauty of family therapy. When a therapist can provide an environment rich in healing potential, families follow. Therapists lend their presence to families until families can provide these environments on their own. Our reliance on underlying family therapy principles and our understanding of queer theory have helped us create these environments.

BEGINNING THERAPY

When a parent who is concerned about a youngster calls, we ask the caller who else is helping raise the youth and whether the parent believes that she or he can give us an accurate sense of how she or he sees the problem with the other caregiver in the room. If the parent indicates that that would be possible, we ask that the caller come to therapy with whoever else is raising the youngster. Together they can give us a detailed sense of how they understand the problem, and as much historical information about the youth and their relationship with the youth as possible in one session

(Wachtel, 1994). We tell the caller that we ask parents to come without the children because we want to give them a chance to explain their concerns without having to worry about what they might say in front of the rest of the family. We also tell the caller that we will then ask the youth to come in by her- or himself, if the youth wants to, to give us a sense of how she or he understands the situation. Then we see the family together and go from there.

Our underlying family therapy principles inform the manner in which we start therapy. We attempt to send a message, as early as possible, that we will create a crucible to contain family members, that we have an inherent sense of relational dynamics, and that we respect the hierarchy in parent-child relationships, as well as the developmental trajectory of adolescence. In creating a *crucible* for families, we can confirm developing relationships, contradict relationship dynamics that are no longer useful, and continue to support family members in the process. We cannot, however, create true *refuge* for all families in therapy without also integrating queer theory into our work.

Queer theory reminds us that everyone we see in therapy enters the therapeutic encounter organized by unspoken rules around gender and sexuality, heterosexism, and homophobia. It is not enough to create a crucible that contains a family without also opening space for new ways to think about these organizing principles. As therapists, we must remind ourselves, despite how people may appear, that not everyone is heterosexual and that we are all constrained by traditional gender and sexual norms. In order to create space for people to allow themselves fuller access to self and other, we must try hard to close the door on our cultural mandates and welcome the family into therapy without them.

RESPONSIVENESS

To create refuge, we must first be responsive to the experiences of our clients and challenge the simplicity of those experiences so that they have ways to think differently about them. Responsiveness is the state of being both empathetic and stimulating. Responsiveness is different from mere confirmation. When you respond, you both confirm and simultaneously stimulate people toward more complexity. Queer theory argues that we are all far more complex than we behave. By embracing queer theory, we are able to help people view the same event or situation in different ways.

In addition to queer theory, Bloom's (1997) work with traumatized patients in inpatient psychiatric facilities has helped us define the necessary ingredients for therapeutic responsiveness. Bloom detailed the chronic hyperarousal that children experience in traumatic situations.

> One of the most essential functions of parenting is to provide children with external modulation for their internal states. To develop normally, children require exposure to environmental stress sufficient to promote skill development and mastery experiences combined with sufficient buffering to prevent them from becoming overwhelmed. Only gradually and with the responsive care of adults do children develop the ability to modulate their own level of emotional response to both events that come from outside and events that originate within their own bodies. Children cannot always soothe themselves and therefore the capacity of adults to soothe frightened, angry, or shamed children is essential to their development. Without such help, children become chronically hyperaroused and will develop a panoply of destructive symptoms and behaviors in attempts to diminish this insupportable state. (pp. 20–21)

Families with a symptomatic youth in the late childhood or adolescent phases of development, who seek therapy, are usually in crisis. If they are not in crisis, the very act of family therapy—the intense interactions that occur when family members are in the same room together without distraction—often puts them in crisis. When people are in crisis, they may act in ways that are not conducive to loving and intimate interactions. Instead, they tend to be overwhelmed and hyperaroused. To prevent this, we must provide "external modulation for their internal states" (Bloom, 1997, p. 20). To provide external modulation, we must be responsive to what they are feeling and have access to their experiences, whether they are verbalizing them or not. To be responsive, we must be empathetic. "Empathy requires that we vicariously *experience* the trauma that our patients have survived. Empathy is not conscious or willed—it just happens. It is the shattering of a barrier between two human beings that is normally present under the circumstances of our present social structure" (Bloom, p. 111).

Therapeutic responsiveness is not just an empathetic response from the therapist; it is also the stimulation of alternative responses from clients. Responsiveness requires the experience of empathy and the knowledge of individual complexity. When therapists have access to the experience of empathy and the knowledge of the possibility in the disallowed and unexplored, they can modulate and stimulate clients at the same time. A responsive position speaks to the constraints but also to the multiple possibilities inherent in each individual's repertoire. Responsiveness, in its entirety, says to individuals in therapy:

> I see you. You do not overwhelm me and I can tolerate all of you. I know you have had hurtful experiences and I know you have done things that you consider untenable. I will encourage you not to be harmful to yourself or to others. I will encourage you to move beyond what you think

you can tolerate and to trust that there are other viable ways to be in the world, and I will help you do it in a way that is loving and tender.

Responsiveness, then, is one ingredient required to create refuge in therapy.

THE PETERSONS

When Matthew was 9 and Joey was 4, the Peterson family moved upstate. Tom and Lisa had mutually agreed that they wanted to be closer to family, and when Tom was offered a transfer to an office upstate, they jumped at the chance. They chose to live in a suburb based on the reputation of the school district, found a perfect house in a cul-de-sac, and joined the church around the corner. Lisa's parents lived 20 minutes away and Tom's sister and family lived around the corner. Tom and Lisa enrolled Matthew in Little League, found a piano teacher for Joey, who was already showing signs of great musical ability, and became active volunteers in the local symphony. When Joey went to kindergarten, Lisa got her real estate license and worked part-time throughout the boys' growing years. Tom, an engineer, was promoted to vice president of the engineering firm. Although they had the usual trials and tribulations of raising children, the Petersons called themselves a happy family. When they had problems, they kept them to themselves or talked to family members for support. As far as the Petersons knew, no one in their family had ever gone to therapy, although they joked about a few of their relatives whom they knew could use it.

It was not until the fall of Joey's junior year in high school that his parents started to worry about him. He had always been quiet, reserved, and a bit socially awkward, but his grades were good and his passion for music was strong. After a meeting at the high school to hear about the college admissions process, Joey's parents came home filled with information and excited about the next step in his development. Joey blew up, stating he was not going to college, and left the room. His parents were shocked. Lisa immediately phoned a good friend who referred her to a family therapist.

Lisa called me (LSF) the next morning to ask whether she thought it would be a good idea if Joey came in to talk with someone. Lisa knew Joey would be reluctant, her husband was ambivalent, and she wanted an expert opinion. I asked her to come to therapy with her husband to give a detailed picture of the situation so that she could assess whether therapy would be helpful.

Lisa and Tom gave a detailed history of Joey, their relationship with him, and his relationship with his older brother, who was a sophomore in college. As they spoke, it was obvious that they had always been concerned about him but never enough to seek therapy, which they thought was a drastic measure.

Although Matthew was a "typical boy," Joey, according to his parents, was always a bit different. He did not play sports, had little social life, seemed to be happiest when he was playing and listening to music, and rarely did anything with the family. When asked if he was always like this, Lisa recalled an incident in fourth grade when she thought things began to change. Joey had come home from playing with some neighborhood children and he did not have his bike with him. His father was in the yard playing catch with Matthew. Tom asked Joey where his bike was and Joey said that two boys down the block wanted to ride it and he couldn't get it back. Tom called him a sissy and told him to go get the bike. Joey burst into tears, refused to get the bike, and ran inside to Lisa. Tom then had Matthew get the bike for Joey.

Lisa: I think things changed that day. Tom lost respect for Joey, began to blame me for not pushing him harder, and Joey became afraid of his dad. I'm not saying that this is the cause of his problems, but I think something changed that day in terms of the family—sort of like, Matthew became Tom's and Joey became mine.

LSF: Sometimes these things happen in families, sort of serendipitously, especially when there are two parents and two children. It just seems to make things easier, you know, if one parent is closer or more responsible for one child and the other parent is the same for the other, especially if one child shares a trait with a parent or an interest or a way of being. Often this is done along gender lines in families. So tell me about the gender roles in your family. Would you say you follow traditional gender lines or is there room in the family to explore both your masculine and feminine parts?

92

Lisa: We have tried really hard to not follow traditional gender lines. Tom has been very supportive of my need to be independent and . . .

Tom: And you have been supportive of my cooking. We have tried to raise the kids together, also, but let's face it, even if I am more involved with Matthew because of the sports, you still do the lion's share of the housework and you do much more carpooling than I do and you always know where they are and where they have to be and I can't get to most of the sporting events anyway.

Lisa: Yes, that's true, but I think, psychologically, we share the parenting, you know what I mean?

Tom: Yes.

LSF: How about nurturing the masculine and feminine parts of your sons?

Tom: What do you mean by that?

LSF: I mean, if you see behavior in either of them that is traditionally seen as feminine, are you as likely to nurture that as you are to nurture the behavior that is traditionally seen as masculine?

There was dead silence. I glanced over at Tom, who looked like a deer frozen in headlights.

LSF: Tom, I have to tell you, from over here, you look like a ghost. I wonder what just happened.

Tom: I don't think I have been very good at nurturing their femininity. As a matter of fact, I would say I was more likely to beat it out of them. I don't mean literally, but I certainly do not want my boys acting like girls.

LSF: What's the fear?

Tom: Well, to be perfectly honest, and this is really the very first time I have admitted it to myself, I don't want my kids to be gay. I know I have been afraid of this my whole life. *(Tom is sad and quiet.)* Do you think Joey is gay?

LSF: I have no idea. I have never met the boy. And if he was?

Tom: *(starting to cry)* This is like my worst nightmare. My brother is gay and he is completely alienated from the family. My parents don't talk to him, I have no idea about how he really is doing, we exchange the traditional Christmas and birthday cards but because of how our family treated him, he isn't really involved in family gatherings.

LSF: *(softly)* And you and Lisa can be different. You can be a safe haven for your boys, no matter what their path, and I will help you create this place.

I was responsive to Tom in his moment of clarity and anxiety. This was an intimate moment in that both Tom and I (and Lisa as witness) had new information about Tom and held it preciously. My responsive position, both empathetic and stimulating, allowed Tom to verbalize his anxiety. Letting Tom and Lisa know that I believed that they could create a safe haven for the boys and that I could help them with this helped to create a form of refuge in therapy.

To create a crucible for family members to work toward greater empathy with one another, we must confirm members, contradict certain behaviors, and continue to support them. To keep cultural mandates about sexuality and gender at bay, therapists use responsiveness. We empathize with the meaning that people have about certain experiences and we stimulate increased complexity of this meaning.

Responsiveness in Families

Most families who come to therapy are short on responsiveness to each other. Parents who present with youth as the concern, queer or not, are usually organized by relational dynamics and are hyperaroused (i.e., they have difficulty seeing a youth's behavior except in extreme ways) and overwhelmed (i.e., meaning that they are unable to parent in helpful ways). A youth's behavior becomes a message about self and a message about the youth, and parents are unable to provide a responsive environment that is a refuge for their family. When Joey, for example, did not want to retrieve his bike from the neighborhood bullies, his father took Joey's behavior as a personal affront to his own manhood. He was hyperaroused by Joey's behavior and overwhelmed by his own relationship to masculinity and therefore was unable to be responsive to the needs of his little boy. When therapists are responsive and create refuge, healing environments are modeled.

In families where responsiveness is practiced, parents learn to differentiate their youth's behaviors from their own perceptions of the youth's behavior so that they can stimulate different responses. Something had happened to Joey that made him afraid to confront the neighborhood boys. He was scared. Had Tom been able to create refuge for his son, he would have been empathetic and stimulating. He would have recognized Joey's fear and seen it as just that, not as an indication of Joey's disappointing interpretation of his gender script, nor as a slap on Tom's masculinity. Instead, he would have been able to recognize Joey's fear and work with him in thinking of alternative ways he could get his bike back. As Lisa and Tom began to learn more about themselves and their boys in a therapeutic environment of refuge, they became more responsive and were better able to create refuge in their family.

Ultimately the goal of all therapeutic intervention is to help create a family environment in which refuge is achieved. Family members are exposed to environments of refuge through interactions in therapy and we talk about how to carry out these interactions at home. Responsiveness is a necessary ingredient in the creation of refuge for queer youth and their families, but it alone is not sufficient. To create refuge, an attitude of critical consciousness (hooks, 1994) and a position of witnessing are also necessary.

ATTITUDE OF CRITICAL CONSCIOUSNESS

Queer theory has helped us create a therapeutic refuge for our clients because it has changed our attitudes about sexual identity and therefore about all the ways we are constrained from thinking more creatively. In her germinal work on race and culture, hooks (1984) first coined the term *critical consciousness*, challenging all of us to be hypervigilant in the ways in which we contemplate all cultural messages. For example, in the United States, the cultural message that there are two genders is deeply ingrained in our psyches. To take a critically conscious attitude,

95

we must challenge the assumption of gender dichotomy that we have been taught and accept that it is more complex than that. Not all human beings are born completely male or female, but, by the time they leave the hospital, they have been given this classification. In fact, there are some babies born neither male nor female, some born both, and some born with ambiguous genitalia (Fausto-Sterling, 2000). Because we believe that there are only two genders, our doctors and our families make decisions to perform surgery, to provide hormones, or to overlook the biological predisposition toward more complexity. We leave the hospital male or female.

Although most of us are well informed about the ways in which our culture dichotomizes gender and then devalues most of what is classified as feminine, we are blind to the ways we have internalized and therefore perpetuate these messages. We may be conscious that there are multiple ways to perform gender, but we continue to learn and teach gendered cultural messages. We teach our boys to be boys by not being girls (Rosenblatt, 1994) and we continue to devalue what is feminine. Because we live in a culture that expects us to act in gender and sexually appropriate ways, when we do not conform (and most of us do not conform 100%) we experience shame. To adopt an attitude of critical consciousness so that we can be available to create refuge for our clients, we must confront shame.

Gender Shame

Shame is the mechanism used to help us conform to cultural mandates. We learn to feel ashamed of the parts of ourselves that are in conflict with the cultural mandates and we have been taught, through shame, to silence ourselves. Gender shame is triggered by impulses and feelings we have been taught are undesirable. We learn that certain impulses, feelings, and ways of being are unacceptable, which we then generalize into us being unacceptable, and we experience shame.

Shame is a developmental process. At first, we are socialized to control our unwanted impulses, thoughts, and feelings. "You don't want to wear nail polish to school," I (LSF) tell my 6-year-old son. "The kids will make fun of you." By telling him that he does not want to wear nail polish, I am telling him that his feelings are unacceptable. Even if I use different language, he gets the same message. It is not only wrong for him to wear nail polish to school, *he* is also wrong to want to wear it to school.

At the next stage of shame development, we learn the humiliation of not conforming. "Oh, but I *do* want to wear the nail polish to school, Mommy," my son might say. "I don't care what the kids say." By early adolescence, most kids care very much. "Sissy, pussy, mama's boy"—the process of humiliation is devastating and it happens minute by minute, hour by hour, and day by day. All of us experience this process. The less we fit culturally prescribed descriptions of our gender/sexuality, and the fewer environmental protective factors (family, community, etc.) the more shame we experience. By early adolescence we have all learned how to perform our genders, and we have learned the terror and angst that accompanies unacceptable displays of our true selves. Butler (1990) described this as "gender melancholia."

At the third stage of shame development, we learn to silence the parts of us that are different from others and the parts of us we do not accept about ourselves. My son decides he doesn't really want to wear nail polish. Even if deep down inside we know what we want, or how we would like to behave, we have learned how to hide the unacceptable parts of ourselves and most of us have learned to feel bad about them as well. Because they do not fit, they must be unnatural, wrong, sinful, evil, or just plain bad. We learn then, the final stage of shame development—to numb ourselves from those parts. When we numb ourselves from parts of ourselves, we also numb ourselves from others. The shame we feel about our unacceptable parts transfers over to how we experience other people. My son has now learned that boys who wear nail polish to school are gross.

My son's distaste of boys with nail polish will probably not be a problem for him unless he becomes a family therapist who wants to create refuge for his clients or becomes the father of a boy who wants to wear nail polish. The problem with allowing shame to numb us from the untraditional parts of ourselves is that it keeps us from being completely involved with our clients. When we are ashamed of parts of ourselves that we see in our clients, we experience anxiety, which preoccupies us. When we are preoccupied with ourselves, we are less available to others.

This preoccupation occurs not only when we see parts of others in us that we have been taught are ugly, but also when we experience our own imperfections, ineffectiveness, or incompetence. As family therapists, we are supposed to be enlightened individuals. We are not heterosexist and homophobic. We accept everyone. When we experience ourselves as otherwise, shame takes over. To create refuge, we have to learn to acknowledge the ways in which we feel shame, recognize how we preoccupy ourselves because of it, and learn to accept our own impulses, feelings, and thoughts. A change in attitude requires some self-work.

Toward Critical Consciousness about Homophobia

To be critically conscious and to change our attitudes, we must first examine our attitudes and the internalized ideas about sexual identity that are commonplace among us. Most of us are homophobic and heterosexist, some of us more than others. It is the rare individual who swims in this culture of homophobia and heterosexism and stays dry. To create refuge, we need first to examine our own homophobic and heterosexist ideas and then expose ourselves to more complex ways of imagining gender and sexual identity. When we do this, we are able to challenge the ways in which our clients are organized by the cultural mandates that denigrate queer people.

THE MARNIS

The Marni family had lived in the same city all their lives. Carol met Jack in high school, but they did not start dating until they were young adults, when they met again at church. After abusing alcohol for many years, Jack found Christianity as a young adult. "I should have been left for dead, that last car accident. But something touched me that night, and, although I still want a drink every day, with Christ in my life I have not touched a drop of alcohol in 17 years." Although initially Carol's family was quite against her relationship with Jack, they came to love and cherish him through the years. Carol was an administrative assistant at the local university and Jack was an electrician for the city school district and worked part-time repairing school buses. Throughout the girls' childhood, whenever problems occurred, Jack and Carol took their concerns to the minister and to Carol's mother, with whom Carol spoke at least once a day. When Jana was 15, the school nurse asked Carol to come to the school to talk about Jana. The nurse and Carol had graduated from high school the same year and had maintained a warm acquaintance since then. The nurse was concerned about Jana's weight and general attitude. She told Carol that she should go to a family therapist. Carol was quite reluctant and it was not until the nurse called again a few months later to see if Carol had made the phone call that Carol called me (LSF) and made an appointment. She made the appointment because the nurse told her that Jana had cut a cross on her lower arm, using an exacting knife she found in her father's tool chest.

In the initial session, I saw the parents alone and they gave me a detailed history of their family, and their longstanding concerns about their daughter. I was responsive to both parents, their religiosity, and how they had both tried to be good parents. While our usual practice is to see the adolescent alone for the next session, Jack and Carol agreed that Jana could not be coaxed to come in alone so we agreed to meet as a family the following week.

The family sulked into my office and the only one to make eye contact was Carol. Jana, at 15, was short, overweight, and unkempt. Her bangs were conveniently placed over her eyes, which were already hidden by a pair of dark glasses. In her ears were earphones connected to a CD player, and a school binder covered her studded denim jacket. She could not have been more overt about her desire not to be there if she had a sign painted on her chest. Standing behind her, Jack gently nudged Jana into the therapy room, using her to shield himself in much the same way Jana used her school binder. Though I had asked the parents to bring the entire family, Carol reported that Kim had a cold, so Michelle was home watching her.

As I asked introductory questions in a warm, curious way, the parents began to soften. Jana was pretending to be asleep in the corner, though everyone knew she was listening.

LSF: So, tell me a little bit about how the relationships in this family work, like who is close to who, who hangs out together—those sorts of things.

Carol: Well, we are all close. This is a close-knit family. In terms of personality, Jack and Jana hit it off right away. They are peas in a pod—at least they used to be. They used to like doing the same things together. Both have a true fascination with anything mechanical.

Jack: Yeah, I used to take her to the shop on the weekends with me. She got really good at helping me fix the bus engines.

LSF: Used to? When did that change?

Jack: A few years ago, when she turned 11 or so, I think it was, I had to stop taking her to the shop. People started asking questions and I just thought it was time to stop. You know, it's queer to be a girl and like those things, and we are a God-fearing, normal family.

LSF: (slowly) And tell me, Jack, because I don't get it. What's wrong with being a normal God-fearing family and being queer?

The Therapist's Own Critical Consciousness

I was only able to say this to Jack because I had validated his religiosity in the first session and had begun to create refuge. I was also able to say it because I had worked through a number of my own attitudes about being queer and being "normal."

When I first began to work with queer people, I had to confront my own homophobic and heterosexist attitudes. One cannot live in our culture without some of these attitudes creeping into our consciousness no matter how enlightened one is and no matter what one's sexual orientation. Denying homophobia and hetero-sexism is like saying that when you look at someone you do not see the person's race. The very first clients I saw, over 15 years ago, that I knew were queer were a young lesbian couple. I saw them for about 6 months and as they started to feel better about their relationship, they got very affectionate in my office. I was uncomfortable. I was more uncomfortable with my own dis-comfort than I was with the open display of affection. "Come on," I'd say to myself, "you're only uncomfortable because they are a lesbian couple, so you must be homophobic and they will notice this. You must be an awful person, ineffective as a thera-pist, and not worthy to call yourself a professional. Shame on you."

In reality, I was uncomfortable because I had never seen two women express affection in that way before and because I am uncomfortable when anyone displays affection that is sexually provocative in therapy. But I was so ashamed of myself that I became preoccupied and then ineffective as a therapist. Shame was talking louder than the clients. I was not available to create refuge because I was uncomfortable with myself. My relationship with my own shame was making it difficult for me to be calm enough to see the clients in front of me.

What would have been more helpful would have been the development of a self-loving and critical view, which allows some-one to recognize his or her own discomfort. This is the first step in attitude change. *Okay, you are uncomfortable and preoccupied,* I say to myself. Just like you have been taught that women should nurture, you have been taught that men are sexually attracted to women and that women are sexually attracted to men. Even though you may know that neither of these statements is always true, it is hard not to believe them. When I saw two women express affection, it triggered a bit of panic in me.

Recognize the panic, I now say to myself. *This is unfamiliar territory. This does not make it wrong, just unfamiliar.* At this point, I have a number of choices. I can bookmark my discomfort and return to it later. I can explore the discomfort internally, or I can comment aloud on my preoccupation. The choice you make as a therapist has much to do with your own therapeutic style and the specific situation. In any case, I must ask myself what my discomfort is about. Well, first and foremost, I had never seen this before and anything new produces anxiety for me. And I had been taught that it is not natural for two people of the same gender to be attracted to each other, so it must be wrong and pathological. Also, displays of affection in therapy sexualize the therapy office in ways that I am uncomfortable with. So there are at least three different ideas I must explore within myself to decrease the likelihood that panic will take over the next time something like this happens. In order for me to be able to begin hypothesizing or asking how this behavior has meaning for my clients, I must have a grasp first on what this behavior means for me.

There are consequences to not examining your attitudes. Once we get past the shame of having attitudes that we wish we did not have and recognize that we do have these attitudes, they must be examined. Although family therapists have found ways to help families face denial and identify secrets that have trapped them in never-ending cycles of pain and bewilderment, they have been less successful at looking at the ways in which shame keeps all of us hidden. Our shame keeps parts of us hidden and keeps many of us silent. Our silence inhibits us from creating healing and intimate relationships and perpetuates the myth that what does not get talked about does not exist.

An unexamined attitude often rears its ugly head in the form of being judgmental. Depending on how you process your experiences, this judgment can be about you or about your clients.

When you find yourself judging yourself or your clients in an unfriendly fashion, bookmark it as information that needs reflection. For example, in working with queer youth and their parents, therapists often find the kids much more available to do work in therapy when their parents are not there. When the families come in and the kids sulk in the corner or project hostility, therapists find themselves irritated and judgmental. They experience the youth's hostility as pathology. "You have some serious issues," they may think to themselves. "I wonder whether you really are queer or just acting out to get attention." When preoccupied by frustration, bookmark it. Then ask yourself what you would experience if you looked past the frustration.

THE NOLANS

Julia Nolan came to see me (RGH) after hearing me speak at a community function on sexual minority youth. She was a single parent with two sons, Craig (17) and Devin (15), and was concerned about Devin. She was convinced Devin would never agree to therapy, but she needed help herself. Although soft-spoken and reserved, Julia gave me a great deal of information about herself and her family in the first session.

Julia divorced Craig and Devin's father when Devin was 2 years old, after she discovered that he had stolen money from a good friend of hers. She remarried when the boys were in elementary school. Her new husband was verbally and physically abusive to both boys and made constant references to the fact that they were "sissies" and "fairies." She left her second husband to protect her sons and moved in with her sister for a few years until she was able to buy her own place two doors down from her sister's house. Her boys were close to each other but very different. Craig was more reserved and more connected to his father, whom he continued to keep in contact with, whereas Devin stopped visiting him a few years earlier.

Julia was always concerned about Devin because his flamboyant effeminacy caused great trauma in his life. He was precocious and bossy from a very young age. While at home, he was dramatic, engaging, and practically ran the household, but Julia was always getting calls from the school about his behavior and school performance.

Julia: We've been on our own for quite some time now, so the three of us used to be pretty close, of course, we always had our moments. Recently, Devin, though, has been harder and harder to reach, for both me and Craig. For the last 6 months he has been completely out of control. It started with him skipping school whenever he felt like it to hang out with his friends. The school gave me a really hard time about it and threatened to get social services involved. I got him into counseling and they have been treating him for depression and ADHD. But I don't think that's the problem and none of that has helped. He is getting worse. He is angry all the time, impossible to live with, running away, getting involved with the police. I can't control him.

RGH: You said that you don't think that ADHD or depression is the problem. What do you think the problem is?

Julia: I think Devin is gay.

RGH: Have you asked Devin about this?

Julia: Yes. I told him it was all right and asked him if he would talk with me about it. I think he has a boyfriend, too. He told me once that he thought this one guy at school was really cute. But he just tells me to leave him alone, that none of this is my business and that he is fine. He won't talk to Craig, either, about anything.

At the time, I was cofacilitating a support group for gay, lesbian, bisexual, and questioning teens and gave Julia the information to pass along to Devin, recommending he bring a friend along if that would help him be more comfortable. The very next week, Devin showed up at the group. As he became comfortable in the group, he became very outspoken and gregarious. He shared that he was transgendered and wanted to transition to female as soon as possible. He spent a great deal of time in the group giving fashion advice and voicing his strong opinions about fashion models and the clothing of those in the support group. Though obviously very bright, he would talk of nothing but shallow and stereotypically feminine concerns.

Devin knew that I was seeing his mother in therapy and after 2 months in the support group, he finally agreed to have a session with her. When I went to the waiting room to greet Julia and Devin, I was surprised at how different Devin looked. He was slouched in the chair with a hat over his head and did not pick his head up as we moved into the therapy office.

Julia: I had to threaten Devin to come today and I told him he didn't have to talk if he
    didn't want to.
RGH: Devin, what's going on?

Devin was true to his word. He would not talk. I could not get him to say a thing until I asked his mother to leave the room.

I was frustrated. I felt I had been responsive to Devin and now he was letting me down. I found myself being triggered by thoughts. *Come on, Devin, cut me some slack here. You are making me look like a fool, and now your mother is going to think all queer people are incompetent.* I also started to judge Devin's motivation and began to feel as hopeless as his mother. It was then that I had to evaluate the situation. What was happening for me that was getting in the way of an attitude of critical consciousness? I realized that I was offering Devin something that had never been offered to me when I was young—something that I really could have used. I had created refuge for him in the support group that he did not have with his mother. Once I came to some understanding of that, I was able to see Devin more clearly.

Most kids will not tell you how they have experienced the world; they are more likely to act in ways that express those experiences. If youth stonewall in therapy, it is often because they have the experience of invalidation. We are frustrated because we have an investment in eliciting warmth between family members. When kids do not present us with any available opening in family sessions and continue to dodge parental attempts at engagement, it is a frustrating experience. To create refuge and maintain a full presence in therapy, we have to remind ourselves how invalidated the youth has been throughout her or his short life.

Creating refuge requires the full presence of a therapist who is open to examining all the attitudes that have become commonplace and invisible. Our work affords us this opportunity. We do not have to go looking for it because it comes to us. When we are preoccupied in therapy (and not because of something that is going on in our personal lives) and not available to understand how it is that our clients experience their worlds, we are probably being triggered by an unexamined attitude. Shame has kept us from examining many of these attitudes on our own. Rather than reexperience the awful feeling, we preoccupy ourselves with unhelpful thoughts and feelings. Thoughts like *I am bored, I am an awful therapist,* or *These are incurable people* hide unexamined attitudes.

An attitude of critical consciousness and an absence of shame open our hearts to individuals who are violated. When we are responsive and fully engaged, we experience strong emotions that we have learned to keep hidden and silenced. We experience all of the ways we feel shame about the parts of ourselves that are not traditional. We are reminded of those painful, lonely, and devastating experiences. We are then able to see our clients more fully as loving souls, tortured and confused in the same ways we have been. When we take the time for self-work and look critically at what we think and believe, we are responsive to ourselves and in turn able to create refuge for our clients. However, responsiveness and an attitude of critical consciousness alone are not sufficient to create refuge. For refuge to be created, therapists must also practice the art of witnessing.

WITNESSING

Weingarten (2000, 2003) coined the term *witnessing* to describe a healing process of shared meaning making, which nurtures the development of voice. Weingarten described *voice* "not as an individual's achievement of self-knowledge but, rather, a possibility that depends on the willingness of the listeners that make up the person's community. In this view voice is contingent on who listens with what attention and attunement" (p. 392). The self of the therapist—our attitudes, blind spots, and resources—affects our ability to see, hear, and know others. Therefore, in using the term *witnessing* we do not mean merely being present or observing. Instead, we use the term in Weingarten's sense in order to describe the elements of a therapeutic process where a clinician openly and vulnerably seeks to grasp and then nurture the meaning clients' are attempting to make of their own life experiences. This nurtures our clients' abilities to more fully see, hear, and understand their own lives and the lives of their intimate others.

Witnessing is more complex than confirming. When you confirm, you see and accept people as they present themselves. When you witness, you confirm and you see that what they present is all that is tolerable at present but *not* all that exists. Witnessing is an adjunct to being responsive. Whereas responsiveness is about empathy and the stimulation of different ways of being, witnessing is about hearing what has not been said, feeling what has not been felt, and seeing what has not been seen. Responsiveness creates the space for witnessing to occur, and an attitude of critical consciousness gives the therapist a way to see. So, for example, when a queer youth says it does not bother him when someone makes a gay bashing comment, a therapist who witnesses is able to be responsive to the spoken word *and* experience those words that might not yet be able to be spoken.

The process of witnessing is important in all therapies but particularly important for queer youth and their families because they are constantly being barraged with the usually negative meanings other people make of their lives. Queer youth face two kinds of assaults while attempting to make meaning of their lives. One is an active vocal denigration and ridicule. The second is a process of silencing—being ignored, not seen or heard. The combination results in a process where the meaning of a queer life is constantly cut off at the knees and actively disallowed. In this hostile environment, little room is left for the creation of their own queer voice. Creating refuge allows witnessing the beginnings of queer voice.

These assaults are traumatic for adults, but they are even more difficult for youth who are in the process of identity development. As Jack Marni, for example, made clear: If Jana were queer it would mean she was abnormal, unhealthy, and against God. This vocal denigration led to ignoring and silencing the queer parts of Jana. She could no longer go to the shop, hang out with her father, or in other ways voice or embody her queerness without making those around her nervous and uncomfortable. The meaning she could make of her life changed because of the way those around her saw her—sometimes ignoring what made them uncomfortable, sometimes denigrating her as perverted or sick.

As children, we make meaning of incidents in our lives by watching how others close to us make meaning of those incidents. Kegan (1982), a constructive-developmental theorist whose work we use to help create refuge, wrote about meaning making as the process of human development. He suggested that we make meaning collaboratively and that we need one another to help create and recreate the meaning of our lives. Children learn how to interpret their worlds by how the adults around them make meaning of certain behaviors. When clients come to therapy, they have finely developed ways to understand their lived experiences. There are multiple ways to interpret one event, but our young clients usually experience the ways they have been taught to make meaning of that event as the single truth.

In our homophobic culture, our queer youth learn that there is something wrong with the way they are and subsequently they experience shame. They do not learn that the culture is restrictive—they learn that *they* are wrong. The process of witnessing helps give voice to the shame and deconstruct the messages that youth internalize. By challenging the negative and denigrating meaning that has been articulated about the youth, therapists begin to make room for other ways to interpret the same events.

THE EDWARDS

Chris and Rona Edwards described Tanya as challenging and difficult, and Tanya readily agreed. The family was referred to me (RGH) after they had taken Tanya for ADHD testing and found she did not fit the criteria. Instead, they were told that Tanya had an attachment disorder and could benefit from family therapy. Chris and Rona were great fans of family therapy because they were convinced that therapy had brought them together from the outset. Rona, a school social worker, moved back to the upstate area when Tanya was 6 months old and Chris was in the process of getting tenure at the local university. They met at a hypnotherapy workshop in which Rona was training and Chris was participating. Chris was one of Rona's first clients in this 2-day retreat; he wanted to be cured of his procrastinating tendencies. She cured him and the rest was history.

I initially saw Chris and Rona without the children in order to gather information about the family. I learned that Tanya had a history of losses that she refused to talk about, even though her mother relentlessly encouraged her to process them. I also learned that Tanya was impulsive, quick to become angry, and spent most of her waking hours arguing with her parents. I saw Tanya alone for the second session and she corroborated her parents' opinion of the situation. In the third session, in which everyone was present, I tried to get a better sense of how the family made meaning around particular events.

RGH: So can you give me an example of a recurrent argument in the family?
Rona: I can give you a perfect example because it just happened today. Tanya got off the bus from school fit to be tied. I guess the bus driver yelled at her again, and again (*sarcastically*) Tanya didn't deserve it. So I try to explain to Tanya how she needs to be accountable for her own anger, and she starts to yell at me and we are off to the races.
RGH: Can I get your perspective, Tanya?
Tanya: My mother of course always thinks everything is my fault.

109

RGH: What happened on the bus?

Tanya: Well, my friend Miles was upset because some punk called him a fag so I took it upon myself to make things right. I started yelling at the punk, calling him names and such and the bus driver had a field day. I was just sticking up for my friend but I guess that's just not acceptable in this family.

RGH: So you were trying to support a friend in need and . . .

Chris: This is a great example because it exemplifies one of the many problems that Tanya has. She's always looking for a fight. There is always someone who is a victim that she can right some wrong for, always some crusade she can be in, some anger she can bring up to fight some battle. You'd think she had testosterone or something.

RGH: (noticing that Tanya is getting angry and on the edge of her seat, ready to continue the argument) Tanya, I am curious how you are doing?

Tanya: I'm fine, I'm used to this. It doesn't bother me.

RGH: Okay, well, I need to clarify things at this point. Bear with me, okay? I would like to slow this down a bit because it is really important that I follow this sequence of events so that I can have a clear picture of how things work in this family, but before I do this, I just want to clarify that last comment, Chris, when you said you thought Tanya had testosterone. Was that meant as a critical comment, praise, or something else?

Chris: It was a joke.

RGH: Made at whose expense?

Chris: Oh, come on. It's just that she is so bossy and she's so sensitive about her friends getting made fun of and she fights like a friggin' boy.

RGH: I have to stop things for a moment because I am stuck here on this testosterone comment. I think your utter frustration with the situation at hand and your own pain about not being able to figure out what to do got the better of you and you were hurtful to Tanya. In some ways, sort of the same thing that happened on the school bus is happening in here. You and Tanya both got angry, and were hurtful when you were frustrated with the situation at hand.

Chris: It was only a joke.

RGH: Yeah, but it was denigrating. Let's face it, you're angry and you hit below the belt. I would like to try to create an environment in here in which this doesn't happen. It probably means that I am going to have to stop action a lot but I know this is

110

what you want and what you deserve. You are angry because you don't want to see your daughter self-sabotage and you don't know what to do.

I had witnessed Tanya's experience of denigration even though she and her family were not voicing this experience. Families who raise queer children do not intentionally go out of their way to denigrate their children. Instead, they are often completely unaware of the ways in which they are making meaning of their children's differences. I remember being quite confused about my own family's values regarding sex and gender. My parents wanted me to be strong but not too strong, passive but assertive, not need a man but definitely want one. Just as quickly as she had fought for me to play football, my mother worried that I showed no interest in learning about hair and makeup, and my grandmother was horrified when I said that I had no interest in getting married. My Aunt Dorene showed great anxiety when I mentioned that I wanted nothing to do with proms. It did not occur to them that I was developing my own special brand of queer femininity. They just thought I was lazy, scared, or depressed. They did not know how to witness my queerness. They had to learn to nurture my queerness without role models, cultural support, or clarity about the possibilities.

To create refuge, therapists must be willing to be attuned to witnessing the violation that has occurred around the meaning that has been made about a youth's behavior. Weingarten (2000, p. 39) stated about clients who have experienced trauma: "If I don't tell you what I really think and feel, I will feel disconnected from you. I will end up withdrawing from you. In silence. But, if I do tell you what I really think and feel, you will withdraw from me. What I have to say is so heinous, horrible, toxic, unacceptable that you will not be able to stand me." Silence and acting out are two ways for youth to remain engaged with family members. As therapists, we must witness the meaning that has been constructed about a kid's life, as well as the impact it has, so that we can create environments in which family members can act in more loving ways. Family members often find ways to act loving when they learn how to witness each other.

Witnessing in Families

Most families who come to therapy with youth are short on witnessing. To create refuge in the family, members must learn to be witnesses to each other. They learn how to do this by experiencing a fuller and more complex picture of themselves and each other as they sit in therapy and watch how people talk in the presence of the therapist as witness. As Chris, for example, began to witness Tanya's experience of herself as he was denigrating, he was able to stop himself more readily from being hurtful to her. Often parents are completely unaware of the importance of their words, and they are unaware how they affect other members of the family. Once this is pointed out, and they experience a different way to interact, they are open to trying new behaviors.

Risks of Witnessing

When we witness the unspoken, the unheard, the unseen, and the unfelt, we risk the unknown. When we create environments where people give voice to ideas they have not spoken before, these ideas may be controversial. We cannot nurture queer youth without being responsive to witnessing, but in doing this, we also risk the chance that the families we see will have strong beliefs and views that violate others. These views and beliefs can be devastating. To create refuge, we have to be ready to bear witness to the devastation. We risk that family members fundamentally and devastatingly disagree with one another. We also risk that family members disagree with us, and also that we have done something to damage their relationship with us and with one another.

Further, we risk the possibility that we will get hurt and that we will fail to contain the therapeutic environment of refuge.

RISKING CONFLICTING VIEWS. Witnessing is not fundamentally about agreement. It provides hope when it is an inclusive process that accounts for context, and it moves beyond silencing or debate to make room for a richer understanding of meaning (Harvey, 2002). Although witnessing may not require agreement, it does require acceptance. Witnessing implies acceptance—acceptance that this is a person's life experience, acceptance of its meaning, and acceptance of the beauty of that life. Witnessing does not require agreement about this meaning, but instead demands vulnerability. Witnessing without vulnerability is merely observation, and observation is not a risky proposition.

When we witness, we pay attention to the fault lines that occur in families around intense disagreement. These fault lines provide not only the most threatening of interactions, those most likely to end in disconnection or even violence, but also the greatest opportunities for bridging gaps, for hope. If people who passionately disagree can be more present, open, and understanding of the other position, hope is created.

THE MARNIS

Jana Marni had a keen sense for how machines run and was able, at a very early age, to fix broken machinery around the house. She was also a good artist, loved to draw and paint, and doodled incessantly as a teenager. Her family valued her artistic ability and dismissed her ability to fix broken machines. Although she enjoyed fixing machines, she had internalized the shame around this interest and found it hideous. In the sixth family therapy session, Jana recounted a story from when she was 11 and her grandmother was at her house.

Jana: Remember when the dryer broke and I told Nana that I knew what was wrong with it and I could fix it and she yelled at me, "Jana, stop pretending you are a boy. God made you a girl, how dare you think you are better than God?" and no one came to my rescue? I was left hung out to dry.

LSF: (*watching Carol begin to cry*) What's going on for you, Carol?

Carol: I didn't realize this was so painful for Jana, that she still remembers it and that we didn't do anything about it.

Jack: Nana was just trying to teach you a lesson. Come on, this is not such a big deal. You really shouldn't be upset by this.

LSF: Jack, look at Jana. I understand that you believe that what Jana experienced was no big deal. For Jana, however, and for Carol, as she looks back, this was a terrible experience, one that caused a great deal of pain and continues to hurt Jana and make her feel bad about herself. Can you see this as a possibility? This idea that Jana's ways of being in this family, which could be a real gift to this family, have been rejected?

Jack: Yeah, but she shouldn't be hurt. I agree with her grandmother. It's not natural for girls to be so interested in those things.

LSF: But she is, and when you tell her it's not natural or when her grandmother appeals to God, it makes her feel bad about her interest. She is hurt just like you were hurt when you were told you were too small to play basketball or when your father demeaned you and your mother. You had so much you could have contributed to your family. You know what I mean? You were so valuable, and yet any indication that you were not quote traditionally masculine—you were cut off at the knees. Well, the same thing is happening in this family with Jana. Not only is she being told there is something wrong with her, this family is losing out by not nurturing her gifts. Hey, she could have fixed the dryer, right? And she could probably teach you all a great deal about what it would be like if we didn't have to be organized by traditional stereotypes of how we were supposed to behave. I don't think it is written in the Bible that only men can fix dryers.

Jack: Yeah, I guess I understand how she could feel that way, I just don't think she should.

LSF: I really appreciate that, Jack. You understand. That means you are available to your daughter. You don't have to agree to be available, to really hear her, which I believe you have been able to do right now. Yes, Jana?

Jana: Yeah, I guess so.

RISKING OUR OWN CULPABILITY. When we risk witnessing, we create space for the unspoken, which can then open wounds to which we must attend. Other times the risk of witnessing is in fully knowing one's own culpability. None of us are innocent of gaining privilege from heterosexism and homophobia. Even queer therapists who are active, vocal gay rights advocates have had moments when they have hidden their sexual identity in ways that many of our youth are not doing anymore. There are moments in which we smell danger and keep quiet or we do not challenge a remark because we are tired. Those of us who are heterosexual—blinded to the torturous moments of terror and shame and culpable on a daily basis to perpetuating our privilege—are often unaware of the ways in which we maintain the status quo. To be responsive to witnessing, we must have empathy for ourselves while we challenge our own simplicity by holding ourselves accountable for the ways in which we continue to value the status quo. To bear witness, we must learn to be less preoccupied with the shame that comes from our own culpability and more responsive to our own growth.

THE SMITHS

Michael Smith called my (LSF) office wanting to talk to a therapist about concerns he had about himself. He got my name from a friend in school who had seen me in therapy and felt I was a safe person to talk with. A number of years ago, Michael had been sent to therapy by his parents, hated the therapist, and told him nothing. He did not want to replicate what happened in his early teens. He had also heard that I was a family therapist and thought that he wanted, at some point, to possibly bring his parents and sister into therapy because he did not think he was the only problem in the family. In the first session, Michael revealed that he had been having sex with his best friend, James, and that James had "freaked out" and attempted suicide and was now in an adolescent psychiatric ward. Michael expressed feeling depressed and suicidal himself.

LSF: Michael, what does your family know about your relationship with James?

Michael: We haven't talked about it. I think my mom knows something out of the ordinary is going on but she refuses to see it and my dad doesn't have a clue about my life. And if he knew that I had had sex with James, he'd kill me.

LSF: Literally?

Michael: No, he just has so many stereotypes about gay people and he has already said stuff about James before that makes me sick. Like when he heard that James was hospitalized he said, "Oh good, maybe they can cure him of his limp wrist, too."

LSF: (*chuckling*) Your father has a cute sense of humor.

Michael withdrew into silence.

LSF: What just happened?

Michael: Nothing. I just feel bad about James.

When Michael left the session, I experienced great shame in the pit of my stomach, both because my comment was hurtful, and even more profoundly in this situation because Michael had come into the session ready to work after hearing that I was a safe harbor. Michael's father's remark had been hurtful and denigrating to Michael, and I reopened the wound by laughing with his father. The shame came from recognizing the ways in which I continued to be culpable despite my critical consciousness. I realized that I had been hurtful and that, although Michael had said nothing about it, I had witnessed the experience and the pain that I had caused him. In the next session with Michael, I apologized. He said that he did not remember the remark, and I believed him. I knew, however, that I had to attend much more readily to my own homophobia in sessions with Michael.

RISKING OUR OWN PAIN. Through the act of witnessing our clients, we often willingly assume the risk of heartache, despair, or numbness associated with witnessing. Experiencing the pain of others without also experiencing the awful, traumatic, deeply painful events in our lives, is crucial so that we can bear witness to our clients and not be preoccupied with our own pain. It is a balancing act, however. Witnessing with youth can be even more difficult.

Because the pain can be so omnipresent, the therapist risks losing the youth when that pain is acknowledged. Thus, we must experience the pain but not overexpose the client to it.

THE NOLANS

After the disastrous first meeting with Devin and his mother, in which Devin refused to speak with Julia in the room, I (RGH) spent the next few sessions meeting individually with different members of the Nolan family. In an individual meeting with Devin, he told me about an experience he had with his stepfather, Bruce, when Devin was 11.

Devin: Probably one of the last fights that Bruce and I had was a few months before my mom kicked him out of the house. Craig and I were fighting in the bedroom and it got pretty loud. Bruce came in and told us to shut up and, of course, we didn't. I told him, sass that I was, that he had no right to tell us anything because he wasn't our father. This always pissed him off, so he started to call me a sissy ass baby, like he always did, but this time he started on Craig as well, and the next thing you know, Craig is pounding on me—I mean, really pounding—and I'm getting my ass kicked, and Bruce is laughing and screaming in the corner, "Hit the girl, Craig, hit the girl, Craig, hit the girl." He just goes on and on. And I thought to myself, you know something, Bruce, you're right, you don't even know it but you're right. Something about that gave me great pride, you know, that I knew something that he didn't.

Devin was telling me about a horrendous moment in which he felt great pride. I felt deep sadness for Devin and rage at Devin's stepfather. At the same time, I understood that Devin was telling me this story not so that I would show him empathy and kindness but because he really was proud of himself. He had won. He would not be conquered, despite the beatings and the degradation. The best thing to do at that point was just to witness, which is exactly what I did.

When Devin left the session, I took a moment to cry. I cried because I had witnessed such bravery, degradation, and pride. Devin did not want me to feel sorry for him, nor did he want to experience the pain of the violation, for it was too tender. I was a container for the pain and the resilience, and I felt great sadness. I cried, not just for Devin, but for some of the times I had felt the same way as an adolescent. You handle it—you have no choice—and it hurts like hell.

RISKING FAILING. When you attempt to create refuge in therapy by witnessing difficult moments, you risk the possibility of losing your clients. Therapists always walk the fine line between attempting to create environments that are too different and those that are not different enough in attempting to help families change. This is similar to Friedman's (2004) "Tilt Theory of History." He wrote, "The Tilt Theory states that countries and cultures do not change by sudden transformations. They change when, by wise diplomacy and leadership, you take a country, a culture or a region that has been tilted in the wrong direction and tilt it in the right direction, so that the process of gradual internal transformation can take place over a generation" (2004, p. 9). Sometimes, in our attempt to be helpful, we tilt too much and risk losing the refuge we have created.

THE EDWARDS

In the third session with the Edwards, I (RGH) misjudged Tanya's openness to the process of self-exploration. Although she seemed quite sophisticated in her ability to claim her ideas about herself, she was still an adolescent in the tender throes of self-discovery. We were talking about how she was treated by her parents.

RGH: Do you ever think about how they would treat you if you were a boy?

Tanya: (*frozen*) Do I what? What the fuck?

RGH: Ugh, that must have felt like I just slapped you in the face. Sorry—it's just that sometimes, when I was growing up, I used to think that I would have gotten more respect if I were a boy, so I was just wondering if you ever felt that way. I didn't mean anything else, I was just relating to you from how I felt as an adolescent, that's all. I'm sorry.

Tanya: No, that's okay. I just didn't know what you meant. I just wish they trusted me more. I wish they knew I was a good kid and all. They have no idea how awful I *could* be, you know?

Although Tanya explained that she did not know what I meant, I experienced her response to me—"Do I what? What the fuck?"—as a moment of panic. The idea that she could be treated as male, that she would identify as male, or that she would be seen as male was too far from how she had been thinking about perceiving herself. I had tilted too far and for a moment our relationship lost its balance. These are moment-to-moment risks we take in the process of creating refuge. When you are open to the experiences of your clients, however, it is easy to tilt back to a place in which you are safe once again.

SPECIAL ISSUES IN TREATMENT: OUTING YOUTH

We walk a tightrope in family therapy with youth because they are in the throes of identity development. We do not want to produce a tilt so drastic that we overexpose youth to something they cannot tolerate about themselves, and we do not want to tilt so little that we underexpose them by not asking questions that help to create refuge. With young children, we can play, which allows them access to tender and vulnerable places without overexposing them to content that is too overwhelming to tolerate. I (LSF) worked with a 7-year-old girl who had a small puppet turtle rage at a large puppet bear because the turtle was left at the picnic table by herself. The turtle berated the bear, told him what an awful animal he was, and told him that she hated him. The young girl had been adopted at 6 months old, had recently witnessed the psychiatric hospitalization of her father, and was sent to live with an aunt for 3 months while her mother attempted to find work and housing. When I asked her directly about the impact of these recent separations, she said she was happy because her aunt had a swimming pool. In reality, I suspect, she was scared and angry. Both feelings were too terrifying to face head on because she was so vulnerable and had very little control over her own destiny. It would have been useless to discuss this with her because it would have been too big a tilt.

Once children move into late childhood and adolescence, they are less likely to use play in therapy as a method of dialogue. With youth who are coming in to the knowledge that they are different, this knowledge is sometimes too terrifying to acknowledge. We believe that tilting too much and asking youth whether they are queer is disrespectful, useless, and potentially harmful to the creation of refuge in therapy. To not ask, however, when we have a sense that youth are wanting to tell us, can be equally disrespectful and potentially harmful to the relationship. How, then, can therapists walk this tightrope when their therapeutic intuition is that being queer is an important part of the issues being addressed in therapy?

We recommend an indirect form of questioning that is in between play and direct forms of expression. Naturally suited to youth who are transitioning from childhood to adulthood, this indirect questioning probes identity development in a way that is respectful and curious, yet leaves youth with the ability to remain in control of how much they expose to themselves and to the therapist. We have asked youth in our practices at varying times in therapy the following questions:

- What would you recommend a teenager do when she has a secret about herself and she wants people to get to know her but she is afraid if she tells the secret, they won't like her?
- What do you do when you know that you are different, you want to talk to someone about it, and yet you also think that if you talk about it, you will be really hurt—that somebody won't like you or accept you or something even worse?
- Is it okay if a boy is attracted to other boys?

- Do you have any gay or lesbian friends?
- Do you and your friends talk about homosexuality?
- Have you ever had anyone come out to you?
- What do you think your parents would do if they found out someone was a lesbian?
- Have you had sex with Cindy?
- I used to think about having sex with my best friend. Do you?

Generally, we do not ask youth direct questions about their own sexual identity, but we have asked them direct questions about their sexual practice. Adolescence is often a time of sexual exploration and youth have a keen sense that exploration may be just that and are therefore able to discuss sexual practice quite openly. Youth can be open about sexual practice in ways that are easier to tolerate than sexual identity. Even if youth tell us that they are having sex with someone of the same gender, however, we would not label them. Instead we would ask how they understood this experience and what labels they are using to identify the relationship and themselves.

Coming out discussions may be different with youth who are gender variant. Because most people merge gender and sexual identity, feminine-acting male youth and masculine-acting female youth are exposed to questions about their sexual identity in ways that gender typical youth are not. Gender variant youth are often targets of harassment and have learned how to defend themselves—sometimes in helpful ways, and sometimes in ways that make it more difficult for them to be true to themselves. Gender typical youth, on the other hand, may not be exposed to introspection that is triggered by outside curiosity or attack.

As therapists, we must create a space for all youth to tell us about their burgeoning sexual identity. In some ways, this may be more difficult for gender typical youth. We have found that gender typical youth, when they come out, are often met with shock, surprise, or mistrust. Female-identified lesbians, for example, are told that they don't act masculine, so they must be wrong. Parents claim that this is a passing phase because they always liked to play with dolls and weren't tomboys. Gay young men are reminded that they always loved sports.

For gender typical youth, then, creating space for discussions around sexual identity may be more difficult, and therapists must listen for indirect forms of expression that may go unnoticed. When youth talk about particular friends with some intensity, for example, asking questions about what these friendships mean, or about how these friendships are opening new ways for them to think about themselves, may create space for youth to tell us more about their burgeoning identities. When youth talk about shame, feelings of inadequacy, knowing that they have dangerous knowledge that other people cannot tolerate, or just being secretive in general, we must give them the space to explore these experiences in deeper ways. In all circumstances, however, we believe that not rushing to ask directly about sexual minority status is a form of respect. Creating refuge is about helping youth label themselves and allowing them to try on differing definitions in a crucible of tolerance.

We do not advocate honesty at all costs in our work with youth and their families, and we are up-front with our families about this. We advocate a nontoxic environment. We often see people individually so that they can share some of their toxic thoughts without hurting others. Sometimes we are able to work on those thoughts so they do not get in the way of intimacy with others. Sometimes certain thoughts, feelings, opinions, and behaviors are best kept silent so that family members can live together until it is time for adolescents to leave home.

We learned, for example, during the early part of therapy with the Marnis, that Jana's father thought that homosexuality was a mental illness and that homosexual people should be hospitalized or jailed so that they were not a menace to society. We recognized that this was his first response and not his only response, and we hoped that in the years to come, his views would change as he got to know his daughter differently. However, at the time of the therapy, Jana was 15 and living under his roof, and it was not in her best interest to come out to her father.

Creating refuge opens the possibility for complex and difficult dialogues for families. It does not mean that all information is shared or that everyone bares all. Instead, it fosters a process in which individuals find a voice for themselves together. When you create therapeutic refuge for queer youth and their families, you develop a great appreciation for the complexity surrounding the coming out process. Unfortunately, there are no hard and fast rules about when it is safe for youth to come out to their families. We never recommend that youth come out to their families; we always follow the youth's lead. We tell youth that this is *their* process and we will walk with them but not in front of them. We trust that they will know when it is a good time to tell someone and we are there with them to handle the consequences. In most instances we have found that this process is out of our control. Most therapeutic work in families occurs outside the therapy office. We advocate being on the side of "safe, not sorry" and protecting youth from further denigration, devaluation, and rejection. We have had a great deal of experience with the coming out process, and we do let youth know that the process is probably both smaller and larger than they think it is, and that we will help. When you have created refuge in the therapeutic relationship, you have opened the door for containing all that comes your way.

CONCLUSION

Creating refuge is the process of organizing a therapeutic environment in which family members are able to have access to their burgeoning thoughts and feelings about themselves and others so that they can grow and develop in intimate relationships. Family therapists create crucibles so that family members are able to experience support as they struggle to grow. When working with queer youth and their families, the crucible is necessary but not sufficient on its own. Therapists must also create refuge, a therapeutic environment as free as possible from cultural mandates about gender and sexual identity. We do this by being responsive to our clients, seeing how it is they experience themselves and the world, and stimulating more complex understandings of those experiences. We also challenge ourselves to continue working on our own attitudes of critical consciousness. Finally, we witness the full experience of family members—spoken and unspoken, simple and complex.

CHAPTER 4

Difficult Dialogues

Difficult dialogues peel away layers of misconceptions, lies, unspoken knowledge, and damaging interactions to help family members develop new appreciation for each other so that they can love, respect, and nurture what they never did before. These dialogues are fraught with tension, fits and starts, crying, yelling, leavings, and returns. With queer youth and their families, this is frequently how change occurs. Often when families come into therapy, the youth is so distant from the parents that they are no longer available to help the child develop. The family has ceased to be an environment that confirms, contradicts, and continues in relationship to its youth. The family is not providing the necessary ingredients for growth and development, and problems erupt. We need to reintroduce family members to one another, and this is both a challenge and an opportunity.

Difficult dialogues are a struggle, and it is in this struggle that something shifts and the relationship develops. If the relationship moves forward, the struggle resolves and the relationship changes. A different level of intimacy exists until the next opportunity for transition. At each stage of successful relationship development, individual development occurs. Each person in the relationship develops a new appreciation for the other, which happens simultaneously with the cessation of the struggle. As family relationships develop in a successful manner, members move toward intimacy with self and with others. This paves the way for youth to be more open about themselves, and it paves the way for their family members to embrace and respect them. In short, it helps families get back on track in helping kids grow and develop (Stone Fish, 2000).

CREATING REFUGE FOR DIFFICULT DIALOGUES

Difficult dialogues are best attempted within the crucible of refuge created in family therapy. Once we have recognized our clients and confirmed the ways in which they make sense of the world, as well as created a refuge in which they can hold on to us and feel like they will be taken care of and that their needs will be met, they are more able to tolerate change. When family members learn new information about each other that challenges the way they are accustomed to seeing the other, they experience disequilibrium. If they feel supported, the disequilibrium is less dramatic, and they are able to integrate the information they learn about each other more easily. "When disequilibrium is weathered it can begin to lead to a new, more articulated, better organized construction of the world which differentiates and reintegrates the understanding of the prior balance" (Kegan, 1982, p. 266).

Difficult dialogues occur when family members attempt to be more open or honest with themselves and with each other. These dialogues happen frequently between youth and their parents in therapy because youth are developing a sense of identity that is newly articulated. If that identity creates some disequilibrium for the youth and the family, it may be quite difficult to articulate it. We have heard many times in therapy about youth who have tried to tell their parents about themselves but clearly get the message that their parents do not or cannot hear what the youth has to say. In much the same way, parents complain that youth do not listen to them, and that they no longer have any influence on their children's burgeoning identity or activity. Creating a crucible for difficult dialogues to take place is the process of helping family members tolerate a more complex understanding of themselves and each other.

DIFFICULT DIALOGUES AND QUEERNESS

The refuge in which difficult dialogues can take place is not created solely to help queer youth come out to their families. In fact, sometimes the creation of a space for difficult dialogues reveals that the family cannot be a place of refuge for a queer youth. Difficult dialogues are used to explore the unexplored in each other and ourselves, and sometimes the unexplored turns out to be a place that does not tolerate sexual minority status. Queer youth who know this about family members are better off than youth who have to guess. Unlike queer adults, who do not have the same dependency on family members that queer youth have, youth are in great danger of losing all security if they guess wrong.

We believe that acceptance (or lack of acceptance) of queerness usually exists on a continuum. Most family members, when confronted with the possibility or probability that a family member is queer, show some level of acceptance of the family member. Some, when they hear that the youth is queer, never mention it again. There are others who initially are intolerant and then come around to some level of acceptance, or accept some parts and not others. In therapy, for example, one father, at first outraged about his teenage daughter's sexual identity disclosure, ultimately expressed acceptance as long as she did not "flaunt it in front of him."

For some family members, however, queerness is completely unacceptable, and viewed as a pathology that must be cured. This does not mean that therapy has failed, and it does not have to mean that youth cannot continue to be in relationship with their families. It often means the establishment of an uneasy truce in which youth learn to hide parts of themselves or some families agree never to discuss it in order to stay in relationship. Queer youth who have had difficult dialogues in a crucible of refuge can stop guessing what other members think, are more aware of what other members in their family can tolerate, and, with guidance from the therapist, can learn to have their own opinions and remain in relationship with their families.

As noted earlier, a family member who does not accept sexual minority status may request conversion therapy. When this comes up in therapy, we ask questions about the request. Sometimes people just want to know what the options are and whether conversion therapy works if the youth chooses this option. Others want to try conversion therapy before they think about accepting their youth. Still others want nothing to do with acceptance and will only tolerate the youth if she or he tries to be different. Youth themselves may also ask about conversion therapy because they want to know if it is possible for them to change. Family members who believe they have to choose between their communities and accepting sexual minority status are in a very difficult bind and need options.

We are open about our beliefs and we engage family members in difficult dialogues about these beliefs. We do not try to change anyone's sexual identity, nor do we believe that we have that kind of control over another human being. We think conversion therapy exists only because of institutionalized homophobia and heterosexism, and that *this* is what needs to change, not the sexual identity status of individuals. We also tell people that the evidence of conversion therapy's success is inconclusive and we recommend that they do their own research on the studies that have been done. After we give our opinion, we inform people that if they would like to pursue this option, their religious leaders may be able to help refer them to people who practice conversion therapy.

Difficult dialogues can take place and growth can occur despite some members' intolerance. In some instances, growth occurs in particular dyads because they face together the unacceptable views of another. In other instances, youth learn about themselves in relationship to the family member's intolerance— lessons they would not have learned had they not had difficult dialogues in which they experienced a family member's honest and open view. Once queer youth come to understand how they have received the knowledge that sexual minority status is unacceptable, they are more open to examining it themselves.

DIFFICULT DIALOGUES AND RELATIONAL DYNAMICS

If we as therapists are to promote difficult dialogues to enhance growth and development in relationships, it is helpful to have an understanding of the complexity inherent in these dialogues. Our understanding of relational dynamics alerts us to how challenging it is for family members to be open and honest with each other. We help create crucibles for difficult dialogues by meeting with members individually to develop a sense of how they interpret events when their family members are not around. Adolescents, when feeling held and accepted rather than judged, will give you a great deal of information about themselves and their activities. Adults, often more wary than adolescents, will give you a great deal of information about how rigidly they adhere to their beliefs and how supportive they will be about their children being different from what they anticipate.

When difficult dialogues occur in therapy, differences emerge that may not have been previously discussed because the discussion itself was intolerable. Many of the families we see in therapy have not been able to create a therapeutic crucible that contains intense discussions which confirms family members, contradicts certain behavior, and continues to be stable. Family members are dependent on one another and most find it difficult to risk sharing information that may be too intense for the relationship to handle. Parents, partners, and youth are all concerned that, if the discussion gets too intense, someone will leave. The fear of being left is also the fear of no longer being loved and being cut off from human contact, shut down, violated, abused, and not tolerated. These fears are real and must be respected when creating crucibles for difficult dialogues.

Relational dynamics are catalysts for misinterpretation because a message that is sent about oneself is also sent about others and about the relationship. This makes difficult dialogues even more challenging with youth and their families. Youths use their relationships with their family members to develop into adults. If a friend rejects an adolescent, the adolescent can find another friend. If her or his mother rejects the adolescent, the stakes are much higher. If a queer youth who is in to herself but not out to anyone else hears a friend and her mother say something homophobic, she is more likely to challenge her friend than her mother. She can tolerate her friend's rejection but not her mother's. Because of this, she is more honest with her friend. Being honest with her mother may mean loss of love, security, and life, as she knows it.

The complexity inherent in family dynamics intensifies the difficult dialogue. Family members develop a sense of how much they can share of themselves in their families without risking the loss of the relationship. Youth, then, are often known more completely and complexly by their peer groups than by their parents. The lesbian, known to herself but not to others, has practiced active exploration of identity development in her peer group, even while hiding. She may challenge homophobic remarks, bring up same sex attractions, ask others about their identities, and engage in conversations that pave the way for her disclosure. It is easier to have difficult dialogues with her friends than with her mother.

The life giving and life-threatening importance of family relationships make difficult dialogues—dialogues in which people share more about themselves in relationship than they have shared before—even more difficult.

THE CRUCIBLE OF DIFFICULT DIALOGUES

Kegan's (1982) principle of *natural therapy*, which describes environments that are conducive to individual growth, informs the therapeutic crucible we attempt to achieve. The three crucial ingredients of these environments—confirming, contradicting, and continuing—allow family members the space to explore the unexplored parts of each other so that they can get back on track toward having successful relationships. Families who come to therapy with youth who are queer have had problems providing an environment in which to guide the youth toward growth and development. Youth are alienated, withdrawn, or angry, and parents are confused, worried, outraged, or clueless. They do not know how to talk with one another about what is happening between them, although, despite some protestation, each family member longs for these conversations. Cushioned by a therapist who has created refuge, family members learn how to tolerate increased intensity in their relationship with one another and so can have difficult dialogues.

Kegan's concept of a natural therapy environment comes from his understanding of the necessary ingredients for raising children. For children to develop into adults, they must be confirmed in the stage of development that they are in, contradicted so that they can move toward the next stage of development, and assured that their parents will continue to be in relationship with them. From childhood to adulthood, youth pass through early to late adolescence. For most youth, this is a developmental period in which they are intensely self-focused. Parents confirm this focus on self and at the same time they contradict this focus by holding them accountable for being in relationship with family members. It is okay, for example, to be completely involved with friends, but the youth still has to be nice to his sister. It is these types of messages that help youth develop into self-sufficient adults who are also responsible in relationship and that make the maintenance of familial relationships so crucial for youth.

Youth develop into self-sufficient adults while in relationship with family members who change in response to the youth. Youth continually adapt to changes in response to family members as well. The crucible remains and family members continue their relationships, but the relationships change so that they can contain newfound individual experiences. Parents have a responsibility with youth, as they move toward greater independence, to continue to be involved in their lives but to be involved in very different ways. The families we see in therapy have not been able to maintain a natural therapeutic environment for youth to grow and develop. We create this environment in therapy so that families can do the same for their individual members.

Confirming

Most children learn at a very early age what will pain their parents too much to hear. They stop sharing painful experiences because it so hurts their parents that the parents are unavailable to help them in their time of need. Kegan noted, "When we respond to the person in her experience of pain rather than in order to relieve the pain, we testify to our faith in the trustworthiness of the motion of evolution, to our faith in the trustworthiness of life itself. . . . The mother who can hold her infant unanxiously when the infant is itself anxious is giving the child a special gift. She is holding heartily at the same time that she is preparing the child to separate from her" (1982, p. 126).

Unfortunately, many parents are unable to do this for their children, especially when their children threaten the cultural mandates under which they live.

THE SMITHS

Michael Smith would never have agreed to family therapy meeting if he had not felt like I (LSF) could hold him and his family at the same time. He knew that the therapy environment would demand honesty, and he had learned that his mother could not tolerate honesty from him. A number of years ago, Michael had told his mother that he felt like killing himself. He had no plans for suicide, but he felt desperate and without hope. His mother became quite upset and preoccupied. She tried to come up with all sorts of solutions for him, which only made him feel more desperate and alone. He learned at that point that she could not tolerate his pain without becoming quite anxious herself and unhelpful.

Most queer youth learn early on what their families can tolerate about their behavior. They learn to hide the parts that are unacceptable so that they can fit in. They have learned that honesty breeds contempt, disappointment, and disgust. Usually, by the time they come to therapy, the hiding has taken its toll. Creating refuge paves the path towards honesty. It is necessary that clients believe they can be honest with family members in therapy in order for the environment to hold difficult dialogues that will take place. In order for this to happen, the process of confirming must occur. This should happen simultaneously with creating refuge or even before it. The process of confirming is similar to the process of holding an anxious infant in an unanxious way. I recognized Michael and I was not anxious. I had been able to hear about his desperation, and the ways in which his very being as a queer young man was constantly invalidated and I did not try to anxiously fix something for him. I simply held his truth and believed in his ability to cope. Having the experience of being *known* allowed Michael to gather the strength to have difficult dialogues with his parents in therapy.

Contradicting

The second ingredient in a crucible that allows for difficult dialogues is the therapist's ability to contradict clients in a way that does not alienate them. Contradicting is the process of limit setting. Therapists contradict certain behaviors so that environments are created such that people in those environments change. This is similar to the strategic therapist's adage—in order for clients to change, you must make the environment more difficult for them to stay the same. The process of having a difficult dialogue is the process of letting go of the way things are so that new parts of people can emerge and relationships can develop. This cannot happen, however, if the therapist has not already created refuge. As Kegan stated when discussing developmental transitions: "When I feel recognized and have a sense that you understand how I am experiencing my experience (whether this is how you experience it or not), I can find your limit setting tolerable and even a relief; if I do not feel recognized, I resent it as a violation of who I am—which is just what it is" (1982, p. 181).

THE EDWARDS

I (RGH) saw Tanya Edwards alone for the fourth session, after having supported her in her fight with the school bus driver the week before. She reported that her stepfather had been trying all week to be nice to her.

RGH: Tanya, you were really brave last week in the family session and I just want you to know how much I appreciated you. Your father was furious and said things that hurt you, and rather than retreat or leave the session or yell back, you stayed, you listened, you participated, you were really mature, and I really appreciate it.

Tanya: Yeah, well, he continues to make me sick. He wants so badly to know what's going on in my life. He comes into my room and sits on my bed and asks me questions about my day, like I really want to talk to him about what's going on with me.

RGH: Well, I bet you are mixed about that. You want to be close to him but you don't want to be hurt. So, you know what? I think you give him mixed messages. On the one hand, you tell him to butt out, but I think you really want him to know you and I believe, honestly, that he wants to know you. I think that's probably why you fight so much. He may not know how to do it well, but he definitely wants a better relationship with you and I keep seeing all the ways you keep him out.

Tanya: But if he really knew me, he'd be disappointed. I don't want him to be disappointed.

RGH: In what ways would he be disappointed?

Tanya: Well, I do things that he doesn't approve of, so if he knew, he would be disappointed.

RGH: I want to talk more about that, but I just want to get back to this point I was making about the mixed messages that you give him. You really don't want to disappoint him; I understand that, because his opinion of you is really important, right?

Tanya: Yeah.

RGH: Well, how come?

Tanya: Well, he is my dad. I care a lot about what he thinks of me.

RGH: Great, that's what I mean. His opinion of you is really important, as it should be. You care a great deal about him and it is obvious he adores you, but you continue to act in ways that keep him out of your life. You know what I mean? You're like a porcupine with him—don't get too close to me or I'll hurt you. You know?

Tanya: Yeah.

RGH: So, what could you be doing differently?

In asking Tanya what she could be doing differently, I both support and challenge her. I let her know that I understand her and I encourage her to be different. I recognize and affirm her view of how she interprets things, and I encourage a different view as well. Of course, this only works if you are encouraging all members of the family to see the world differently, each according to her or his abilities. In the process, the therapist becomes a just leader and helps create an environment where everyone is held and held accountable.

Continuing

Continuing, the third aspect of the crucible, is the therapist's creation of an environment that remains stable despite the turbulence that occurs among family members. It is as if the therapist says to family members, "I can tolerate what you have to dish out. I will remain steady and stable despite how awful you feel the world is. You can count on me being here, continuing to hold the hope that things can be better." Equally important is the family's sense that the therapist will encourage them to be different but not so different that someone in the family will leave the relationship and not continue.

The family's relationship with the therapist is important, but it pales in comparison to family members relationships with one another. For family members to engage in difficult dialogues, they must be assured that their therapist will not push them or other members to places that the relational dynamics cannot tolerate. Family members must be able to trust that therapy will not make things worse. Though relationships may be inadequate, family members, in order to be more honest with each other, must believe that the relationships will continue to function. This means that the therapist is sensitive enough to relational dynamics to know when and how to challenge people to be different, and when to slow down the process so that family relationships stay viable.

THE NOLANS

Though Devin Nolan had told some of his friends and the GLBT support group that he was transgendered, he had not told his family. He began to use the Internet to learn about transgendered individuals and discovered a great deal of information about physically transitioning from male to female. He had read that his transition to female would be easier if he blocked male hormones while in adolescence. As he learned this information, he began to become anxious and demanding, because he decided that he wanted hormones and he wanted them immediately. In a session that included Devin and his mother, Devin was quite agitated because he was afraid that he was going through a growth spurt and worried what it would do to his future.

Devin: This one site that I have been on says that I gotta get some blockers, so I need to know what to do here, am I doing it right? Am I going about this the right way? I'm starting to panic here.

RGH: Julia, do you know what Devin is talking about?

Julia: No, I have no idea.

RGH: Why don't you ask him?

Devin: She won't understand.

RGH: Try her.

Devin: Mom, I don't want to be a runway model in drag, I want to be a female runway model. You get it? I hate my body. I fucking hate it. I get up in the morning and I see my body changing and I want to throw up. It doesn't fit. Something is very wrong. I am in the wrong body and I know now that I can change it—they have ways to make my body right, to change me into a girl. It is what I am and I have to do it now.

Julia: Wait a minute here, Devin. I . . . I don't understand. I . . .

Devin: (*standing up*) I knew you wouldn't understand. You just don't love me. You never understood, you're so busy trying to . . .

Julia: What the f . . .

RGH: Okay, let's see if we can understand what's happening here. Devin, can you sit down? Okay, both of you are upset and for very good reasons. This is difficult, really difficult, and you guys are trying really hard to work this out, but this is difficult stuff. We're in new territory here. We'll make it through, but this is new ground, so we have to slow down a bit and look at the territory. Devin, you have been looking on the Internet now for months, and you have all sorts of information that your mom doesn't have—this is all very, very new to her. This is the first time you have even mentioned anything to her about transitioning or even about being

137

transgendered, right? I understand your urgency, but, Devin, you gotta cut her some slack here. And Julia, we know this about Devin, when he gets anxious, he tends to pressure you, and you fight like kids instead of reminding yourself who the adult in this relationship is. You've been unbelievably understanding so far, we all know that. The two of you are in a great place in your relationship. You are trying to work together and I will help you. First things first. Julia, what's going on for you right now?

Both Devin and Julia were struggling to stay in the relationship, to speak to each other and to be listened to, and both were reacting to the desperation each was feeling in relation to the other. Devin was dependent on his mother's support and Julia was so frightened that she would lose her child that she was unable to listen to him. Therapy became the crucible that contained each of them enough so that they could calm down and be present for each other. I confirmed their views, contradicted their volatility, and continued to maintain the importance of their relationship. The focus of therapy at this point was not to change Devin's identity, or to help him transition to a female, but to help both Devin and his mother deal with the day-to-day issues of gender variation.

The crucible of difficult dialogues is maintained throughout therapy. As relationships change and individuals develop, members come to acknowledge that growth can occur through challenging conversations that are cushioned by the therapist. Some families chose not to have these conversations during the week and wait for therapy, while some continue the conversations outside of therapy and repeat back what happened during the week so that the therapist can help smooth over the rough spots. Sometimes life with youth is one long difficult dialogue, and therapy is used to cushion the process so that the difficult dialogue becomes a fruitful place for growth to occur.

THE FAMILY'S DEVELOPMENTAL TRAJECTORY PROCESS

Parent-child relationships are organized around the development of the youth in those relationships and, ultimately, in the launching of those youth. In each stage of development, a relational process occurs in which the youth develops and the family must accommodate to the developmental change. In families that are responsive, this process occurs continuously. The family confirms, contradicts, and continues, and the youth grows while the family accommodates to this growth. The accommodation is in the direction of relating to youth as more independent than before. This independence does not occur in one leap but rather in minor transitions throughout development.

Usually when youth develop, there is a minor relationship struggle, and it is in this struggle that perturbations occur and the relationship develops. The struggle, however slight, occurs because people are used to treating each other a certain way. When people change, relationships must change to accommodate. If the relationship moves forward, the struggle resolves. A different relationship develops—one that is more developmentally appropriate to the life-cycle stage of the youth. At each stage of successful relationship development, individual development occurs embedded in a responsive relationship.

THE MARNIS

While meeting with the Marni family, Carol, Jana's mother, relayed a story about her oldest daughter, Michelle. She used it to describe how she felt her relationship with Jana was different from her relationship with Michelle. Michelle was developing like a "typical" girl, according to Carol. Carol knew all about Michelle's friends and activities, whereas she knew nothing about Jana's. At 13, Michelle wanted to hang out with a group of friends at the mall and she didn't want to tell her mother every detail of her trip.

Carol: At first I demanded the details and then Michelle calmly explained that she was getting older and she didn't want to share everything with me anymore. She said, "Mom, I have another best friend now and I tell her everything, okay?" I was taken aback for a moment because she was so honest and forthright, you know, and then

I realized that she was changing, that she was becoming a teenager and she needed some privacy. When I went to bed that night, I was sad that she didn't want to be as close to me anymore, but I began to appreciate that she could tell me that and also that she was more grown up now and I had to cut her some slack. You see, she talked to me, so I understood what she was up to, whereas Jana doesn't say a word. I can't know how to respond to her if she doesn't tell me what's going on.

In relationships that are responsive to a youth's developmental trajectory, perturbations happen continuously and they help children with the task of growing up. When Michelle became pubescent, she demanded that her mother treat her differently. Her mother had continued to treat her like she was a child, and she now demanded different respect. There was a struggle, but the family accommodated and eventually developed a newfound respect for her growing womanhood. In these struggles, each person in the relationship develops a new appreciation for the other, which happens simultaneously with the cessation of the struggle. Although we don't know Michelle's side of the story, she probably appreciated that her mother listened to her and gave her the privacy she desired. With this newfound appreciation comes a change in the hierarchy and growth in the individual.

THE FAMILY'S DEVELOPMENTAL TRAJECTORY PROCESS AND QUEER YOUTH

Although many families get off track in nurturing the development of their youth, it is, unfortunately, more common when the youth is queer. In families raising queer youth, the developmental trajectory process for the youth may be more difficult. Sometimes the youth are hiding and no one is looking for them. The youth's development and her or his relationship with family members are neglected. Take sexuality as an example. Whereas straight teenagers' burgeoning sexuality allows ample opportunity for difficult dialogues that help families grow to accommodate their

140

youth, with queer and closeted youths' families, kids are some-times perceived as asexual. Because they hide their sexuality, their families are not confronted with their development. Sometimes youth hide by pretending to be straight. In these cases the family is also living a lie, attempting to accommodate to youth who are pretending. The youth are not in close enough relationship with their parents to use the developmental trajectory process to engage in growth.

In the stage of development in which youth come in to them-selves about their sexual minority status, they come to recognize, if they have not already recognized, that they are different from their families. Because they know they are different, youth are quite aware that the family environment is not conducive to knowledge about themselves. They may not use the family, then, to explore identity, which then makes it more difficult for families to remain engaged in the developmental trajectory process.

Youth are not the only ones who may become derailed from the trajectory process. Because of life circumstances or rigid adherence to how things are supposed to be, in some families the members are severely out of sync with one another. Put simply, when parents recognize, knowingly or unknowingly, that their child is different, it creates a crisis. If the crisis leads to such dis-tance that they are no longer available to help the child develop, the family is not providing the necessary ingredients for growth and development, and problems erupt. Queer youth often grow up loved but unknown. Unlike other minority populations who grow up in families with the same minority status, most sexual minor-ity youth grow up in families who do not know them and cannot provide the necessary skills for their burgeoning lifestyles. The family's developmental trajectory process is easily derailed.

Not all families who are raising queer youth experience this. We have seen a continuum of families with queer youth over the years, ranging from families who come into therapy actively and positively engaged with each other (on track in the developmental trajectory) to those who are either highly conflictual or not involved with each other (off track of the developmental trajectory). Although all families are in the life cycle stage of a family with children and adolescents, some have gotten derailed and fail to nurture their youth in growth-producing ways long before they come into therapy. Some families are derailed because life circumstances have made it difficult for them to nurture. Others are off track because they so rigidly adhere to culturally prescribed ways to behave that they are unable to care for their queer youth.

GROWTH THROUGH DIFFICULT DIALOGUES

Growth occurs through difficult dialogues in family therapy as members are confirmed and contradicted by a therapist who also continues to engage them in a place of refuge. The goal of therapy, at this point, is for family members to be more open and honest with each other in ways that are devoid of relational dynamics and cultural attitudes that get in the way of their seeing each other. When youth express themselves in ways they have not been able to express themselves before, therapists remind parents that a message about self does not have to be a message about other, and that the family does not have to be constrained by divisive cultural attitudes. When cushioned by this place of refuge, family members are able to use their own developmental trajectory process to continue growing in relationship with one another.

FAMILIES ON TRACK IN THE DEVELOPMENTAL TRAJECTORY

Families who are able to be responsive to individual differences in their children without pathologizing those differences or cutting off from relating to the children because of those differences, continue nurturing their development even though they may not be aware of their youth's burgeoning sexual minority status. Meetings with individual units of the family will often give you a good sense of whether a family is on track. Families that are on track often interpret the importance of events similarly, offering the same information about themselves, although from differing perspectives. In other words, they seem to know one another. One week you hear about an argument that the parents had with the youth, and the next week the youth tells you about the same argument. A parent shares a concern about a teenager's drinking, and the day before that the youth told you about a party he attended with kegs of beer. In going into difficult dialogues, then, therapists have a general expectation of how sessions will go, although the unexpected always happens and you learn to roll with the punches.

THE PETERSONS

After meeting with Tom and Lisa Peterson in the first session so that they could explore their concerns about their son, I (LSF) saw Joey individually in therapy two times before he broached the subject of his sexuality. The subject had already come up in my initial meeting with his parents, when Tom talked about his fear of Joey's sexuality, but we had not had a family session yet because Joey was not ready to have one, and sexuality had not been discussed at home. Whereas some adolescents share their news about their sexual identity in layers, stating that they don't know whom they are attracted to or that they have questioned whether they are attracted to the opposite sex, Joey just told me that he was gay. I told him how honored I was that he shared this with me and he said that he could tell I already knew (although I had not known). He was not ready to tell his parents, and although I had a sense that his parents would be both upset and supportive, I did not challenge his decision. Youth must follow their own timetable in the coming out process, based on their own sense of what fits for them. Two sessions later, Joey relayed a fight he had with his mother.

Joey: I was on the computer and she walked into the room and I turned the screen off. She was pissy about me being secretive. I was reading about gay heroes when she walked in. I wish I could tell her that I am gay.
LSF: Her or both your parents?

143

Joey: Both of them, and my brother, Matthew.

LSF: How can I help?

Joey and I talked about his fears, his wishes, his relationship with his parents and his brother, and how things would change if they knew. Matthew was home for the summer and Joey was feeling that his relationship with Matthew was beginning to get close. He was concerned that his disclosure would ruin the beginnings of a warm relationship with his brother. We went over the pros and cons of whom to tell first and whether he wanted to use the next therapy session to tell anyone in the family. We decided to schedule a family session the next week and I told Joey that I would follow his lead.

The next day, Lisa called at 8:00 a.m. in tears. She relayed the following story. While cleaning Joey's brother Matthew's room the night before, she found a letter from Matthew's friend, Brian, which detailed a loving sexual encounter they had together. She couldn't say anything to Matthew because she should not have read the letter. She was afraid to tell her husband because she thought it would devastate him, and she was embarrassed that she had violated her son's trust and did not want to share her guilty act.

Lisa: (*crying*) We thought Joey was the gay one. Now I come to find out it's Matthew. I can't handle this alone.

LSF: The truth can be devastating, but you can handle it and you can do this together with Tom because you have vowed to have a relationship based on honesty with your husband. You have a good, loving relationship. Shame should not keep you from sharing this with him. Speak with him and let me know if you want to change our appointment and meet earlier in the week. We will work through this together.

The following week, all four family members were sitting in the waiting room of my office and looked as if they were ready for root canal. As they moved into the therapy office, silence choked the air.

Joey: (*after about 3 minutes of dead silence*) I want you all to know that I am gay.

Lisa started to cry.

Tom: (*in a barely controlled and angry voice*) What?

I immediately moved my chair close to Tom and Lisa and used my warm, authoritative voice.

LSF: Guys, Joey just shared an intimate part of himself with you because he trusts that you will treat it carefully. You are loving and wonderful parents. You have done a magnificent job raising your boys. You can handle this. It is really, really important that you be careful with your words here. This is a difficult time and in a moment of crisis, people sometimes say things they regret later. I trust that you will be very careful with your words. And Joey (*turning to look at him*), I am really proud of you. You have done something that very few kids your age are honest enough to do.

Tom: Yes, I agree. I am just a little surprised. It is going to take some time to get used to this. Are you sure? How do you know?

Joey: Dad, I've known since I was 10. I just know, okay? I mean, how do you know you're straight? (*Everyone chuckles a bit*)

Tom: Good point.

Matthew: Joey, you're braver than me.

Lisa: What does that mean, Matthew?

Matthew: Well, just that I have been having passing thoughts about being bisexual and I never would have thought about coming out to you in high school. You're a really strong kid.

Tom: You know, I'm in shock but I have to agree with you Matt, I feel really proud that you told us. We'll work this through. It'll be difficult, but we'll work it through. We always do.

Lisa then got up, hugged both her sons, and told them that she loved them.

The difficult moment passed. Of course, there were others. In some ways, they were at the cusp of understanding how their lives were different. What happened in that moment, although smoother than some difficult dialogues, had all the necessary ingredients for growth to occur. There was tension and fear. I respected the family's interpretation of events and also offered contradictions. The family was holding onto old definitions of how they related to each other while struggling to adapt to new ones. The transition occurred and each member had a new appreciation for each other. The difficult dialogue produced growth in the family.

Growth occurred because the family was able to use the naturally healing developmental trajectory process to hold each other in relationship. I had created refuge, which cushioned the family to be more open and honest with each other. I confirmed Lisa's fear, contradicted her desire to act on it, and let her know that I would continue in relationship with her to help deal with the consequences.

Cushioned by a crucible of refuge, this family's members were able to support each other in their attempts to be more honest with one another. In this case it was Joey who contradicted the status quo in his attempt to be honest about himself, and the family continued engaging in relationship with one another. Joey came to the recognition that he wanted his family to know he was gay. He was growing and he wanted his family to be responsive to his growth and stay on track in the family developmental trajectory. There was a struggle, and in the resolution of that struggle, not only did his family develop a new appreciation for him, but it also allowed his brother, Matthew, to grow in relation to the family.

THE EDWARDS

I (RGH) saw Rona and Chris Edwards alone a few times, had two family sessions with the parents and all the children, and had a few sessions alone with Tanya. Just meeting together, and being encouraged to listen to one another, seemed to help the family share their opinions more openly and be less aggressive. The family was able to develop a shared vision of Tanya's emerging maturity, though she had not yet shared her sexual minority status with them, and they reported that things calmed down at home. Then Tanya and her parents came into the following session acting as if all the changes that had occurred had gone out the window.

RGH: So, what's up?
Rona: (*to Chris*) You start.

Chris: (*to Tanya*) No, you start.

Tanya: No, you start.

Rona: All right, I'll start. Two nights ago, Tanya left her computer on so I could read her screen and . . .

Tanya: I did not leave it on so you could read it, I left it on by mistake.

Rona: Well, that is certainly not how I see the situation. You knew I was coming in there to get the scissors and you could have closed it but you left it right there on the desktop for me to see.

Tanya: Whatever.

Rona: So I read what was on her computer.

Tanya: And what happened to privacy in this family? It's all such a farce.

RGH: Tanya, since this was your computer and something that you had written that's troubling all of you, maybe you could tell me the story?

Tanya: I'd love to. So, I was talking to Keisha on-line and she asked me to send her this poem I had written a few weeks ago, so I had the poem open on my desktop when my mom came in and she read the poem and totally freaked out. She starts yelling at me and telling me I'm a basket case and gets all bent out of shape and everything and it's really no big deal.

RGH: What's not a big deal?

Tanya: Well, in the poem I talk about being bisexual. I mean, what's the big deal. I'm attracted to girls and boys. It's not like I killed anybody or anything, or like I'm into heavy drugs or flunking out in school. You'd think I shot the president. So, anyway, she starts asking me about it and starts making all sorts of generalizations like I'm going to get AIDS and I'm a slut and I can't tell my grandparents and shit like that.

Rona: Now hold on a minute—that's not exactly what happened. I was really surprised, that's all. I mean, I read this thing on the computer where she talks about kissing another girl's breasts and I sort of freaked out. I thought we were doing so well and now I think she's starting to act out again. After we had this argument she went into Robert's room and started swearing, and I had to ground her for the weekend.

RGH: Can you help me understand your reaction, Rona? You say you were surprised, that you sort of freaked out—help me understand.

Rona: I just think this bisexuality thing is another plea for help—you know, like, first it was ADHD, and then this. It's a distraction from what's really going on in her life.

RGH: Okay, well, that's one possibility. But for a moment, let's just put that possibility in the background, okay? Let's say that she really is bisexual, that she is attracted to both girls and boys, like she said, and that isn't a distraction but something that is really going on in her life. Then what?

Rona: (*after a moment of contemplative silence, where she looks at Chris, and then at Tanya*) Well, we'd work it out. I mean, I don't want her to be sexual now in any shape or form, but as a lifestyle thing, that would be cool, it would be okay. I mean, it would certainly take some getting used to, but if that is what she wants, it would be fine.

RGH: And for you, Chris?

Chris: Well, you know, Rona and I have talked about this as a possibility, I just don't know. (*His voice starts to shake*) I love Tanya and I will do whatever I can to raise her up right, so that goes without saying, but I gotta tell you, in my community, and in the community of her grandparents, which is who Rona was talking about, she would just not be accepted, you know? So, I mean, if she wanted to live with a woman, well, that would be okay but she'd have to keep it quiet, you know what I mean? I mean, we could know, but I don't want anyone else to know.

Tanya: (*tenderly*) I guess I'm a bigger problem than you thought I was going to be.

Chris: Tanie, you're no problem. They're the problem.

Tanya: (*sincerely*) Well, thanks, Dad.

RGH: (*after a few moments of silence*) I notice that you've all calmed down and there is a great deal of warmth in the room. I want to go back, Rona, to the conversation you had with Tanya when you found out that she was bisexual. I would like you to revisit that conversation. (*I stand and put my hand on Rona's back*) Can you switch chairs and sit by Tanya and talk with her now about it?

Rona: I don't know what to say.

RGH: Well, why don't you start by looking at your daughter.

Rona: (*Rona puts her hands out and Tanya takes them*) Honey, I don't know what to say, I mean, are you really struggling with, like, being a lesbian or something?

Tanya: Mom, I'm not struggling. I'm bisexual.

Rona: So, what does that really mean?

Tanya: Well, like, for instance, I think Keisha's hot, and I think Dan is hot, and it feels about the same to me. Sometimes I think I might just be a lesbian but I don't know yet, 'cause I'm not sure about the boy part but I'm sure about the girl part.

148

Rona: How long have you known?
Tanya: For a long time.
Rona: How come you didn't tell me?
Tanya: 'Cause I knew how you'd react.
Rona: I'm sorry, Tanya. I'm really sorry.

Tanya and her mother hugged, and I leaned over to make sure that Rona was the one doing the hugging. In this moment, it was important that Tanya get hugged, not that she felt the need to take care of her mother. Rona nodded to me to indicate that she understood what I was doing. The hugging lasted a long time.

Through fits and starts, this family was able to stay on track in the developmental trajectory process by growing in relationship to one another via this difficult dialogue. There was a critical moment in therapy in which Rona struggled to see her daughter in the way that Tanya saw herself. For Rona to see her daughter as bisexual, she had to privilege her daughter's definition of self and not the relational dynamic that privileged her view of her daughter. She also had to look past homophobia and heterosexism to see her daughter. The therapist had to contradict Rona's interpretations so that she could be present for the new discovery about her daughter. This new discovery softened Rona's responses to her daughter and encouraged her to be a crucible for her daughter's development.

Because the Peterson and Edwards families were positively and actively engaged with their adolescent children, the new information about their children's sexual identity was, although challenging, incorporated in a reasonable fashion. Family therapy provided a context in which people were affirmed, introduced to new and challenging information, and enveloped in a supportive environment. The youth themselves wanted to be known and trusted the therapeutic process enough to sense that their information would be treated as sacredly as possible. The families were on track to begin working toward nurturing their children's burgeoning queerness and integrating this difference into an expanded vision of family life.

FAMILIES DERAILED FROM THE DEVELOPMENTAL TRAJECTORY

The difficult dialogue process is more laborious in families that enter therapy derailed. Therapists begin to develop a sense of how stuck a family is in their developmental trajectory by observing the ways in which individual members perceive the reality of the family differently. During individual sessions with members of families who are derailed, you may feel as if you are talking to people who live in entirely different households. A youth, for example, will detail an aggressive and hurtful argument he had with a parent in an individual session. The same week the parents will mention nothing about the argument during their individual session. In other instances, youth and their parents will describe an incident together in therapy and it will seem as if they are talking about completely different events. Youth in these families often feel completely misunderstood and acknowledge that they have given up trying to find support from their families.

THE SMITHS

The difficult dialogue process with the Smith family progressed in fits and starts. In a session alone with Michael, he gave me (LSF) a detailed history of some of his life experiences of which his family had no knowledge.

Michael: I think things started to go really bad in seventh grade. In health class, I learned about sex and thought there must be something really wrong with me because I thought girls' breasts were really gross. So I said something to this kid, Brandon, who was a friend of mine, and he started to call me a fag. It caught on and all the kids started calling me names. It was bad, real bad. I was a real freak.

LSF: Did you tell your parents?

Michael: No, they would have just blamed me.

LSF: What do you mean?

Michael: Well, like, one day, I get off the bus and somebody trips me. I'm bleeding, and the bus driver yells at me like it's my fault. Anyway, I'm walking home kind of slow and when I get home, my mother is hysterical. She doesn't even notice that my pants are ripped or that I'm bleeding—she is just yelling and screaming at me because I forgot to be home to let my sister in the house and my sister is crying and I'm sent to my room because, of course, this is all my fault. When my dad gets home that night he comes into my room and starts yelling at me. So, no, I didn't tell my parents.

Over the course of the session, Michael relayed many experiences growing up that he did not share with his parents. Each experience further isolated him from his family as he moved through the developmental trajectory. He had few friends and spent most of his time on the computer. Surfing the web, he encountered lots of pornography sites and discovered that he was sexually attracted to men. As he got older he partied with a peer group that was isolated and rejected like him. Somehow, at one such party, Michael found himself alone with an older boy in an upstairs bedroom wrestling on the bed. Michael was aware that he was having a great time—in fact, probably the best time of his life—and then it quickly turned ugly. The boy raped Michael. Michael believed he had brought this on himself, that it was his fault, that he could not tell anyone, and that he was a sick, perverted, and disgusting human being.

A few weeks later, Michael told his mother that he wanted to die. She found an individual therapist for him to talk with. Because he saw how anxious his mother was, he complied with her request to seek help but only if she promised not to tell anyone. Michael spent 3 months in weekly therapy sessions and never told the therapist a thing about himself. It was easy for Michael to pretend that he was doing okay for the next few years. His grandmother's health, his parents' marriage, and his sister Emily were distractions in his family. He squeaked by in school by being quiet and he was discreet with his marijuana use, so his parents never discovered his daily habit. In his senior year of high school, Michael befriended James, another rejected high school student who smoked pot, liked computer games, and was not a distraction to others. Their sexual relationship started while they were looking at pornography together on the Internet. Around the time they started becoming sexually interested in each other and romantically involved, James had a bad fight with his father and attempted to hang himself in the basement.

Michael was 12 years when he and his family disengaged from the developmental trajectory process and 17 when we started the process of difficult dialogues toward reengagement. Because Michael was quiet and did not cause trouble, his parents and sister basically left him alone. They neither confirmed his growing identity nor contradicted his isolation and loneliness. Instead of relating to one another and struggling with new definitions of youth development, they got derailed.

Difficult dialogues must occur in derailed families before the family is involved enough with one another for growth to occur, and they must continue if the family is to stay involved. In sessions with families like the Smiths, who are not positively and actively involved in their youth's lives, difficult dialogues may take many months of fits and starts. The stage of difficult dialogues is organized to reinstate parent-child relationships so that natural growth and development can occur. Michael's family had no clue as to what was occurring in his life. Like many queer youth, his queerness hid him from his parents. We have to help these families get back on track and become visible to one another.

GETTING BACK ON TRACK

Difficult dialogues take on a staged progression in families that have been derailed. First the family members become positively involved with one another again, and then the family must relearn the importance of staying involved. The therapist's task at the beginning stage of difficult dialogues is to encourage family members to take an active role in one another's lives despite the overt messages they are receiving from one another that they don't want to be involved. The therapist must ignore these messages and continue to remind her- or himself that the people in the room want nothing more than to be loved, valued, and accepted by one another. Most have been hurt deeply and are protecting themselves from being hurt again.

While the therapist encourages family members to be more involved with one another, she or he must also ensure that they not lose the ground they have made so far in the therapeutic process. This is a bit of a balancing act. You want to encourage family members to be honest with each other but not hurtful. Because we can never be sure how someone will react to what someone else says, or be sure what someone else is going to say, therapists must be keenly attuned to each member and also ensure that the process goes slowly enough that everyone remains involved.

THE SMITHS

After a few sessions alone with me (LSF), Michael decided that it would be possible to bring his parents, Rose and John, into therapy to talk with them about his depression and to attempt to be more honest with them. He had a feeling that his mom knew about his sexuality but it was not something they had spoken about. He was convinced that his father did not have a clue and also that he would never talk to Michael again if he knew. We agreed that his depression, not his sexuality, would be the topic of conversation for this session.

After a few initial pleasantries in the beginning of the family session, Rose turned to Michael.

Rose: Why don't you ever talk to me? Why don't you tell me what is going on in your life?
Michael: Because you'll just lecture me.
Rose: Well, maybe that is because you deserve to be lectured to. You say you are going to do something and then it doesn't get done. Your room is a mess and a few months ago we had a deal that you would clean up your room and maintain its appearance

by putting your clothes away and getting rid of containers and paper and all the things on the floor and put away your equipment and rearrange your computer desk and take care of the money that is just lying all around your room, and in exchange for doing that, I would take you driving and teach you how to drive a stick shift. I kept my end of the bargain but you have not kept yours. You just sit around depressed all day and don't do a damn thing. You don't even attempt to keep yourself or your room looking good anymore. You don't give a damn. I am trying to teach you about responsibility because when you leave this house you will have to be responsible for yourself. You will have to learn how to pay bills and have a checking account and organize your money and know which bill to pay which month and then how to save and whether you should save this month or pay a bill. And you will have a boss who will expect you to be responsible and only think he has to ask you once to do something and then he expects that you will do it. I have so much to teach you yet and you say you are independent and don't have to listen to me.

LSF: (*turning toward Rose, with my hand on her knee*) Do you see him? Stop for a moment. Good, now take a deep breath. Okay, good, I want you to look at your son. Shhh. Slow down, take another deep breath; now look at your son. Okay, okay. Shhh. Michael, I want you to turn your chair around and let your mom see you. Good. Slowly, let her look at you. Good. Now, Rose, tell me, what do you see?

Rose: I see an obnoxious, spoiled teenager who doesn't . . .

LSF: Okay, can you slow down a bit?

Michael: (*standing up and yelling*) You are a fucking bitch, that's all I see.

John: (*in a whimper*) Calm down please, Michael.

LSF: Rose, he is your son and he's very confused, and he needs your help and you can help him. Right now you see how he treats you, you see him as a reflection of you or maybe your husband or your parenting, I'm not sure what yet. I know you can see past that, I know you are capable of being able to see past that. I know you want to see past that. You want to know him, really know him. You can. You are courageous. You can do it. You can take the first step. Michael, do you need to take a break or can you sit back down?

Michael: I can sit down but it is not going to do any good. They don't give a flying fuck.

LSF: His anger masks his pain. Something is wrong. He is hurting. He is hurting bad. He needs to feel like you love him, that he is loveable. He needs that from you and you can give it to him because you are brave enough to take the first step.

John: She's always harping on him. She won't leave him alone. You know, when you're a kid, you need your space. She treats him like a God-damned toddler.

LSF: Right now I am less concerned with how you all got so distant and more concerned with changing it. Later on, when things calm down and you all are more on track in raising this boy of yours, we can talk about your differences. So, what's your sense about why Michael is hurting so bad?

John: I don't know.

Rose: Me neither. But we wouldn't be here if we didn't want to know. We do, we really do. Do you know that Mikey?

This was a difficult dialogue that was used to encourage the Smith's to get back on track in the developmental trajectory process. Michael was an early adolescent when the family stopped growing together, and his parents were still treating him as if he were that young. When Rose suggested that Michael was a spoiled teenager, she failed to see that he was a late adolescent struggling with identity development and very unhappy.

To reengage families in the developmental process, parents must learn to see youth as they present themselves in their families so that they can be open to beginning to see parts of them that they are not sharing. To help families get back on track, therapists may make the covert overt by confronting stereotypic notions of gender and the ways in which these notions are keeping them from engaging with one another. In families that encourage traditional gender roles, a youth's not fitting the stereotype can make it challenging for members to know how to engage with one another. Sometimes these youth are derailed at the beginning of adolescence and must be put back on track via intervention from the therapist and reengagement with their families.

THE MARNIS

The following difficult dialogue occurred as a family was in the middle of the course of therapy. Carol and Michelle were discussing a recent shopping trip that Kim had wanted to go on. Carol was explaining to Kim why she hadn't taken her.

LSF: I'm curious why Jana and Jack are not involved in this conversation.

Michelle: (*snickering*) They both hate shopping.

LSF: Well, why is that? How is it that you understand that you, your mom, and Kim like to shop and that Jana and your dad don't?

Kim: Jana thinks shopping is stupid.

LSF: I've noticed that there seems to be a fence around Dad and Jana, although they're at opposite ends of this enclosed area, and the fence is separating them from the rest of the family.

Carol: That's not true. That's not true at all. Jana does not like to shop—she has made that perfectly clear. I mean, what is the point of bringing her, begging her to come, when she hates it and makes everyone else miserable in the process? I learned long ago to leave her alone. When she doesn't want to do something and you make her do it, well, she just wrecks everyone else's time. Isn't that right?

LSF: That's exactly what I mean, about a fence separating you. This fence has been erected by everyone in the family. It's a family thing, no one's fault, just the way the family has organized. Humor me for a moment, but I think it has something to do with girl and boy interests. Even though everyone doesn't want to admit it, when Jana is interested in things that boys are usually interested in, or she's not interested in things that girls are typically interested in, she gets punished.

Carol: Well, I wouldn't say she gets punished. She punishes herself—we don't punish her.

LSF: It is certainly not something that happens intentionally, and I don't mean to imply it is something you or Jack and the other girls set out to do. I just mean, she is isolated, left out, not part of the family. She is sort of . . .

Carol: Like she doesn't belong anywhere? Yeah, I know what you mean. It's painful to watch.

Michelle: Well, she is a girl. I mean, it is a little embarrassing to have a sister who so obnoxiously doesn't want anything to do with you.

Jana: That's because you just want to hang out at the mall with your girlfriends. That is the last thing I want to do.

LSF: How come you aren't helping each other through adolescence?

Michelle: She doesn't want my help.

LSF: Yes she does.

Jana: No, I don't.

LSF: Isn't that what families are for? To help each other? I wonder what happened in this family that made it so you all stopped helping each other grow up? I can't help but think it has something to do with the way you've been constrained about what sort of interests certain people are supposed to have.

Jack: Well, if only Jana liked to do things that the other girls like to do . . .

Jana: (*standing up and starting to scream*) You know something, Dad, I don't! Okay? I just don't and I am so sick and tired of having to pretend to be somebody I'm not. I am so sick and tired of it. (*She starts to cry.*) Everybody wants me to be something I'm not. Everybody wants me to be just like Michelle. Well, I'm not like Michelle, I can't help it. I'm not perfect and you keep expecting me to be, you keep expecting that I am going to wake up one day and just be a perfect little Barbie doll. Well, it's not going to happen.

Jack: (*compassionately*) I know, honey.

LSF: (*after a moment of relieved silence*) I'm impressed. Jana, you really needed to say this. You have been feeling for a long time like you can't win in this family. If you are who you honestly are—someone who happens to have different interests from the other girls in the family and interests more like your father's—you are punished. You get punished either by not being involved with the rest of the family or you get punished because you are told that your interests are wrong. Now, I know no one says this just like that, but those are certainly the messages that I am picking up. And Jack, I am really impressed that you are listening to Jana. You see that she is hurting and you see that she feels helpless. She wants so badly to be involved with the family and she wants to be valued. So what are we going to do about it?

Kim: I can play with Jana.

The process of reengagement is the process of engaging members in difficult dialogues that have not occurred outside the therapy room. The therapist's responsibility at this point is to keep the family moving in a direction of more involvement but not lose sight of the ways in which people can get hurt by each other. In other words, while we help families get back on track, we must continue to be aware of the relational dynamics that may have made it difficult for them to stay on track. When I said that there was a fence around Jana and Jack, I hurt Carol and she responded by defend-

157

ing her position. I had to make sure that she knew that I was not blaming her but rather suggesting that it was a family problem, or she would not stay involved in the conversation. When Jana was yelling at her dad, I was enthused that she was saying what needed to be said and also concerned, both that she would get so angry that she would leave the room and that he would get so angry that he would say something mean or not come back to therapy.

Therapists also help families get back on track by encouraging parents to take charge of reengaging their youth so that they can begin to influence them again. Parents who are able to maintain a natural therapeutic crucible for their youth in which they confirm, contradict, and continue have great influence over their youth because they are engaged in their development. Youth who are derailed are left to figure out their developmental trajectory on their own.

THE NOLANS

In the middle of the course of therapy with the Nolans, I (RGH) had individual sessions with Devin's mother, Julia, and with Devin. I encouraged Julia to be more actively engaged with Devin by reaffirming her role as his mother. We discussed ways in which her fear of losing Devin kept her from expressing her opinions to him. In individual sessions with Devin, he expressed his desire to have a closer relationship with his mother. In family sessions, we worked on reengaging their relationship with one another. In a family session, Devin was frustrated and complaining that the process of transitioning was going to take forever.

Devin: (*to his mother*) If you loved me and understood me, you wouldn't make me stay in this body one more day. If I start transitioning now, it'll be easier for me for the rest of my life. I can't take it anymore—I can't—and you're standing in my way. You think you're being helpful but you're not. I've never wanted anything like this before and I really need it. I don't know what I will do if I can't get hormones now. It's like what's happening to me now is making me go crazy. I look in the mirror and I see hair on my face and I feel nauseous. I could be so gorgeous. I know exactly what I need to do. I can take care of making all the appointments, I can pay you back. It's not fair that I am too young to sign for all of this myself. This is so unfair, treating me as if I have no rights.

RGH: Okay, I understand that Devin is frustrated right now, right? I wonder, what's going on for you, Julia?

Julia: I feel like he's bullying me.

RGH: Tell him.

Julia: You're bullying me. (*She looks back at me.*) This whole thing scares me a lot. I don't know what to do. This is his life we are playing with here—this is real stuff, you know, and it scares me. It just scares me. This is final, this is major, I can't make these decisions by myself, but he is too young to be making these decisions by himself. This is permanent and he is only 15.

RGH: You need to make Devin understand how it is you think about this. Talk to him about it.

Julia: Devin, I know what you want but I think you are too young to . . .

Devin: Mom, listen . . .

RGH: (*moving quickly over to Julia*) Julia, you were saying . . .

Julia: No, you listen. I have supported you throughout this whole thing—you know that. I will continue to support you and love you no matter what happens. I will love you as my son and I will love you as my daughter. I will. (*She starts to cry.*) But I will not let you make these decisions before you are legally able to do them by yourself. I have been reading, too, you know, and there are plenty of people who say you should wait—even doctors who say it's not good for you to fool around like this because they don't know the long-term consequences for teenagers. When you are old enough, you do what you want, and I will support you, and so will Craig, you know that. But right now that is my decision.

Devin: Then you leave me no fucking choice.

Julia: (*firmly*) Devin, you are threatening me now and I don't like it.

Devin: No, I'm just saying that I'm going to have to do something desperate. I'm not threatening you, I'm just telling you the truth.

Julia: You know what, Devin? I'm not going to put up with your bullshit anymore. I am not signing papers. I love you, I support you, but I am not signing papers. I have to live with myself. I am your only mother and you'll have to learn to live with me.

Devin: (*getting up to leave*) No, I don't.

RGH: Devin, you can stay here, I know you can. This is really difficult, this is intense. But you guys have to talk about this stuff.

Devin: This is bullshit. I don't have to listen. I don't know how to fucking get through to her. She's so fucking stubborn. (*under his breath*) That's why everybody leaves.

RGH: Your mom has really tried hard to listen to you, right? These are the kind of conversations you have wanted, where you're both honest with each other. But when you are honest with each other, you may disagree. It is really hard for her to say these things to you because she adores the ground you walk on—you know this—and she is trying hard to be a good mother, and at this point, she has to make the decisions for both of you. This is a really big dilemma, probably one of the biggest dilemmas you and she have faced. Well, now that I think about it, you and she have faced some other really big dilemmas before, haven't you?

Julia: (*chuckles with a bit of relief*) Yes, we have.

Devin: How do I get her to listen?

RGH: To be perfectly honest, Devin, I think she is listening and she understands. She just doesn't agree.

Devin: (*loudly*) How can she understand and not sign the fucking papers?

RGH: She understands your perspective and she has her own perspective.

Devin: Yeah, but it's my life.

RGH: When you are in relationship with others, it is not just about you. That's just the way it is. There are good and bad things about being in relationship with other people. When it is good, you get love, support, money, you know, and when it is bad, you have to compromise your position. It doesn't mean you won't be able to have hormones or the surgery. It just means you can't have them immediately.

Devin: Well, it seems like forever.

The relief in the room was palpable. Although Devin was extremely disappointed, I think he was also relieved to have his mother be actively involved in his life. Julia, too, was relieved, both to be able to make a decision and stick by it, but also because Devin stayed in the room, did not escalate his threat, and seemed to calm down and be resolved.

Decisions about how to transition are major and are best made in process with other people who care about the youth. Although the dialogue is difficult (particularly when being understood does not mean absolute agreement) there is always a sense of relief when everyone knows where they stand.

When we create an environment in which difficult dialogues occur, we reengage family members in the process of nurturing each other. While we are encouraging people to be different, we must remember to witness the ways in which they are experiencing themselves and each other. Although we may wish that family members change more rapidly, it is the process of conversation that ultimately holds the healing needed. Once we have reengaged members in the developmental trajectory process, the therapist's task is to maintain the therapeutic crucible so that family members can stay involved with one another.

STAYING INVOLVED

Difficult dialogues must continue to occur even after families have gotten back on track, if the family members are to remain engaged with one another. Family members avoid many difficult dialogues because they hold toxic material. It often seems as if all members of the family have a natural tendency to find ways to maintain the status quo for fear that they may bump up against material that because of relational dynamics, is challenging to tolerate. Negative cultural messages, troubled marriages, and the youth's own developmental trajectory toward independence all work toward maintaining the family's tendency toward derailment. Diffiuclt dialogues used to help get back and stay on track may be difficult if a marriage is in trouble, but if parents are able to work together in any shape or form, it must remain a goal. To keep families on track, therapists have to have tunnel vision, they must keep focused on the goal of helping parents get closer to their adolescent children. Therapists must remind families to keep their eye on the ball and stay positively and actively involved with each other.

THE MARNIS

I (LSF) saw Carol and Jack Marni alone after the session in which Jana told her father how angry she was at him for not appreciating that she was not a typical girl. They

161

reported that Jana, Michelle, and Kim were getting along much better and that Jana seemed happier in the family but that she was still withdrawn and sullen.

Jack: I'm still very concerned about her and think she has some serious problems that Carol is pretending don't exist.

Carol: What do you mean by that? Are you blaming me again?

Jack: No, I just think you want to throw all of her problems under a rug, like you do with everything.

Carol: And you think everything is a crisis and the world is going to end tomorrow.

LSF: (jokingly) Now, maybe I'm in left field here, but I kind of notice some marital tension here.

Carol: We don't agree on anything.

LSF: Well, you have agreed to come to therapy and you have agreed to work on your relationship with Jana. I have sensed, from the beginning of our relationship together, that you are both pretty lonely in this relationship. This is something we can certainly work on in therapy, if you are interested, after we get Jana launched. Right now, I want to keep focusing on Jana's loneliness because I get the feeling that she's still pretty desperate and I really believe you can help her right now, both of you, regardless of how isolated you feel in the marriage. Am I wrong about this?

By asking the parents to wait to work on their relationship, I am asking them to put aside their troubles so that they can be present for their daughter. You have to work with what you have. In some families, putting marital problems on hold is not possible, but for others it is. Paradoxically, sometimes asking parents to wait to address their relationship problems, eases some of the tension between them. Also, when they are successful at reengaging their children—and share that success—it helps heal some of the tension between them. We used to believe that successful couple relationships bred successful children. We have come to recognize over the years, however, that good relationships with children can help couple relationships as well.

Difficulty in the couple relationship isn't the only thing keeping families from staying involved with each other. The adolescent contributes her or his developmental trajectory as well. Many parents have to be educated about the importance of being involved with their teenagers even when their teenagers are making it quite obvious that they have no interest in being involved with them. As therapy progresses, parents will make moves to reinvolve their children, only to be rebuffed and sworn at. In therapy, parents often talk about ways they can increase their involvement with their children and then come back the next week with stories of belligerence and withdrawal. This is why it is so important to continually remind parents of their role in the relationship. They may have no control over how their children will respond, but they cannot let their children not relate to them. Being self-focused is one of the tasks of adolescence, and it is the parents' job to keep them other-focused as well.

THE SMITHS

About 6 months after therapy with the Smith Family began, Michael's boyfriend, James, was released from the psychiatric hospital. Michael wanted to visit James and asked his mother if he could use the car. Rose asked him where he was going. Michael did not want to tell his parents where he was going, and Rose started to lecture. Michael stormed off to his room and put his fist through the wall. When his father came home from work, he tried to talk with Michael but got no response.

Michael had told me (LSF) about the incident in my individual session with him that week. When the family came in for their session a few days later, we discussed the blowup as a group.

John: Michael, I don't know what to do anymore. I am really worried about you. I want you to feel like you can talk to me, and I don't know how to get that to happen.

Michael: It's done. It's over. I'm just biding my time until I can leave this house and be on my own. You say you're so worried about me, but you don't have a clue and you don't really care. Somebody told you it was time to worry so you started to worry. And if you really did care, you'd hate what you saw.

John: What do you mean? How can you say that I don't care? All I've been trying to do the last month is show you that. See, this pisses me off . . .

LSF: (*looking at John*) Okay, now I want you to listen to me for a minute. Turn your chair around and look at me. You want Michael to talk to you and he just did. So, now you have to listen. He told you something here. It was in adolescent speak, but still, he told you that he is worried about your really getting to know him because he thinks you would hate what you saw.

John: How can he say that? He doesn't give me the chance. He's locked up in his room or ranting and . . .

LSF: Are you interested in hearing what he has to say? You have asked him to talk to you and he is talking to you. Now, are you interested in what he has to say?

John: (*sulking*) Yeah, I'm interested.

LSF: It doesn't seem like you are. If I were Michael right now, attempting to have a relationship with my father, attempting to do what my father has asked me to do, I certainly would not think that you were really interested in hearing what I had to say. I know you are. I know how much you care and how hard this is for you and that you don't have any role models to show you how to do this. You've been burned a number of times in your attempts to be close to your son. I know that, I have seen it happen in here. You have been trying really, really hard and you have been doing a phenomenal job. But, John, this feels different to me. It seems as if Michael has something important that he wants you to hear, okay?

John: (*calmly*) Okay.

LSF: (*looking at Michael*) Now, your dad's not perfect, Michael.

He is filled with anxiety about being a good dad. We have talked about this before, you know? But he wants to hear you. He really does. So go ahead.

Michael: It's just that usually when I try to talk to him . . .

LSF: Talk to *him*, Michael. Say, "Usually when I try to talk to you . . ."

Michael: Well, when I try to talk to you, you get so loud and pigheaded. And I suck as a son.

LSF: (*No one is moving so I move my chair closer to John.*) Why don't you ask him why he says this. Can you get closer to him?

John: You know I don't think you are a terrible son. I think you are a great kid.

LSF: Ask him why he thinks he is such a terrible son. You really want to know him and he wants you to know him, so ask.

John: I don't think what you did with the wall was great, obviously, but other than that, you don't cause many problems, you know.

LSF: (*I move closer to John and look him straight in the eyes.*) John, you're doing a great job. You are warm and loving and it is obvious that you care a great deal about Michael. But John, you don't see him. You know what I mean? You know him as the little boy he was, but he is not a little boy anymore and he is telling you that he wants you to see him. But you have to look and listen. You have to ask questions.

John: So, why'd you punch the wall?

LSF: Okay, that's a good start. But before he can answer "why" questions, and most people can't, maybe a question about his statement about you or about his position as your son. I know it is a bit more tender to ask those kind of questions, but I think you are up to it. He said that he sucked as a son. Do you know what he meant?

John: (*curiously*) What did you mean?

Michael: Just that I disappoint everyone all the time.

John: You don't . . .

LSF: (*interrupting*) Go on, Michael, in what ways are you disappointing? These are some of the things we have been talking about in therapy and I think it is great that you are able to say these things and that both your parents are present and wanting to hear more from you. Go ahead.

Michael: If you *really* knew me, really knew me, you would hate me. And don't say that you wouldn't, because you would, I know it.

LSF: So, you hide from them because you are frightened that they will disapprove so much that they will stop loving you.

Michael: Yeah.

LSF: And you couldn't tolerate it if they stopped loving you because they are so important to you.

Michael: Well, yeah, they are my parents.

LSF: I know, I know.

Rose: Michael, you are scaring me. I mean, what could be so awful that we would hate you? What are you, a mass murderer or something? Your father and I will never stop loving you. You are our son.

LSF: Michael, do you mind if I talk here? (*Michael nods.*)

LSF: Michael has knowledge about himself, about who he is, what has happened in his life, how he feels, what he wants to do and be, and he wants to share it with you

165

but he is afraid that you won't be able to tolerate it and you will stop loving him. Now, I have worked with many families around these issues and I know that your bond as parents is really strong. You have a deep, unfaltering love for Michael that I know will last forever, but he has good reason to be afraid to share with you all of himself because you may be disappointed. You will get over it, but you may be disappointed, and that is really hard for a 17-year-old to take, one who is trying so very hard to be a good son and a good man.

John: I'm not perfect either. We want to get to the root of the problem or else we wouldn't be here. There is nothing you could say that would get me to stop loving you. Okay? So we'll be disappointed. We'll get over it, okay? You know what I mean? What's most important now is that you feel like you can talk to us about what's going on in your life.

As parents soften, youth talk. They talk about the desire to be valued, loved, and respected as they struggle to define themselves. The Smith family was reinvolved with one another on the developmental trajectory process toward Michael's transition to adulthood, and they stayed involved. The difficult dialogues that ensued in therapy helped Michael move toward independence even though he had not come out to his parents. They did not know everything about him and yet they were reengaged in the process of parenting him and attempting to provide a crucible for his growth. Families have a lifetime to develop relationships with one another that can contain open and honest dialogue. As therapists, our responsibility is to create refuge so that families are able to get back on track toward developing those relationships. Difficult dialogues tilt those relationships so that the natural therapeutic environment can reemerge. We do not expect miracles, just perturbations that lead to more satisfying relationships.

SPECIAL ISSUES IN TREATMENT: DANGEROUS SITUATIONS

Dangerous situations—such as suicide attempts, homelessness, or violence—may arise when working with queer youth and their families. Although most queer youth learn early on what their families can tolerate about their behavior, there are those who misjudge what their parent's reactions will be. Some youth misjudge because a level of dishonesty has permeated the relationship and the youth have absolutely no way of knowing how their parents will react to certain changes that have occurred. Other youth do not misjudge their parents reactions; rather, they are well aware that what they are going to do and say will upset family members, and they intentionally act in these ways because they are angry. This anger turns into recklessness, creating dangerous situations. Sometimes, as youth move into adolescence, they may tolerate or be less able to hide their identity, which exposes them to volatile adults. Dangerous interactions can also occur when family situations change. A single, open, and accepting parent, for example, may get involved with a rigid, controlling partner who decides it is time for the youth to learn lessons about life, and all hell breaks lose.

Those of us who work with youth in family therapy sessions know that regardless of how much experience we have or how much information we possess about a family, we are constantly challenged with unexpected situations in which we have to react and react fast. With queer youth, therapists may be called upon to respond to violence to self or others that has occurred outside the therapy office, in-session threats of cut-off and violence (if not violence itself) and in-session intensity that occurs when discussion explodes in front of you.

Whenever someone tells us that a youth has been physically abused by an adult, we call the county child abuse hotline in front of the family and, without identifying the family by name, explain the situation and ask if it is reportable. Although most situations we discuss are not reportable, this act itself shows the family that we take this very seriously and leads to a discussion about discipline and arguments without the use of force. We use the same direct, intense approach when youth say that they are going to commit suicide. When youth tell us that they are abusing drugs, sexually acting out, or self-mutilating, we honor these self-disclosures and spend many sessions exploring the meanings of these behaviors and finding alternatives. We explore their knowledge of sexually transmitted disease, the risks of HIV infection, and strongly encourage safe sexual practice. If youth tell us in session that they have plans to commit suicide, we take a different approach. First, we take them very seriously. If the parents are not there at the time, we call them, with the youth in the room, and tell them that they must take the youth to the emergency room to get evaluated for hospitalization.

In taking such extreme measures, we sometimes lose the opportunity to continue to be helpful to families because they do not reschedule visits with us. Often the parent who was abusive is furious with us and the youth who was threatening suicide refuses to come back into treatment. Sometimes the family waits a year to pursue contact with us; other times, we never hear from the families again. Every once in a while, years later, we receive e-mail messages, phone calls, or letters from families who have prematurely terminated therapy that thank us for saving their lives. Just recently, I (LSF) heard from a college senior I had seen when she was a freshman. She wrote that although at the time she was enraged that I told her parents to take her to the hospital, and that the hospital had been a horrific experience, she credited my intervention for getting her parents to take her seriously for the very first time. She thanked me for hanging in there with her during the worst period of her life and credited my harshness for saving her life.

When dangerous interactions occur or threaten to occur in the therapy office, therapists are called upon to maintain refuge. Sometimes, when parents learn of a youth's sexual minority identity, either by accident or because the youth tells them, they threaten to kick the youth out of the house, lock the youth inside the house, leave themselves, cut off the youth's contact with friends, put youth in boarding school or boot camp, stop paying for college, stop all contact between the youth and his or her siblings, and so on. In other words, parents threaten to make things intolerable for their child, creating a dangerous situation. Sometimes these are idle threats and sometimes they are not. In all cases, parents are really saying that they are overwhelmed, feel out of control, and need help.

When parents threaten to cut off family support, youth are often outraged, and, you, the therapist, find yourself in the middle of an intense screaming match in which no one is listening to one another and the yelling is escalating. In these cases, we compassionately and firmly stop the conversation. We acknowledge what we think people are feeling and we work toward finding solutions in which the family can take a break from one another. This break may mean having someone sit in the waiting room for a while or conducting a discussion about ground rules for communication. Often we recommend that families not talk to each other until they come to therapy again, and we schedule more meetings than usual during the week. Sometimes we recommend that someone leave the house for a while until things settle down. We may also suggest that the family call in a relative to provide respite for a youth, or have the youth stay with a friend. If the youth is prone to or threatens to run away, we acknowledge the youth's need to take a break and find ways for him or her to take that break in a way that is safe and allows for contact with some member of the family.

Sometimes in therapy you cannot stop an explosion from taking place, and the intensity gets so high that someone storms out, loses control in the room, hyperventilates or dissociates. It can happen so fast that you are left speechless. I (LSF) was in a second family therapy session in which I was attempting to discover if any of the adult children attending the session had problems that were hidden from the parents because the identified patient was, figuratively speaking, taking up too much room. The 20-year-old college junior told us that she was a lesbian and, out of the corner of my eye, I noticed that her mother had started to hyper-ventilate. I asked the father to put his arm on his wife's back and I ran outside to get the small paper lunch bag in which I had car-ried my lunch to the office. I had her breath into the bag as the father rubbed her back. By the time the mother had caught her breath, two of the siblings had left the session and the two that remained were crying. The parents asked that the session be ter-minated. I never saw the family again.

Other times, a discussion explodes and therapy progresses. Whenever possible, we attempt to help people calm down in ses-sion so that they can continue being in relationship with one another. We encourage people to touch each other, we teach peo-ple how to self-soothe, we pull our chairs closer to them and soothe them ourselves, and we remind people that this is really hard work, that they have made a great deal of progress already, and that not being able to tolerate something does not mean that love is gone. We sometimes stop sessions when they become too intense and encourage family members to take a break. Mostly, we remind ourselves that therapy is really hard work and that fami-lies are wonderfully resilient resources for individual growth and development.

CONCLUSION

Family therapists encourage difficult dialogues between family members so that family members can continue to support one another's growth while remaining meaningfully connected to each other. Parents provide environments for youth to grow toward increased independence by confirming youth where they are, con-tradicting stages of development that are no longer useful, and continuing to stay in relationship with them. The developmental trajectory process, in which small changes occur and relation-ships adapt, is one that family therapists encourage by creating a crucible to hold difficult dialogues. Families that come to therapy on track in this developmental trajectory process are often able to engage in difficult dialogues that allow sexual minority youth to disclose their sexual identity, if that is what they want to do.

Families who are derailed are encouraged to have difficult dialogues to reengage youth in the developmental trajectory process. For youth to be in meaningful relationships with family members, they must come to feel both confirmed and constrained in those relationships. The confirmation encourages youth toward identity exploration while the constraint holds youth accountable for their impact on others. Family therapists encourage difficult dialogues by being aware of relational dynamics that get in their way, by having tunnel vision, by challenging cultural stereotypes that distance family members, and by challenging family members to stay involved in relationship with one another.

Coming out to one's family is a dramatic process because relational dynamics in families are usually life-altering. For youth, the dynamics are even more dramatic because, until they are launched and independent, their very survival is dependent upon some support from their parents. For some queer youth, then, therapy is not about coming out to family; it is instead about getting back on track in the developmental trajectory process so that they can be parented, in spite of the fact that they must continue to hide their sexual identity. Therapy has set the stage for difficult dialogues to occur and for people to remain in relationship with one another. We trust in the developmental trajectory process and in family members' inherent desire to be loving with one another, and we hope that youth will eventually be received in loving ways.

Difficult dialogues in therapy pave the way for a more intimate and loving view of family members. Although family members, and the youth themselves, may accept sexual minority status, because most queer youth are growing up in heterosexual homes, most have no role models and parents do not have a clue about how to help. Once the family members are providing an appropriate developmental context for the youth, they must then learn to nurture their children's queerness. Therapy, then, becomes a place where youth can explore their identities, where parents can continue to develop relationships with their youth and learn to cherish the gifts their youth have to offer, and where everyone can learn how to nurture queerness.

CHAPTER 5

Nurturing Queerness

The final stage of therapy is the process of helping families nurture their children's burgeoning queerness and integrate their youths' identity into an expanded vision of family life. In short, it is a process of queering the family. Queering expands the family's worldview in unexpected ways. Some parents question the gender stereotyping they have done and work hard to change the dichotomous ways they think about gender. Some question their religious beliefs and others become more religiously identified, having faith that only God knows the truth. Some vigilantly challenge the heterosexism and homophobia they experience in daily life and become activists in their community. Many say, after their initial negative reactions, that their lives are enriched by their family member's minority sexual identity.

We liken this change to the invention of the game of rugby. Rugby was created when William Webb Ellis was playing in a soccer match and picked the ball up with his hands and ran with it. The plaque that commemorates Ellis praises him for his "fine disregard for the rules of soccer." Imagine being at that soccer match. The players and fans were engrossed in the game and suddenly some guy comes along and picks up the ball. Everyone there had an investment in the status quo; many people really liked the game of soccer, some were thoroughly enjoying that specific match, and some were very good at soccer and wanted to leave well enough alone. Most were probably afraid that changing the rules would mean the end of soccer as they knew it. At the time, they probably were not able to see that there is room for all types of sports that end up enhancing each other.

These same experiences occur when a family is introduced to the possibility of a queer youth. At first, families are invested in the status quo. They usually liked thinking of their family as heterosexual and were happy leaving well enough alone. Then they become afraid that changing the rules means the end of life as they know it. Once they can recognize that life will be different but also the same, that the youth is queer and also the same person they have always known, they finally can begin to nurture queerness.

Nurturing queerness is not just for families who have accepted that the youth is a sexual minority. We understand acceptance on a continuum, and in rare cases an individual is on the extreme end of the continuum. Those in the middle are encouraged to experience the possibility of alternative ways to view gender and sexual identity, and are tilted toward being more nurturing than they were before therapy began. If family members are unable to tolerate the possibility that their youth are queer, therapists can still create an environment in which queerness is nurtured. We continue to hold hope that we will tilt them enough to begin to tolerate the possibility, and we therapists can be a place of refuge for the youth.

Nurturing queerness happens in individual sessions as well as in relational therapy sessions. We use individual sessions to allow people to explore parts of themselves that relational dynamics prevent them from being able to share with the rest of the family. We see youth individually to help explore their sexual identity in ways they are unable to do when their parents are in the room. We are often able to be more supportive of youth because we have less invested in them than their families do. We also see youth individually to continue to create refuge for them from the homophobia and heterosexism they continue to face.

Relational sessions are used to allow family members to nurture one another. Sometimes we see dyads in sessions without the whole family being present. These sessions are used to increase intimacy within the dyad. Other times we see dyads so that people can talk honestly about their concerns without hurting others who are not in the room. Sometimes we see dyads in session without the rest of the family present because other issues come up through the course of therapy that are not directly related to the youth's sexual minority status but still have an impact on family member's ability to nurture queerness.

Nurturing queerness, like the process of difficult dialogues, sometimes happens in fits and starts. We may see a family in therapy, for example, for a year and then, 3 years later, see individuals or dyads from that family alone. The first portion of family therapy is used to get over the crisis of the coming out process. After the family has tilted in a direction of more complexity, other issues emerge that require facilitation. Sometimes youth who felt supported by us in the coming out process call us a few years later and we are able to nurture their burgeoning sexual identity status in ways that were not possible in the first round of therapy.

There are a number of ways to nurture queerness, and our list is not meant to be exhaustive. To begin with, nurturing queerness is about encouraging the active exploration of identity formation in youth. It is also about encouraging family members to express their negative feelings with the therapist so that we can begin to understand their investment in maintaining the status quo. Nurturing queerness also occurs when parents develop a new appreciation for their youth and embrace the gifts that their child has to offer. Last, nurturing queerness is about broadening the family's center to include complex views of gender and sexual identity, and involving them in a community larger than the one they had before.

ACTIVE EXPLORATION OF IDENTITY FORMATION

Difficult dialogues help family members be actively engaged in the developmental trajectory process toward launching their youth. Once members are actively engaged with each other, they can be confirmed in their identities, contradicted when those identities are challenged, and maintained in relationship with one another. The developmental trajectory from childhood to adulthood contains an active exploration of identify formation. Youth become self-focused and seek to understand who they are in the world. Individuals who come out during this time of exploration are able to integrate their sexual minority status with the rest of their identity. Rather than seeing themselves and being seen by others as one-dimensional, youth can be for example, queer and avid readers who love bologna and don't clean up their rooms— not just queer. When queerness is nurtured in families, children are able to grow up being more than just their sexual identity.

When my son (LSF) was 5, he wanted to be a lion when he grew up. When I asked him why he wanted to be a lion, he said that it was because saber-tooth tigers were extinct. He had a vision of a lion. Lions exist; therefore, he could grow up to be one. Although queer youth certainly see more visions of themselves in the media than they did 10 years ago, they nevertheless have very few visions of future identities. Some youth are lucky enough to have positive models in their communities, but most of the youth we see are not. They grow up in a world where gay marriage is not a possibility, where most religions do not embrace and value queer lives, and where everyone they know is assumed to be heterosexual. We encourage the families we see to actively seek media representation, positive role models, and community resources, and we actively encourage youth to create visions for themselves around their burgeoning identities.

IDENTITY EXPLORATION WITH YOUTH WHOSE FAMILIES ARE LESS ACCEPTING

Exploration of identity formation is challenging for queer youth whose families are less accepting of sexual minority status. Often, in the stage of difficult dialogues, therapists come to an understanding of the ways in which family beliefs about differences get in the way of people's accepting and appreciating queer youth. During these intense discussions, it is important that youth, whether they are closeted or not, believe that the therapist is on their side while also able to respect other family members' viewpoints. Many youth living in families who are intolerant of sexual minority status also receive intolerant messages from the institutions in which they are involved. Therapy is another institution, and unless therapists actively and lovingly challenge family members to embrace more complex views of gender and sexual identity, youth will be unable to trust that the therapist can create refuge and a safe space to explore identity. Individual sessions with youth are often great vehicles for active exploration of identity in families who are less tolerant of their queerness.

We advocate the exploration of their sexual minority identities in environments that are conducive to that exploration. Family therapy, when everyone is present, is about attempting to create such an environment, but it is not always possible. Sometimes youth are only able to explore themselves alone with a therapist. At the same time, the therapist must work toward creating an environment in the family that is conducive to the youth's exploration. As noted earlier, we never encourage youth to come out or act in ways that would put them in danger. We follow their lead, and we find, more often than not, that they are more open, honest, and brave than we might advocate.

177

THE MARNIS

I (LSF) had begun to develop a nice working relationship with Jack and Carol, and their three daughters. Through many difficult dialogues, they were beginning to come to an understanding of the ways in which the family's beliefs about Jana's differences were getting in the way of their appreciation for her. After meeting with the Marni family several times, I asked to see Jana alone. So far, the institutions she was involved with were anything but supportive of who she really was and I, at the beginning, was just another institution. When she was able to see that I was on her side, and saw that I challenged her family, in a loving way, to see her differently, I knew she would be willing to entertain the possibility of seeing me alone. She came in, sat down, and began to cry. She cried for a while and I sat quietly.

Jana: (*talking about a particular incident in school with a teacher*) He says, "Marni, you are disrupting the class again and I will not tolerate it. One more sound out of you and I will send you to the principal's office." Everyone starts to snicker and laugh at me, and I get pissed off and I tell him that it wasn't just me talking and we get into an argument right there in front of everybody.

LSF: You said that you got pissed off. Was it because the kids were snickering or because the teacher was embarrassing you in front of everyone and picking you out when everyone else was also talking? I mean, they both sound absolutely horrible, but which was worse?

Jana: (*quietly*) I guess the kids snickering.

LSF: That is absolutely the worst. I mean, you have the teacher yelling and no one is supporting you. Not only are they not supporting you, but they seem to be enjoying it that you are getting singled out.

Jana: And all my mother sees is that I get sent to the principal's office.

LSF: Your mom is trying really hard to understand—I've noticed that over the course of our therapy—but she keeps missing you, doesn't she?

Jana: She always thinks everything is my fault. I know my mother thinks there is something really wrong with me. I am not what she imagines a daughter should be like, not like my sisters certainly and not like anyone else she knows.

LSF: And how about you? What's your idea about what a daughter should be like? I mean, like if you could really be anything you wanted to be with her? If you weren't constrained by how she thinks about you, and you could be really who you are and you knew she would love you and accept you no matter what?

Jana: (*crying softly*) I'm so fucking ugly.

LSF: Help me understand.

Jana: I disgust myself.

LSF: So, you've internalized some messages about how you're supposed to be and they don't really fit who you are? Because you're like your sisters and your mother and the other females in your community, but you're also different and you have always been different.

Jana: Yeah, and those things are evil and disgusting and I can't get rid of them no matter how hard I try.

LSF: What things?

Jana: Well, you know, I'm afraid that I think too much like a guy, and what that might lead to, you know. Like I have to constantly stop myself from having those thoughts, but, you know, they keep coming up, they won't go away.

LSF: What thoughts?

Jana: Well, you know, like, I'm worried that these feelings that I have, you know, if I keep thinking about them, keep fueling them . . . well, you know that story my dad told about the guy and the wolf? if the guy keeps feeding his wolf, then he keeps getting angry, you know, and so I try not to fuel them but they keep coming up and so I just get mad at myself. But of course that helps nothing. And then I know God knows anyway, so what's the point of denying them, you know—he knows everything anyway, even if I try to pretend.

LSF: Yeah, I know, you keep pretending. But sometimes when you're honest with yourself . . . is that when you think you are gross? Is it that you have these thoughts and feelings that you know are yours, that you know about yourself, but when you have them you feel gross?

Jana: Yeah, so I keep telling myself not to have them. I mean, sometimes I have visions of myself that aren't gross, that I like, even if other people don't, but some I worry are just disgusting.

LSF: And they keep coming anyway?

Jana: Yeah.

LSF: Okay, just play with me for a minute. What if, just for a moment here, what if you tried not to get rid of them but to sort of think of them as neat, you know?

Jana: I'd be excommunicated. Burned at the stake, all that shit.

LSF: Jana, this is just between you and me—and God, of course. You're having thoughts and feelings but you are in control of who you tell. Just because you are having thoughts and feelings doesn't mean, number one, that you have to tell anyone about them, or two, that you have to act on them unless you choose to do so. No one else decides that, just you. Right?

Jana: Yeah, that's true. (*thoughtfully*) Well, really what I'm worried about is that I might be a lesbian.

LSF: Uh-huh, and what makes you think that?

Jana: Well, I've got this mad crush on Meg, and I don't think it's normal.

LSF: Normal, shnormal. So, you like her?

Jana: Yeah, but I mean, *really* like her, like I can't get her off of my mind, I think about her all the time, like I'm obsessed, you know?

LSF: Yeah, I know.

Jana: Then I get worried, you know, and I think about what would happen if I really was a lesbian. You know, my life would be *over.* I mean, really over. I would be excommunicated, I'd be kicked out of the house, everyone would hate me, I'd hate myself—so then I just get depressed and . . .

LSF: Jana, you are in control here. You make the decisions, you decide. There are all sorts of ways to play this and you have plenty of time, okay? First and foremost, I guess, I just want to thank you for telling me. It says a lot about you. It shows how thoughtful you are and also how much control you have over the situation. You see pretty clearly, you know? I've always appreciated that about you. So, you're thinking you're a lesbian and then you start to feel bad about yourself, right?

Jana: Yeah.

LSF: Because you've been told all your life about what you should be and you've tried really hard to fit in, to please everyone, to follow everyone's expectations of yourself.

Jana: Yeah, and I can't.

LSF: But you haven't had time to explore who you want to be. Instead, you get disgusted because you have internalized messages from other people. But they don't have to define you. That's one of the fun things about growing up.

Jana: Well, it's probably just a passing phase.

LSF: Yep, it could be that, and I'm still glad you told me.

As youth begin to voice their vision of themselves in individual sessions with a therapist who also sees the family, the therapist is able to use sessions with other family members to explore the possibility that they can nurture queerness. Therapists can have individual meetings with other family members to help create a container for youth to be held while they get more comfortable sharing themselves in the family. For example, in an individual session, Jana's mother, Carol, was able to express that she felt that Jana's nonstereotypical gendered behaviors were a rejection of her and her mothering. When she was able to let go of those feelings, Carol was able to begin to see Jana's struggles and pains as less of an extension of Carol and more as a reflection of a struggling young woman caught by expectations around traditional femininity that she could not meet.

IDENTITY EXPLORATION AND THE COMMUNITY

Youth long for potential visions of themselves as they explore their burgeoning identities. This is more possible than ever before, but there are still many youth who do not *know* that they know another queer person. Part of forming an identity as a queer person means finding role models. In many communities, this is close to impossible because queer adults whom youth interact with, like teachers and coaches, may be closeted. We know many teachers who live vibrant queer lives outside their professional ones but who fear the community's response if it were to find out about their alternative lifestyles. This means that youth do not have access to those who potentially could be valuable resources.

Although youth may not know any teachers who are out, we encourage them to find supportive adults in their schools and communities, if possible. We brainstorm with them about how to identify people who are safe and people who are not. Most youth have a keen sense of this already and we help them fine-tune that sense by exploring how it is they know and when and how to approach different people. Some high schools have alliance clubs for different oppressed minorities and we encourage our youth to get involved. If it is too dangerous for them, we encourage them to find the adults involved in those clubs and see if they can develop relationships with them.

It is helpful if therapists know about community resources available to help support sexual minorities. If there is a college nearby, we encourage youth see if it has a center devoted to sexual minorities. At these centers, youth are often welcome to hang out, volunteer, fundraise, and borrow written and videotaped material they may find helpful. There are many events on campus that youth can attend that further introduce them to queer role models in their communities, including queer film festivals and outside speakers. Many communities also have HIV/AIDS clinics that provide support and education to all sexual minorities. Some even have support and educational groups for queer youth and their families. Some communities have active PFLAG organizations, with a wealth of information helpful to youth. We encourage youth and their families to use the resources available in the community. The more people who can support a youth, the better able the youth will be to create a positive identity.

Although youth need to be advised about safety guidelines, we also encourage youth to read first person narratives and to look on the Internet for community (although we don't advocate chatting with anyone they do not know). There are great books and Internet sites written by proud queer people that can help youth develop positive images of themselves. We are also aware that when we ask the youth themselves, they have often found resources on their own that they love to tell us about. When they discover that there is a community beyond their own that is waiting for them and is active, vibrant, and accepting, they begin to believe that they are not the only people in the universe who experience the kinds of things they have experienced. When they can share this information with you, it helps develop that identity further.

IDENTITY FORMATION AND THERAPY

In therapy with youth, it is helpful to ask questions that authenticate our curiosity about how they identify themselves. With curiosity, we acknowledge that the formation of identity is both subjective and fluid. Queer youth are often limited in exploring different identities because there are few role models with which to identify and because once they come out as queer, they and their community assume things about them that may or may not be true. Whereas queer adults are often able to explore gender roles and sexuality within their own communities (and sometimes in ways more complex than their heterosexual peers) queer youth usually do not have the same opportunities.

For example, a heterosexual teenage boy has many friends who act as role models about how boys talk about the girls they are attracted to. The boy can choose to be the extroverted type who talks openly about these things, the introvert who never talks about them, or the type who talks about them only to a few close friends. The lone adolescent boy who is out and open about his homosexuality with his friends, however, does not know if he wants to talk with them about whom he is attracted to. If he doesn't share his thoughts how much does that have to do with his introversion and how much does it have to do with his homosexuality? More importantly, whom can he trust to understand if he does talk about these things?

Regardless of whether they are supportive, the families that raise queer children and the communities in which they are embedded are limited in their experience of minority sexual identity development. Because most people have limited exposure to those whom they know are queer, they have certain expectations of how queer people are supposed to behave. Any deviation from that causes people to become confused, judgmental, and questioning. Many youth who come out find that people expect them to behave a certain way because they are queer. For example, friends and family may wonder why a male youth who says he is gay is also good at sports, or why a female youth who says she is a lesbian likes to wear dresses. They often confuse sexual identity with gender identity. They may also question youth about dating practices and ask inappropriate questions about sexuality that they wouldn't ask a straight youth. Therapy, then, may be one of the only places in which queer youth are free to explore identity formation in a way that is nonthreatening.

THE EDWARDS

After Tanya came out to her family as bisexual and felt supported, her parents were less worried about her and they terminated therapy. Three years later, when Tanya was 17, her mother called and asked if I (RGH) would be willing to see Tanya alone for a few sessions, at Tanya's request, because she was going away to college and was concerned about the transition. She had, according to her mother, regressed back to being argumentative and difficult. I agreed to see her alone and we had four sessions before she left home.

Tanya: I guess my family has been supportive of me and all, but it feels like they have me sort of stuck in this box about being bisexual. It's like that's all they see. That's how they see me and they think they're so hip and all, but they have all these stereotypes and some of them just don't fit.

RGH: Can you give me an example so I can see if I understand?

Tanya: (*thinking*) Well, like, last night, my brother Robbie was telling a story where he was telling someone about his sister, and I asked, "which sister?" and he said, "I only have one real sister," meaning Jen, of course.

RGH: So he was saying that you weren't a real sister because you are attracted to girls?

Tanya: Yeah, exactly.

RGH: That must have hurt.

Tanya: Well, it's not that it hurt, necessarily—just that It's wrong.

RGH: You're a real sister.

Tanya: Yeah, I'm a real sister. I'm a girl, you know?

RGH: What did you say?

Tanya: Nothing. They think I'm too sensitive anyway and that I'm always looking for something to pick a fight about. No one would understand.

RGH: I understand. (*I'm silent, waiting for Tanya to respond.*) I had a kid in here last week who had the same problem. He is open in his family and a few friends at school and he sort of regrets that that he told his family because they see him now as gay, and that's all. His room is messy and his mom said that she was surprised that he would keep such a messy room, being gay and all. And they were so surprised when he tried out for the lacrosse team. It's like he can't just be a normal kid who goes through normal developmental stuff now that he has come out.

Tanya: Yeah, like when I started dating this kid, Jared—when my brother found out, he was like, oh, does Jared know about you?

RGH: It's like you're not allowed any flexibility to try on different identities.

Tanya: Yeah, that's exactly it.

RGH: You know what, Tanya, this is not your problem. I know that's easy for me to say, because I don't live in your house and you have to, but really, this is your brother's problem, not yours. But soon, and maybe even as soon as next year, in college, you will meet people who will understand, who will nurture your sexuality in ways that your family just can't, not because they don't love you and support you but just because they can't. And later on, to continue to be in relationship with you, which they really want to be, you will teach them. And you know what. They will learn.

Tanya, like most queer youth, was thirsty for information about how to be different in a family which, while supportive, had no clue how to be helpful. She also felt trapped in her family's definition of her and unable to explore her own complexity. Family therapists, knowledgeable about the developmental trajectory of sexual minority identity, can help youth explore their own identity by sharing information about other youths. We can use our relationships with youth to mentor them because we have more information about the exploration than most people in their lives. In addition to reading material and community resources, we can talk about our own experiences, both as therapists with this population and, when appropriate, as sexual minorities ourselves.

Tanya: Can I ask you a personal question? Are you gay? I'm mean sometimes in sessions, my gaydar goes off.

RGH: I am more than willing to answer that if you are sure you want to know. Have you thought about what it would be like to hear the answer?

Tanya: Well, if you say no, I'll feel like an idiot for asking. I guess I might feel lonely or lonelier. Which I don't want. If you say yes, well, then I won't feel like an idiot and I won't feel so lonely.

RGH: So you're really wanting to not feel so alone. What's the loneliest part?

Tanya: Just feeling like no one knows how hard this is. How confusing it is to be in these boxes people put you in and wear the labels that make it easier for them to deal with you. Even my friends don't totally understand. Many of them call themselves bisexual because that's what we all do. It's hip and cool. But when they talk it's obvious that they are visiting the place where I live. They try it on like clothes. And I just feel more confused.

RGH: It sounds like in addition to being lonely you are confused because everyone has some beliefs or assumptions about sexuality and none of them are fitting for you.

Tanya: Yeah . . .

RGH: It also seems like you are not totally sure who you are yourself yet, and then you have all these different friends and family telling you who they think you are or should be based on the label "bisexual."

Tanya: Yes. I'm not sure either, I guess. But I know what they are saying is not right either.

RGH: So back to your question about me. If you still want me to answer, I do not want to be another person who tells you who they think you should be. Because I do not think that would be helpful to you. Sexuality is very wonderful and complicated and tricky. And you will find your own way through this. You will learn for yourself what feels and seems right for you. But you have to keep trusting your gut instincts about this.

Tanya: Well, I still want you to answer.

RGH: Okay. Well I have a long-term partner who is a woman. And If I had to put a label on myself the label I would use is "queer."

Tanya: Queer?! Why that word? I hate that word. It's so corny.

RGH: I'm sure you've heard it used as an insult.

Tanya: At school everyone uses it to mean corny or stupid. Or to harass kids they think are gay.

RGH: Well, the reason I use it is that I don't feel so boxed in by it. As you are finding out, people make many assumptions when they hear labels like lesbian or gay or bisexual. They also make assumptions when they hear "queer." But they aren't as clear about what that means. To know more they have to ask me. Of course, that means I have to be able to explain how I think about it. So it makes me work harder, too. And it makes me feel more free of those other labels that feel more rigid and defined.

Tanya: But "queer" sounds so horrible and gross. And I'm not sure what it means.

RGH: I think what you are saying is important. Some people have had such horrible experiences with the word *queer* that they are completely uncomfortable with using it at all. It can feel degrading. I am respectful of that. But remember, I told you that this was complicated. And for me personally, this is the label that fits best, partly because I see sexuality as constantly evolving and changing. So what it means changes as well.

Tanya: I still don't like it. I wouldn't use it myself.

RGH: I understand. The label you feel most comfortable with is "bisexual," yes?

Tanya: Well, I guess so, except that I'm not sure what that means and everyone else seems to think it means things that don't make sense to me. But being queer sounds even worse.

RGH: Well, I think there is some power in reclaiming words. Words that were insults, like *queer*, lose much of their power when they are reclaimed and used as a positive way of referring to the people they were intended to hurt. Could you think of how you might reclaim the word *bisexual?* And make it your own, something you are proud of?

Tanya: I never thought about that. How could I do that?

RGH: I'm not sure. It might be helpful to start with your own definition of bisexual.

Tanya: I don't know how I define it. I like the idea of taking what was an insult and turning it around. It would feel powerful to not be so afraid of it.

RGH: Well, what would it be like to ask some people around you how they define it? Your brother for instance. You could ask him to define bisexual and then stay curious and ask him to clarify. Does he think that being bisexual makes you less a sister and more of a brother? Does he mean that you are not as much of a girl, or more like a boy, or both? Do you think you could tolerate the answers he would give you?

Tanya: It would be hard because I think that's stupid. And it would make me feel like he doesn't understand me.

RGH: On the other hand, it might help you understand yourself better. At least you'll know what you don't think is true about you. It might really help you clarify and better explain who you think you are and are not. And at some point, when he's older or more open, you'll be able to let him know who you think you are. But you would have to be careful to take care of yourself when asking people. You may get answers that are really hard to hear. What would help you?

Tanya: It helps just to think about it as their opinion. To keep a bit of distance and remember that the goal is to help me get clear about me. It would also help to know I could talk with you or my friends about what I was finding out. And how it made me feel.

I used this opportunity in therapy to encourage Tanya to be open to the process of defining herself in her active exploration of identity development. I also encouraged her to talk with other people about their ideas and to think about language differently. When youth hear how it is that others experience them, if they are able to be critical, they can use the others' ideas as a way to understand themselves. So when Tanya's brother said that she was not a sister, Tanya could try this on for size—seeing which parts fit and which parts don't, and come to a better understanding of her definition of sister.

We learn a great deal about ourselves by the ways in which others see us. If we help youth understand that part of the process of identity development is in the claiming of that understanding for ourselves, we are nurturing that development.

Therapists can help youth actively explore their identities by sharing stories about themselves, stories about other queer people they know, and stories about clients, as long as they protect their identity. Decisions about how you use yourself in therapy are beyond the scope of this book, but because queer youth are looking for role models, we encourage therapists, if they are comfortable, to share stories that will help youth explore their identities. We have had many youth tell us that different stories we have told about ourselves and other people have helped them know they are not alone and also helped them embrace more complex ways of being queer.

EXPLORING THE NEGATIVE

As difficult dialogues are successfully resolved, family members come to see that more honest and open recognition of each other makes for more satisfying relationships. Most importantly, family members recognize that their youth are more engaged in life. The youth are easier to live with, less disengaged from the family, and less angry. Parents see that their youth were in trouble and that when they allow more flexibility in their youth's behavior while holding them accountable in relationship, they have an impact. They also come to recognize that they are happier and more comfortable expressing themselves more fully.

While helping family members actively engage in the developmental trajectory process towards launching their youth, difficult dialogues encourage people to be more honest about themselves and each other. In this way, they are more able to nurture queer youth because they know them better. Honesty, however, brings not just love, but also negative feelings that need to be explored. Although exploring the negative does not appear to nurture queerness, when people can investigate the full range of their worry, disappointment, anger, and sadness, they are able to let it go and be available to their children. We have seen this time and time again. When parents and siblings of queer youth are able to express their concerns openly to us, they more often than not move on to loving positions. It is almost as if their worries, fears, and homophobic ideas lose steam when they are voiced.

189

When family members are more honest with each other, they are more open to the fears they have about homosexuality and the possibility that their youth is queer. They are also more open to thinking about the religious beliefs that get in the way of them fully accepting that queer youth. Family members, when more honest with each other, also come to find that they disagree in important and profound ways. Although all of these variables— fear, religious beliefs, and profound disagreement—threaten the developmental trajectory and the possibility that queer youth will be nurtured, when explored, they lose much of their power.

Exploring Fears that Get in the Way of Nurturing Queer Youth

Some family members are afraid to share their worries for fear that they will be hurtful. Others express their concerns with no awareness of how they may be hurtful.

Those who are afraid to be hurtful may worry that everyone else will get the wrong impression of them—that everyone will think that their concerns are all that they feel. As therapists, we have to be conscious of the trap of political correctness. We must be able to normalize homophobic bias and simultaneously challenge it, seeing our clients more complexly than their homophobia or political correctness. We therefore explain to families that it is important to share their worries and negative feelings so that they can get rid of them. We also acknowledge that having homophobic and heterosexist biases is a natural part of living in this culture and that we all have these biases regardless of our sexual orientations.

For family members who are not aware of the ways in which they may be hurtful, we help explore this issue in therapy. When someone makes a negative statement, we process it until the member understands the impact of the statement. Often what happens is that someone says something hurtful, and when it is pointed out, the member explains that it was not her or his intention to be hurtful. We acknowledge that intentions are important and it was hurtful, whether it *was* intended to be that way or not. We then look at the origins of the intentions, which are usually based in some fear that the member has, and we explore that.

Because we alternate between seeing entire families and seeing individuals and dyads, we have ample opportunity to explore negative thoughts and feelings in individual sessions. Parents, for example, often feel more comfortable exploring the negatives when their children are not in the room. Children seem to feel the same. In sessions with their parents youth may put up a good front about a stress-free lifestyle, but inside they are more frightened than they let on. Worry, disappointment, anger, and sadness are natural feelings in a homophobic culture.

THE SMITHS

In a marital couple session, Rose was having concerns about Michael that she wanted to discuss with me (LSF). James, Michael's boyfriend, was out of the hospital and Michael was starting to spend time with him again.

Rose: I'll tell you what I think. I think something is going on with Michael and that James. I think they have a sick relationship. I don't like it at all.

LSF: What do you mean? What is sick about their relationship?

Rose: Well, I think James is, ah, well, not right. I think he is a, uh, homosexual, and I think he is making Michael into one. Michael is so lonely and James is nice to him and I am afraid that Michael is going to be a faggot just to keep this friendship. It worries me sick.

LSF: What worries you sick? That Michael could be gay or that he is doing something that is not him so that he can keep a friend?

Rose: Well, both, really.

LSF: All right, let's start with the gay thing. What worries you about the possibility that he might be gay?

Rose: Where do I start? He is our only son and it is so wrong, you know? They're so dramatic, so flamboyant, so . . . odd. I mean, he didn't play with dolls or anything, we always treated him like a boy. I don't know, it is so unnatural.

LSF: It's not really unnatural—it's as natural as being a heterosexual. It's just that most people are heterosexual, so we sort of make the assumption that everyone is when, in reality, we all aren't heterosexual. Some of us do prefer the same gender, you know?

Rose: I know, I know. I have a brother who thought he was homosexual. He was clinically depressed and committed suicide when he was 28. I just never thought I would have a son that was gay as well. My brother's life was a living hell and (*starting to cry*) I really don't want that for Michael. He is such a baby. I don't want him to be hurt and it is so bad out there for gay people. Just the other day I heard about some kid getting beat up at school because someone thought he looked gay.

LSF: I know, it is a war zone out there and lots of homophobia exists. We need to be active agents to fight that kind of hateful behavior. Many of the schools are doing that now, you know? So, you worry about Michael being gay because you think it is unnatural and because there is so much prejudice out there. Why else?

Rose: Well, obviously, I worry that people will think it is my fault—you know, everyone always blames the mother. And then I worry because it means I won't have grandchildren, and what if he becomes a drug addict, like my brother, and it would kill my mother if she knew—ugh—and what if he gets AIDS . . . oh my goodness, my worries would be endless.

LSF: They feel endless now, but they aren't endless, except that you are a loving mother, so in that way they are endless. But let's see, so a number of things now—that it is unnatural, that there is prejudice, that you are at fault, and that he would develop unhealthy practices, not take care of himself, and get AIDS. Right? Oh, also, that it would kill your mother if she knew, and what else?

Rose: That I wouldn't have grandchildren, although I know that is changing. It's just that, gosh, I just never thought, you know? I mean, when you are raising your kids, you don't think about the possibility that they would be gay. My brother was so depressed all his life, that's why I thought he was gay, and Michael was really a very happy child and not at all acting like a girl. My brother was always into dolls and acting like a girl, crying all the time and afraid of everything. Michael wasn't that way.

LSF: So really, if Michael were gay, you would have to mourn the boy you thought he was, or so you think. I mean, in reality, whatever his sexual orientation, he is still Michael, you know what I mean?

Rose: Yeah, I guess so.

LSF: Well, he would be. In the families I work with, where someone comes out of the closet, there is always this assumption that coming out means a completely different person, like a Jekyl and Hyde, when in reality, the coming out process is smaller and bigger than we think it is going to be. That is neither here nor there right now, but some family members have this assumption that everything is going to be different if they discover this quote secret about their kids. Anyway, whatever Michael's sexual orientation is, you will love him and be there for him like you always have, right?

Rose: Oh my God, yes, he is my son. I am not that kind of person—I would never be that kind of person that disowned their kids, no matter what.

LSF: You are such a good mother. John, what are you thinking? You have been kind of quiet.

John: Well, I mean, I don't know. I guess it would get some taking used to, you know. I mean, I never thought about it before. It would be a shock. But he can't tell yet, can he? I mean, he is only 17. Don't you have to be much older? I mean, a lot of boys do . . . you know . . . do stuff with other boys, but it doesn't mean they're gay.

LSF: Yes, that's true. It is quite common for kids to experiment with their neighbors and friends. But the issue of whether he can know now about his sexual orientation is pretty specific to each person. Some kids know they are gay or straight long before they reach adolescence, some kids know during adolescence, and some not until adulthood. Then, also, some people change their sexual orientation and some people's stay stable their whole life. So, this thing you said, that it would be a shock and would take some getting used to, how would you respond, do you think, if you discovered that Michael, or, for that matter, Emily, was not heterosexual?

John: Emily, forget it! She is a real girl. Michael, I really don't know. I guess I'd be disappointed.

LSF: First of all, just an aside, I'd have to disagree with you when you said that Emily is a real girl, because lesbians are also real girls, they are just attracted to other girls. You know what I mean? I think what you mean is that she has already shown strong interest in boys, right? It's just that we make assumptions about people's behavior based on all sorts of stereotypes that aren't always entirely true. Anyway, to get back to your disappointment with Michael, in what way would you be disappointed if you discovered that he was gay?

John: Well, I mean, who wouldn't be? For all the reasons that my wife mentioned.

LSF: Yeah, but what about your own reasons?

John: Hmm. I'd be embarrassed to have a son parading around like a girl, I guess. I just wouldn't be proud of him. He'd be a freak, you know what I mean?

LSF: So you would be afraid that he would be outrageous and embarrass you? And whom would he embarrass you in front of? I mean, when you think about yourself having a homosexual child, and people knew, who comes to mind?

John: I guess I don't really care what other people think, I think it's just that I would be embarrassed.

LSF: Because it is a reflection on your own masculinity? Like you weren't masculine enough to have a heterosexual son? Would you feel sort of like Rose—that in some way, even though someone's sexual identity is totally an individual thing, and most people talk about it not as a choice but as a biological given, that you were responsible for it happening? If you had just played catch with him one more time? (*Both John and Rose laugh.*) What other sorts of thoughts do you have when you think about the possibility that your son might be gay?

John: Now that you put it that way, I think, in the back of my mind, I always thought he might be gay. I remember when he was 5—remember this Rose?—there is a guy in my office, Bob, who's sort of a friend, and he's gay, and I was talking with him about Michael once. Something had happened that made me wonder, and I was talking to Bob about it, remember? And I asked him then what he thought.

LSF: Wow, I'm impressed. It's not every father who can be so vulnerable with his male friends to discuss his concerns about his child. That's impressive. So, it sounds like on some level, you would be shocked, but on another level, you wouldn't be. How about what Rose was saying about being there for him? That even though she would be disappointed, she would never disown him and she would accept him no matter what. Do you feel that way as well?

John: Oh, yes. He is my son and I will always be there for him. I have learned, in this therapy thing, that I've been pretty distant as a father, but I certainly think that Michael knows how much I love him and that I want to be there for him no matter what he has to tell me.

Exploring the negative in this couple session was a way to help begin the process of nurturing queerness. The Smiths, like most families who are exposed only to cultural mandates around homophobia and heterosexism, were steeped in fears about their son's homosexuality. Rose carried the extra burden of having a depressed brother whose homosexuality appeared to be problematic. Fears create anxiety that keep people disconnected from their youth and from each other. Some people think that if they do not explore their fears or their negative attitudes, those attitudes will not influence them. We find just the opposite, however; unexplored fears and negative attitudes greatly influence people and their ability to nurture one another.

Once family members explore their fears openly, they come to recognize that they can handle them. When people say homophobic things, like homosexuality is not natural, we challenge these statements. When they talk about their fears around homophobia, we challenge them to become activists in the fight against it. When they share their worries about their children, we witness their experiences. When they discuss the relational dynamics that are getting in the way of seeing their children, we challenge them to look critically at these dynamics and to not be organized by how their youth's queerness is a reflection of anything but their youth's queerness. When parents are able to explore their fears and negative attitudes, they are able to remind themselves how loving they feel toward their children. This creates the needed space to nurture queerness.

THE SMITHS

The Smith family cancelled the next two sessions. When I called to reschedule, they said they were too busy and would call back when their schedules opened up. Rose called 3 months later to ask to see me by herself. She said she wanted an individual appointment and did not want to be seen with John. Rose was concerned about her marriage and wanted to talk about that in therapy. As she was discussing her concerns, she casually mentioned Michael's homosexuality. I was shocked and asked Rose to take a detour for a moment.

LSF: Rose, wait for a minute, the last time we met, a little over 3 months ago, you and John were talking about your reactions about Michael if he were gay, and now you are talking as if you know he is. Could you fill me in?

Rose: Oh, yes, well, Michael came out to us over dinner one night a while back. This feels like yesterday's news. He said you knew so I didn't think it was any big deal. He and James are just good friends, although they had a sexual relationship. But he was careful, he says, and he says that he is not going to have another relationship until college, so for now he is just focusing on his schoolwork. He's certainly not as lonely anymore and he and Emily have gotten closer. So anyway, as I was saying about John . . .

A space was created for Rose and John to share their negative attitudes, which paved the way for them to be ready to hear about their son's sexual identity. Somehow, Michael knew this about his parents and came out to his family. Youth usually come out to their families outside of the therapy room. Often adolescents elicit our help but then do it on their own. This is certainly our preferred way of working, as it is important that they be in the driver's seat. Also, if we have created the kind of atmosphere in the family that elicits this kind of disclosure outside of the therapy room, then we have been successful.

Exploring Religious Beliefs that Get in the Way of Nurturing Queer Youth

Some people believe that sexual identity is a choice whereas others believe it is biologically driven. Still others believe that it is a combination of the two. We have found that some family members who belong to religiously conservative congregations fall on the choice end of the continuum when it comes to understanding their youth's sexual identity status. Because scriptures state that homosexuality is sinful and we have free will, they argue, even if individuals have homosexual thoughts and feelings, they can control their behavior. Homosexuals can choose to control themselves just like heterosexual people can choose to control themselves. Some argue that sex should not occur outside the marital relationship and because homosexuals cannot be married, they must abstain from having sexual relations.

We do not dispute this position—unless a client solicits our opinion, of course—but we encourage conversation about these different positions in families. We want to have these opinions voiced so that people can listen to each other, hold differing opinions, and still be loving. Usually what occurs is that a family member will talk about choice and a youth will report that it doesn't feel like a choice to him or her. "Why would someone choose all this pain?" is frequently the response. We often use this opportunity to attempt to enrich intimate interactions in families. We remind them that intimacy does not mean that everyone always agrees with everyone else but rather that everyone has enough comfort to voice a dissenting opinion.

In families in which religious beliefs get in the way of youth's coming out to their parents, difficult dialogues have ensued over the course of therapy and family members get back on track in the developmental trajectory process. Parents often become less rigid regarding what they can tolerate from their youth and also more aware of the ways in which their youth may be unhappy. As they get to know their children in this stage of development, they begin to have an awareness that the child is hiding her- or himself from them. Sometimes this leads them to explore the possibility that their youth may be queer.

THE MARNIS

I (LSF) saw the Marni family intermittently until Jana graduated from high school. As Jana became more comfortable experimenting with behaviors that felt more congruent with her own sense of who she was, I coached her parents and sisters to be support-

197

ive. When they saw the results—i.e., Jana's relaxed and kind behavior at home and the improvement in her grades—they recognized the ways they may have been hurtful in the past. The family allowed and even began to encourage Jana's non-steriotyped gender behavior and Jana appreciated their support by helping around the house and being easier to live with. As they became less preoccupied with their concerns about Jana, the parents began to work on their marital relationship in therapy. I recognized that, for Jana to come out to her family, I had to explore both parent's thoughts and feelings about homosexuality as well as how much tension the marital relationship could tolerate. After a particularly intense session with the entire family, Carol asked me if she could see me alone the next week. In the individual session, Carol relayed a story from home that troubled her.

Carol: We were watching TV and some show was on that said something about a homosexual and Jack said something in his nasty way about fags and I happened to look over at Jana and I saw how upset she was and I realized how I have spent my life trying to protect those girls from Jack's rages and that I haven't really done a good job, because she was scared to death sitting over there. And it also hit me like a punch in the gut that Jana might be thinking she was one of them, if you know what I mean. Like she was thinking she might be gay or something. And if she were, if she was, it would absolutely, positively kill Jack. He would never get over it and he would hate Jana and our life would be ruined. He'd never want to see her again. I don't think I would be able to hold the family together after something like that.

LSF: And how would you feel if Jana was a lesbian?

Carol: Well, I'd get over it. I will love my daughters no matter what. A mother's love is different from a father's love. It is much less conditional. I will never stop loving any of my girls. But Jack, he has this way of just deciding that something is wrong, and that is it, he never looks back. And as a Christian, you know, he has all sorts of support for his position. Oh my, he'd never let her go back to church. Oh, I just don't want to think about the consequences.

LSF: And how would you feel if you discovered that Jana was a lesbian? Or if Kim or Michelle were lesbian?

Carol: (*softly crying*) I think Jana is a lesbian. I think she is. I mean, maybe she'll get over it, but I have a feeling that she is thinking about it now. I'm getting some hints from her that she is worried about it. Oh, it's awful.

LSF: Tell me more.

Carol: She's been asking me questions about the Bible and how much I believe everything that's in it. You know, whether it is the word from God or just a man-made version of it, and what would happen if God made a mistake? She said the other day, something like, if God is always right and He makes someone in His image that is sick or perverted, then does that make that person right? I think she is really struggling with this evil inside of her and she is looking for some answers. I certainly can't send her to church with these questions and I don't know what to say.

LSF: What have you been telling her?

Carol: Well, I told her that God does not make mistakes. Men make mistakes, but God doesn't ,and if we are confused it is because we haven't figured it out yet and we should pray harder for clarity. I also told her that Satan was in all of us and that we had to fight hard to not listen to him.

LSF: And do you believe that Jana would be succumbing to evil if she were sexually attracted to girls?

Carol: You know something, even though I don't want her to discover this about herself, like if she has a choice to not be a lesbian, I want to give her all the encouragement I can give her to choose to be normal. But if she is a lesbian and God made her that way, then I don't think it is evil. We tried so hard to knock the boy out of her for all these years and we only made her depressed and the family miserable. I've talked to God about it. I think He wants her to be happy and if her calling is to be a lesbian then that's how she was made and the only thing we can do about it is to make her miserable.

LSF: Carol, you continue to amaze me. You are a wonderful mother. You try so hard and you care so much. The girls are lucky to have you. Do you realize that?

Carol: I mean, I have all sorts of questions, you know, like would it be something permanent? How would she know it now? Can it be something that she can change?

After Carol explored her religious beliefs with me in the context of thinking about the possibility that her daughter was a lesbian, she was open to exploring what this all meant. A few months later, Jana told her that she was sexually attracted to girls. Jana also told Carol that some of her friends knew and that she had been trying to get advice from Web sites for Christian homosexuals. She knew she had homosexual desires but she wasn't sure yet whether she was going to act on them. Jana asked Carol not to tell anyone, and said that she wanted to control who knew and when. Carol told Jana that she would love her no matter what and also promised that she would let Jana decide how, whom, and when to tell. I knew from my meetings alone with Jana that she had already been sexual with a friend and was much more comfortable with her identity than she had indicated to her mother; she just knew that her mother was not yet ready to hear the whole thing. She said that she was preparing her mom so when she came home from college with a girlfriend, she would be okay with it.

The experience I had with Carol was similar to many experiences we have with parents who are struggling with two principles that are completely contradictory and therefore inhibit of any sort of resolution. On the one hand, Carol was firmly and lovingly engaged in conservative Christian religious principles around homosexuality while, in direct contrast, she was firmly engaged in the knowledge that her daughter, whom she loved, was being hurt by these principles. She knew that God did not make mistakes, that he wanted her daughter to be happy, and that he had made her a lesbian. She also knew that he did not approve of lesbians. Once she was able to hold these principles together in her mind and struggle with their inherent contractions, she was able to come to some sort of resolution. Because God made her daughter this way, it must not be evil.

When parents explore the religious beliefs that get in the way of their ability to nurture queerness, they are more open to exploring sexual minority status. The question then becomes how much they really want to know their children. As they open themselves up to seeing their children they also open themselves up to seeing how their children fare living in the direct center of these contradictory principles. They become much more sensitive to the pain their children are experiencing and begin to understand how traumatizing it is for their youth to struggle with identity development in the midst of such profound contradiction.

Parents make decisions all the time about how much information they can tolerate knowing about their children, and they make these decisions automatically, without thinking. In a therapeutic space of refuge, with access to more awareness, parents are encouraged to make conscious decisions about how they want to parent. We make it very clear that this is their choice and only they can know what they can tolerate. We also make it very clear that, even if they can tolerate knowing more about their children, children may not want to share everything (or anything) with them. In these cases, we urge parents not to pry, snoop, or do anything to get information that involves lying or deceit. We encourage them, instead, to tell their children what they see, whether the children want to hear it or not. We find that when parents are open and ready, youth generally will allow them access to self, and parents can nurture with knowledge.

Exploring Profound Differences that Get in the Way of Nurturing Queer Youth

When family members have had difficult dialogues in therapy, they are challenged to explore differences about fundamental ways to be in relationship. For some family members, this challenge exposes differences about the acceptability of sexual minority status. We encourage family members to explore these differences so that they do not prevent those who can nurture queerness from doing so. We challenge the members who are willing to nurture queerness to do it openly and to not let other members' views get in the way of their relationships. We also challenge family members who are not willing to nurture queerness to continue to tilt in that direction.

THE MARNIS

Carol, Jana's mother, was getting closer to her daughter and her daughter was sharing more information with her outside of therapy sessions. The dilemma became how much Carol wanted to know her daughter. This was a decision she had to make and there was

201

no right answer. She knew Jana was struggling with her identity, the church, and how she felt about herself. Jana could continue to talk with her mother about these struggles or she could shut down. That was up to Jana. But some of this was in Carol's control and depended on how open she was to hearing about the struggles. Carol met with me (LSF) individually to talk about this dilemma.

LSF: This is something that you should probably make a conscious decision about, even if it is not in your control. Jana struggles so much with her own fragile sense of being okay and particularly what you and Jack think about her that I don't think it would be helpful for her right now to share thoughts and feelings about herself that you find evil. It is absolutely fine for you to say, I cannot handle knowing her completely, and it is way too much for me. It would ruin my marriage and my life if I found out that she was struggling with this possibility.

Carol: It infuriates me that I have to worry about how Jack will feel about this, that we can't do this together, that I have to worry about him blowing up and ruining my daughter's life, you know what I mean?

LSF: Yes, I understand. I really do. We can work on your relationship with Jack so that you feel like you have more access to him and that you can have an impact on his thoughts and feelings. He is opinionated, but he has also shown a remarkable ability in therapy to change his opinions, right? I mean, look at how he first came in and look at where he is now.

Carol: Yes, you make a good point.

LSF: And I also noticed that it was convenient for you to think about Jack's thoughts and feelings and you have avoided the question that I posed about 15 minutes ago about your thoughts and feelings about Jana and whether you really want to know her and whether you can tolerate what she might tell you.

Carol: I do want to know her; I want to be a good mother. Jana deserves that. I just don't know whether I could tolerate knowing that she was a lesbian. I guess as I really think about it, I would be fine with it, as long as I didn't need to tell anyone else. I mean, if that's what's going to make her happy, well, it's her life. I have chosen Christ and I always told myself that I wanted my children to chose Christ, that it has to be an active choice, not something pushed down their throats because then it is not a choice and I do believe in free will and that, in order for you to be saved, it has to be something that comes from inside of you, not something that someone makes you do. And I guess she could still choose Christ, I know there are plenty of homosexuals in the church, she would just have to find a progressive church and all. I just can't see Jack knowing or even wanting to know.

LSF: We do know that Jana is happier, more successful in school, easier to live with, and seems to have much higher self esteem when she is acting in ways that are congruent with who she really is. Both you and Jack know that. She was really in trouble a few years ago and because both of you, and I mean *both* of you, have been more flexible in allowing her room to voice who she really is, she is much less depressed. The cutting was a grave expression of pain and it could have become a habit but it didn't because you all gave her room to express her pain and express herself more fully. You both have done a magnificent job with this. And, you both recognized the ways in which she has contributed to the family now, as she is freer to be herself. I don't just mean helping out around the house, but in teaching you all how to more comfortable with different ways to be yourselves.

Carol: I know, but it is one thing, letting her be more masculine; for Jack, being gay is evil. We have talked about this. He said very clearly, many times, that it is something he could definitely not tolerate. Right now, there is no give on this one.

LSF: What would it do to your relationship with your husband if you allowed your daughter to share herself with you and then you had information about your daughter that you could not share with your husband?

When family members differ in how much they are able to tolerate their youth's sexual identity status, it gets in the way of their relationship with each other. For Carol, for example, to be fully engaged with her daughter, she had to challenge her relationship with her husband. Couple therapy is beyond the scope of this book, yet it is highly recommended when the couple relationship is getting in the way of nurturing youth. We often find that partners usually believe they are polarized around certain beliefs when, in reality, each person's view is more complex than they let on in the couple relationship. By this stage in therapy, the family has gone through a *queering* process, in which simple definitions of gender and sexuality have already been challenged. This process helps partners remember that they are more complex than they present and it cushions the couple therapy process so that members can discover new ways to be in relationship with one another. This becomes one of the ways in which queer youth are gifts to their families.

GIFTS

Queer youth are gifts. They are gifts because they have something different to offer their families. They are also gifts because those who come out to their families while still living at home have trusted their families with valuable information about themselves, which increases intimacy in relationships in the family. They are also gifts because they recruit parents to be appropriately involved with them on the developmental trajectory process toward independence. Queer youth are also gifts because they teach their families and their extended communities about the joys and pain of life lived, from a very early age, with the knowledge that everything is more complex than it seems.

Part of nurturing queerness is helping parents acknowledge the gifts their queer youth have to offer. With the help of a crucible of refuge, some families move from difficult dialogues to nurturing queerness rather quickly. Families change the way they see homosexuality by being confirmed and recognized for their present position at the same time that their position is being challenged. Family members begin to see their child's sexual identity as a gift to the family. We explain the concept of relational ethics (Boszormenyi-Nagy & Spark, 1973) to families in order to highlight the role of giving in a person's self-worth. When youth are able to give to their siblings, parents, and extended family members, it enhances youths' self-esteem. Sexual minority youth open all family members to different ways to be in the world, to different communities, and to different lifestyles. When that difference is appreciated and affirmed, both the family and the youth benefit.

The gift is not just about expanding the family's experience of the world, but also about expanding the nature of family communication. When a child shares this intimate information with the family, it is a gift. Even if the information is shared in a roundabout way—so that parents find out rather than being told—just the awareness itself is a gift. Despite the fact that youth are coming out younger than ever before, they still are more likely to wait to share information about themselves with their families until after they have left home. Families that know about their child's minority identity while the child is still living at home have been given a tremendous gift. We let families know that this says a lot about their dynamics: The child feels safe enough to share, despite the difficulties inherent in the process.

The gift, given during youth, enhances the developmental trajectory process. The task of youth, of course, is to separate from the family of origin while also staying connected. When youth are developing, parents do not just leave the field; they stay actively involved in the promotion of independence and interdependence. Parents must be careful not to be over involved or under involved. A sexual minority youth who is out to her or his family promotes appropriate involvement. Parents cannot be too involved as they come to respect that the youth has a sense of self that is separate from the family understanding of the youth, and they cannot be too uninvolved because the very act of coming out creates a level of intimacy that keeps families involved.

Parents must follow their queer youth's lead in a number of ways they may not have had to do if their child was on a different developmental trajectory. Because this is new territory for everyone in the family, they must learn together about how the youth will grow and develop. Although parents can be supportive, they are not experts on queerness in the way they are about heterosexual life. Most parents still believe that they know what is best for their youth, based on what they went through and based on information they think they have about their child. By simultaneously respecting that ultimately the youth will have to learn what is best for him- or herself and maintaining a loving and supportive relationship, parents help youth mature.

When parents come to nurture queerness in their youth, they begin to see that sometimes this *queer* view of the world is interesting in itself. Because many queer youth have experiences of not fitting in, they have knowledge both about how the world is structured in confining ways and how to be in relationship with that structure while also knowing that things are more complex. This can lead to seeing the world differently—an expanded vision, that, when nurtured, can shed new light on old structures. When family members are able to appreciate youth and begin to think about their youth as having something to offer the family specifically because the youth is queer, they are nurturing the youth in immeasurable ways.

THE PETERSONS

After Lisa and Tom discovered that both their children identified as gay, they met several times as a family and quickly moved from difficult dialogues into nurturing queerness.

Tom: I realized, as I was thinking about how we started this process, Joey, that I went from being drop-dead worried about you to feeling such happiness for you. I was worried that you were going to be miserable the rest of your life and that it was my fault. What I've learned in therapy, however, is that you won't be miserable if you can be truthful to yourself. You have a great head on your shoulders and you know what is right for you. And this thing about fault, well, other people might blame me for you being gay, you know, because our family is so close. Well, I think to myself now, so what? Blame me if you want. I'll take the blame, because I think it is great. You have so enriched my life with this gayness thing. You have opened up for me a whole new way to appreciate the world. It's like, the world used to be so simple and now it is filled with so many different possibilities. The other day at work, Charlie was talking about his son getting married, and you know what? I started feeling sorry for Charlie, that his life is so narrow.

A refuge is created in the family when queer youth are nurtured. The shift is seen in the queer youths' sense of comfort. Once their family has become a refuge for them, youth are more secure in their own identity. They move on with the developmental trajectory process and other areas of their lives. Once the stage of nurturing queerness is activated, it is almost as if sexual identity is on the back burner. Of course, extrafamilial oppression will continue to have an impact, but the youth has a refuge now to fall back on in times of trouble.

BROADENING THE FAMILY'S CENTER

When parents begin to experience their child's difference as an added bonus to their family, they are nurturing queerness. Once families begin this process, an existential shift occurs that broadens the possibilities in all relationships. People begin to see how limited their lives were before the exposure to queerness in their families and their worldview expands beyond their small family circle. Nurturing their queer youth encourages family members to transform relationships with their extended family, and it also encourages transformation in their communities.

Families in therapy who have extended family members who are queer report renewed relationships with these members, who often have been cut off from the family. Those who have been in therapy have developed an appreciation for the struggles that have kept extended family members who are queer from staying in relationship with the larger family, and they find themselves attempting to mend those relationships. Extended family members who are queer also become role models for queer youth and take a position in the family as an expert in ways they have never been asked to do before.

The whole process of coming out to extended family broadens the family's center. Youth make decisions about how to tell different family members and they often do this in relationship with the nuclear family. Often youth follow their parents' lead on this, respecting the boundaries around nuclear family information and extended family knowledge. Family members, then, together are given the opportunity to think about their extended family in more complex ways. Who gets told first and why? Are the extended family members then told that they cannot tell anyone else? Will members be hurt if someone else knows and they do not? Are there people who should not know? Should we wait for so-and-so to die before we tell anyone? These are all complex decisions that broaden the family's center by encouraging critical consciousness throughout life.

When family members come out to extended family members, they often report receiving support that surprises them. We encourage family members in therapy to tell extended family, and they respond by telling us about the horrific things that will happen when family finally finds out. Although sometimes this is the case, more often than not their worst fears are not actualized. Though initially they may show surprise, extended family members are often honored to be told and appreciative of the gift of closeness. Rather than being cut off and rejected, the extended family becomes a larger refuge for the queer youth to be nurtured and feel valued.

THE NOLANS

After Julia, Devin's mother, stood firm about not letting Devin take hormones until he was old enough to make the decision for himself, they struggled through many difficult dialogues but kept working on their relationship. Devin was doing better in school and had not run away since starting therapy. Julia came alone to one of the last sessions I (RGH) had with the family and gave the following report.

Julia: Vera [Julia's sister and support] and I were talking last night and even she has seen a change in Devin. She said that he—I mean, she . . . I still can't get used to calling Devin a she, but that is what she wants, so we are all trying—anyway, Vera said that Devin seemed calmer and more relaxed—not that anyone would call Devin relaxed. Vera has turned a corner with Devin and I think her whole family seems to accept him, I mean, her. And I gotta tell you, that has made all the difference for me. Just having my family help me share this thing has been huge. I can't tell you how relieved it makes me.

RGH: What changed? How is it that you understand Vera's acceptance now?

Julia: I gotta tell you what she said last week. I almost had a heart attack. She's been praying about it. She said, the other day, when I was having some trouble with Devin wearing makeup or something or other, "You know, Julia, Devin has been different since birth. Remember we used to comment on how pretty he was and he acted like a girl as a baby? I've decided that God has a plan for him, you know, and who are we to mess with his relationship with God?" I was shocked. Here she was, saying that she had decided not to mess with God's plan. She was supporting Devin. I mean, really supporting this gender thing. I was so happy. And for the first time, she asked Devin for fashion advice. She was going to some dinner thing at work and Devin was over and he, I mean, she, came home and said that Aunt Vera had asked for advice about which dress to wear. Devin was all smiles. It's great— it is a relief. I feel blessed.

Although it is not easy, families, with guidance and patience, can develop into refuges for youth, and youth can teach families how to be different. Although members continue to worry about each other, they have grown in their appreciation for each other as well. Youth, knowing they have a refuge at home, can use their families as background in the foreground of their own lives, which is where families belong at this stage in the developmental trajectory.

Broadening the family's center goes beyond extended family to the community. Nurturing queerness helps youth and their families become active in fighting homophobia and heterosexism in their communities. Many families talk about the ways in which they used to turn the other way when hearing homophobic remarks but now actively challenge them. Families find themselves using nonheterosexist language, not assuming that everyone they meet is heterosexual, challenging homophobia, and leaving space in other relationships for more people to come out to them. Some describe this vigilance as a mission of activism in their communities, similar to the way in which Herman (1992) wrote of a survivor mission. She described the process whereby abuse survivors channel their misfortunes into political action by finding political and religious aspects of their experiences. By doing this, they transcend their own victimization. Activism becomes a gift they can give to others, and to themselves.

SPECIAL ISSUES IN TREATMENT: BLINDING RAGE

Hardy and Laszloffy described the stigmatization that queer youth face as a form of violence: "The cumulative impact of having one's sense of self routinely denied and denigrated is a form of violence that assaults children who have membership in socially devalued groups" (2002, p. 9). The injustice and magnitude of this assault can tear at the fabric of young queer lives, damaging protective factors and creating a deep and blinding rage. Without constructive outlets, rage can easily lead to violence against self or violence against others. It is these destructive behaviors that can lead queer youth into therapy for presenting problems that may seem to be unrelated to queerness.

Flamboyance can be an outlet for rage. Most of us have had experience with queer youth who appear to be completely comfortable with the gift of queerness and need no nurturing. They are so comfortable with their sexual minority status that they make everyone else completely uncomfortable. We believe that this is not the gift of queerness—it is the gift of flamboyance!

Flamboyance can be a treatment issue when it is a severe distraction and not a statement of secure identity development. An effeminate young man who flounces around and dares someone to make fun of his attraction to men, who is overtly sexual in inappropriate places, who wears makeup in conservative communities, or who kisses his boyfriend on the couch in his conservative Christian stepfather's living room presents a treatment issue. When the flamboyance enrages others, we believe it is an expression of the youth's rage. Flamboyance can be seen as a rage against injustice.

Trans youth who, though well known in their schools as one biological sex, come to school dressed as another are deliberately challenging our culture's assumptions and daring people to question them. They may be harassed, they may gain respect, they may get hurt, and they may feel unsafe. Yet the flamboyance is worth it because it expresses the rage in a manner that may be more appropriate than violence against self or others.

Violence against others and defiance of authority are ways that rage may also be vented. Gay-bashing (being verbally or physically abusive to queer people) may also help young people struggling with their own sexuality handle the powerlessness and rage they feel. In addition, some queer youth report periods of trying to prove their heterosexuality through promiscuous sexual behavior or by getting pregnant or getting someone else pregnant.

Although there are no statistics for the number of youth who are queer, we suspect that there continue to be more closeted queer youth than queer youth who are open and honest about themselves. These youth pass as heterosexuals either because they are not identifying at all or because they are trying really hard to prove to themselves and to others that they are typical. Some youth passively continue to identify as heterosexual whereas others take a more active route and can be sexually promiscuous, engage in unsafe sex, and be harmful to self and to others. We believe this sexual acting out is an expression of rage. Sometimes this rage is turned in toward the self and other times it is directed at others.

Rage is not in and of itself bad. It is a response to struggle and injustice. It is something that all of us, especially those of us who are members of an oppressed minority, must learn to negotiate. It is a powerful emotion that can feel dangerous and be alienating. As therapists working with queer youth, we must be brave in the face of it. We must first recognize the blinding rage, then help youth connect it with their own experiences of injustice, and then help them negotiate different ways to channel it.

The first step is to recognize the rage that is fueling the destructive behavior in which youth engage. Youth may be unable to verbalize the rage in a way that articulates the effect, because it is a profoundly difficult thing to do, even for adults who have more sophisticated access to language. We use our own affective response to youth to gauge the rage. When youth are destructive in ways that infuriate us and other adults in their lives who are trying to be helpful, we suspect this is an expression of rage. With access to this knowledge, therapists can help queer youth sort out what they are feeling.

It is difficult for youth to name the connection between their own destructive behaviors and their experiences with injustice. We help them understand that they have been done an injustice by sharing with them how we would feel if it happened to us. For example, when youth tell us something horrific that occurred that did not bother them, we express the rage we would have felt. We then explore outlets for the rage. We talk about the importance of the constructive expressions of rage for queer youth and help youth discover those that they have already incorporated. Sometimes flamboyance is one of them. When youth own that it is a form of protest, it can be a constructive expression, for it is in the margins that culture expands and new creative expressions emerge. This is a gift that youth have to offer, if we are brave enough to embrace it.

CONCLUSION

Families nurture queerness when they are open to the gifts that their queer youth have to offer. When queer youth are able to actively explore their identities in environments that encourage that exploration, they are able to begin to develop a positive sense of self. We encourage youth to explore their identities in environments that enrich them, and we help them find those environments. Therapy itself becomes one of those environments, as do the family and the community. Although identity exploration is limited in families that do not accept sexual minorities, there are, nevertheless, many ways that youth can get support from those families to explore more complex ways to be in the world. Family therapists are also resources for queer youth and their families when they inform themselves about support in the community and at large.

When family members are on track in the developmental trajectory toward growth, they are open to embracing increased complexity in their own thinking and the thinking of other family members. This leads to exploration of negative views that get in the way of nurturing queer youth. When family members are encouraged to explore these views in a responsive environment, the views lose much of their power. Fears, religious beliefs that contradict the knowledge that they have about their children, and the profound differences between family members that get in the way of nurturing queerness are, once explored, put in their proper place. It is not that these negative aspects disappear, but rather that they no longer organize family members in such a way that family members cannot see the beauty inherent in their queer youth.

213

Nurturing queerness is about valuing queer youth, not in spite of their queerness but because of it. When family members appreciate the gifts that youth have to offer, they contribute to the youth's positive sense of self. Youth who can give to their families, and are acknowledged for this giving, are blessed with self-respect and value. Once family members nurture queerness, they broaden the center of their family life. Extended family dynamics change and often grow into extended refuge for queer youth. Families also learn to fight against homophobia and heterosexism in their own communities. Family members themselves become active participants in the transformation of their communities.

CHAPTER 6

Encouraging Transformation

What we have proposed, in the previous chapters, is a powerful and decisive transformation of our expectations, feelings, and thoughts about sexuality. We believe that all family therapists have a responsibility to grapple with these issues in the same way the families we see struggle with these issues. We are encouraging adults (e.g., parents, therapists, teachers, doctors) to stop assuming everyone is or ought to be heterosexual and to not be satisfied with oversimplifications about gender, sexuality, and relationships. We are recommending that instead of focusing on trying to control the sexuality of our children that we learn to respect this process and its outcome by choosing instead to influence and mentor rather than punish and control. This stance is a courageous one. It takes courage to relinquish the illusion that we do or should have ultimate control over the sexuality of our children. It takes courage to allow ourselves to be changed and moved by queer youth. It takes courage to take off our blinders and see the beauty of all young people, especially those very different from us. And it is this courage that will transform us as parents, as therapists, and as individuals. The families we have had the privilege to know have taught us a great deal about how to do this work, and their experiences, if acknowledged, can transform the field of family therapy.

TRANSFORMING FAMILIES

There are many unknown variables involved in youths' decisions to come out to their families while living at home, to reveal themselves only much later, or to not disclose themselves at all. The individual characteristics of the youth have an impact, as does the community in which the family belongs. We believe that family dynamics also play a role in youths' desire to be known by their families, and as family therapists, we can directly affect those dynamics. Working with queer youth and their families has also taught us that therapists can, unfortunately, provoke alienation as well as dispel it. As therapists we must make sure that we are not agents of alienation.

When children sense that other people in their family want to know them—*really* know them—and also sense that, although there might be initial disappointment and conflict, they will be valued even if they are different, children are more likely to reveal themselves. We have learned, alongside the parents with whom we have had the privilege to work, that youth have knowledge about themselves that we have not taught them and over which we have little control. With this knowledge comes respect, even awe. Compton (1998) described the practice of alterity as joining with clients in the recognition that you can never know another. When we relate to people from a position of alterity, we retain a respectful curiosity. When therapists create refuge, we are modeling for families how to continually create a curious, respectful environment that honors vulnerability and tolerates the intensity that comes from difficult disclosures. We are fortifying families as they give up the illusion of controlling a child's sexuality and we work to replace the search to control with the desire to influence and then sit back in wonder and awe.

Creating refuge from homophobia and heterosexism helps transform all families, and not just families with a sexual minority member. When we attempt to understand, as opposed to categorize, we help create a space for family members to accept one

216

another in all of their complexity. In therapy, we are modeling the possibility of a safe space for family relationships. Having dealt with something as difficult as dialogue about differing perspectives on sexual minority youth, families have set a precedent to be able to negotiate differences while staying connected.

Transforming families means asking questions that we know are taboo and risking that family members will become alienated from each other and from us. Family therapists may shy away from discussing sexual identity in family sessions with youth because we mistakenly merge sexual identity with sexual practice. We cannot say strongly enough that we are neither promoting sexual promiscuity, nor recommending that young people become sexually active.

Nurturing queerness in youth is not an invitation to sexual practice. It is, instead, about recognizing that youth are developing sexual beings who need validation, support, and protection with this volatile and powerful part of their lives. All youth, queer and heterosexual alike, need adults to do a better job of supporting and mentoring sexual development. They need more honest discussion and role modeling from adults about how to handle love, intimacy, sex, and relationships. But queer youth especially lack this mentoring. There are many cultural rules designed to protect homosexual youth as they explore their newfound adult bodies and navigate the often treacherous waters of sexuality. For example, parents discourage sleepovers with members of the opposite sex, school personnel chaperone proms, and, on school trips, opposite gender people are not allowed to room together. These are ways to let youth know we care, we are watching, and we are trying to be helpful.

Many parents talk to their children, albeit awkwardly, about the trials and tribulations of sex and sexuality. We prepare young people for heterosexual sex, but they are often unprepared to handle what happens when a same sex person makes a pass or is attracted to them. We further prepare our girls for unwanted advances from boys and prepare our boys to be respectful of girls. Yet these protections are obviously not designed with queer youth in mind, and are therefore often irrelevant and even unhelpful to our queer youth. Moreover, proms, school dances, and dating are social scenarios designed to affirm the psychosexual development of heterosexual youths, thus leaving queer youth to fend for themselves. We are neither affirming nor protecting queer youth and they must teach themselves about how to socialize, date, and explore who and what attracts them, and how to protect themselves.

We have learned from queer youth that we need to broach these difficult subjects. Open discussion, even if only about honest disagreement, is better than silence and dishonesty. The concept of difficult dialogues came as much from our theoretical perspective as it did from working through intense family therapy sessions and experiencing the results. When people who care about each other vehemently disagree and openly dialogue about that disagreement, tempers flare, feelings are hurt, *and* good things happen. The fear that people are going to disapprove, cut off, disengage, or punish is with us in the room. When you have helped to create refuge so that people are comfortable enough to disclose parts of themselves they know are unappealing to others, there is always anxiety about how these parts will be tolerated. With enough practice, however, families begin to recognize that there is great wisdom in the process, that people's first response is not always their only response, and that, with time, people change. We must constantly remind ourselves that people long to be in relationship with each other, despite outward appearances to the contrary.

In some families, queer youth challenge fundamental family values and beliefs. Some youth are part of families who continue to believe that the youth has a choice about how to identify sexually. Family members believe that homosexual behavior is amoral and sinful, and that if youth wanted it badly enough, they could change their attractions. The process of instigating difficult dialogues has taught us that family members can hold fundamentally

218

different views and still respect each other. Self-knowledge shared in intimate relationships, regardless of how it is perceived, is validating in and of itself. Many have said, after a difficult dialogue, "At least now I know where everyone stands, I don't have to keep guessing, and I don't have to keep pretending." We recommend, then, that therapists risk starting difficult dialogues, with the knowledge that people may say things that are hurtful to one another. The risk is usually worth the prize.

Honest and open dialogue about disagreements builds trust in a relationship. Youth want desperately to be loved, valued, and accepted for who they are, and, on some level, they will yearn for this their whole lives. Yet they are able to go about their business without it. When they disclose their identities and learn that family members do not accept them, youth may be mournful but they nevertheless come to recognize the limitations of the family member. They also begin to figure out which people will not abandon them even when they disagree with them, and those relationships become more trustworthy. Difficult dialogues make it easier for youth to mature. Some relationships, youth discover, are not trustworthy; they mourn these relationships and eventually move on. This is also a process of developing maturity, as youth come to recognize that they can live, and be happy, even if disappointed in a meaningful relationship. Finally, transforming families is about helping them be open to receiving the gifts that their unique children bring. These are gifts they never expected, talents they do not share, and interests that seem to come from nowhere. When we are open to our children and we are brave enough to see them, we are transformed.

TRANSFORMING OURSELVES

Nurturing queerness, a stance that permeates our therapy, encourages giving and accepting the gift that sexual minority youth have to offer their families. When a family appreciates and values the youth's difference, it is a gift for all. It is a rewarding experience, as a therapist, to witness the warm expression of pride in a youth's body when family members articulate appreciation for the child's sexual and gender expression. Youth visibly relax, for a moment at least, and some are even able to express their gratitude. These moments, too, are transformative for the therapist. When you have helped create a crucible in which minority sexual identity is valued, and youth are loved and known, you can hold yourself partly responsible for this gift of intimacy.

To be able to create these crucibles, therapists must be prepared to handle what their clients share. If you are comfortable exploring your own gender and sexual identity, you will be better prepared to create these crucibles. Think about how you knew you were heterosexual, gay, lesbian, bisexual, or transgendered. Think about how fluid those terms are and how your life would be different if you could comfortably explore all parts of yourself without shame. Think about all the messages you received and continue to give yourself about gender and sexual scripts. Think about how much more complex and rich your life would be if you could fully embrace your own knowledge of self without compromise. You do not have to act on this knowledge or share it with anyone else. It is yours to do what you wish. Risk this exploration with the recognition that *you* decide what to do with it. The more knowledge you have about self, the better able you will be to manage yourself in the stressful situations that continuously occur when you create a crucible of refuge for others.

Think about the constraining messages you give your loved ones. Identify the thoughts and beliefs you have that are organized by heterosexism and homophobia, and attempt to challenge them. When your partner, for example, does something that you negatively react to because it does not fit your definition of how it is she or he is supposed to behave, question whether your negative reaction has something to do with sexual and gender scripts

that you have unconsciously internalized. When you have a negative reaction to something a child does, ask yourself if you would
have the same reaction if the child were a different gender.
Challenge yourself to think about sexuality and gender in more
complex ways, especially as they pertain to youth and the development of identity.

Also challenge yourself to more openly embrace the atypical.
To nurture queer youth, we must embrace new ways of living
instead of recognizing and validating only those that are "normal"
or typical. Different kinds of relationships and different kinds of
life richly exist but only a few are recognized as such. For example, some argue that queer relationships are less valuable because
queer people do not reproduce. This assumption is based on the
idea that biological parenting is the only valid contribution that
one can make. But there are many individuals who contribute to
humanity in other ways. Why do we honor biological parenting
more highly than we honor the care taking of individuals who are
not biologically related to us? Only because we have not been
thoughtful about alternative ways to be in the world and instead
have relied on honoring what is typical.

We encourage family therapists to explore the gifts that queer
theory has to offer. Part of the gift of queer theory is in learning to
explore what has been dispossessed in all of us. Queer people, who
have learned to embrace what has been dispossessed, have a power
and freedom to explore themselves and their environments that
those who fit in often do not have. Of course, where the dispossessed receives more recognition it begins to lose part of its power.
In some ways by recognizing it, and validating it, we take away
pieces of the freedom and power of queer experiences. It is precisely because it develops in a dispossessed stigmatized place, outside of the mainstream, that the dispossessed allows for creativity
not offered to those living in the mainstream. Nevertheless, we
encourage family therapists to explore the dispossessed in them-

selves and in others, with the knowledge that increased complexity leads to the creation of crucibles of healing.

TRANSFORMING FAMILY THERAPY PRACTICE

The move from accepting divergent expressions of gender and sexual identity to nurturing those expressions has been enlightening for us and has changed the way we practice psychotherapy. All our clients suffer from insidiously organized homophobia and heterosexism. They also suffer from shame and an inability to express those parts of themselves that do not comply with traditional gender scripts. We work now on nurturing access to knowledge of gender and sexual identity in everyone. We have found, in working with couples, for example, that gender and sexual expression is thwarted because people are afraid that if they get to know themselves, life as they know it will crumble out from under them. When we are not afraid, we are able—through creating a safe haven and through our own comfort with difficult dialogues and our inherent belief in the process—to nurture self-knowledge in a way that contributes to individual and relational knowledge.

If family therapy embraced queer theory and all family therapists entered into relationships with their clients that were open to nurturing queerness, we might make a difference in the larger culture. Heterosexism and homophobia constrain all of us. We encourage our readers to explore the ways in which they continue to be constrained and then make a conscious decision to challenge themselves. This encouragement goes beyond challenging homophobic and heterosexist remarks. We ask that you explore gender and sexual scripts when relevant in therapy, and help clients move beyond simplistic notions of how they are supposed to be. So, for example, when asking adults about themselves, ask about how they express their masculine (if they are women) and feminine (if they are men) selves, or throw in the question "So, when did you decide to be heterosexual?" Or, when asking an adult about a child, ask, "So, when did you know your child was heterosexual?" If nothing else, it keeps clients on their toes!

Heterosexism and homophobia are being fought in the courts, in the media, in parking lots, in churches, and in universities, in ways that often alienate people from one another. Legal decisions or decrees about social policy often leave some people feeling disrespected. As family therapists, we believe we have a special responsibility to wrestle with these issues in ways that honor relationships. We must learn to build spaces for honest disagreement that can still connect human beings. Of course our beliefs come through in therapy sessions and at times we have to take hard stands. But this does not mean, for example, that I (RGH) cannot open myself, push myself to understand the position of a parent who earnestly believes that homosexuality is a sin. I can sit with this parent in his dilemma: He is stuck between a rock and a hard place, an unenviable choice between his faith and his child. And even if I completely disagree I can understand his hurt and fear. I can respect his belief as imperative and vital to his life while I help him decide what his options are. As family therapists we must be brave enough to witness the dilemmas of those very different from us. We must also risk being affected by their struggle. How can we ask this of the families we work with unless we are willing to undergo it ourselves? It is our belief that these interactions change all of us involved. We are pushed to newer levels of understanding and parents feel seen and heard by someone very different from themselves. The families we have worked with have certainly demanded and deserved this of us, and it has transformed us as therapists and human beings.

TRANSFORMING OUR COMMUNITIES

We encourage you to have conversations with your professional colleagues about sexual orientation, especially colleagues with whom you think you might disagree. If you cannot have these difficult dialogues, it will be challenging for you to facilitate them between family members in your therapy office. Remember that the purpose of these conversations is for you to articulate and further understand your beliefs, and to create a forum for you to understand another's beliefs. The goal is not to change someone else but to seek to understand. After one such difficult conversation I (LSF) had with a colleague, we both came to the profound conclusion that my vision of what heaven would be like is his idea of how hell would feel. We lovingly disagree.

We also encourage therapists working toward nurturing queer youth to develop a community of helping professionals who share their vision. Educate yourself. Discover other therapists in your community who are doing this work. Seek out queer-friendly physicians to whom you can refer your clients. Discover support groups in the community for queer kids, and if there aren't any, start one. Surf the Web. If you are lucky enough to be working with a queer youth who is out, ask your client about Web-based services. Queer youth know what's out there and can point you in the right direction. PFLAG has a Web site with great information. Started in 1982, the organization is devoted to educating and supporting everyone involved in the life of a sexual minority individual. It is an excellent resource and has local chapters all over the United States (see Educational Resources).

Educate your community as well. In small ways, you can transform your community. Speak up. Tell them you have queer kids in your practice and ask them if they are doing anything to educate themselves about this growing population. Encourage your local school district to educate themselves about sexual minority youth. Offer your services to educate teachers and staff about the need for accurate information in the environment in which our youth spend most of their time. Educate your physicians. If you have children, educate their pediatrician. Educate the coaches, youth leaders, camp counselors, and everyone else who has direct contact with youth. A gentle reminder that all kids are not straight does wonders for the encouragement of transformation.

If you are heterosexual, do not expect queer people to do this for you. Although many queer people educate others about homophobia, heterosexism, and the benefits of nurturing queerness, there are plenty who are unable or unwilling to do it. Education of others is not solely the responsibility of queer people—it is a responsibility we all share. We cannot make the assumption that queer people are any more courageous than straight people; as a matter of fact, they may be less courageous if they are afraid of the repercussions of exposure. Additionally, straight people, unfortunately, may be more likely to learn from other straight people about the benefits of transforming community, because they may not trust that a queer person has their best interest at heart.

Educate your family. Talk about queer youth at the dinner table. Tell them that you read this book or, better yet, leave it around the house for everyone to see. Educate your friends and your neighbors. You may learn a great deal about family and friends that they have not shared before. Clients often report that once they tell someone about a queer family member, they are surprised to learn that the other person also has a queer relative or friend and has never shared this with them. One youth, still in the closet, challenged a friend about a homophobic remark. The friend said that he had never met a homosexual and that until he did, he would keep making those remarks. A few years later, when the youth was out, she reminded the friend about their conversation and how hurtful it had been. If we were having regular conversations about these issues, some of the hurtful comments could be avoided.

Become an advocate of queer youth, not just an ally. An ally is someone who supports queer youth but only when called upon to do the task. An advocate is someone who supports queer youth even when not called to the task. Unfortunately, it is much more

225

difficult to be an advocate because you must pay the price of people's extreme discomfort when you assert viewpoints that are rarely discussed. Sexual identity is a difficult topic and is made more difficult when it involves youth. Yet youth, a vulnerable population, host the topic more often than adults. The vulnerable are the first to get attacked. When we advocate for nurturing queer youth—in family therapy practice, at our dinner table, at school meetings, at churches, or any other time—we are a refuge in unimaginable ways.

The beginning years of the twenty-first century have witnessed increased media attention about gay marriage, and people have spoken out for and against civil rights for gay and lesbian individuals and couples. The debate about homosexuality in this country continues to heat up and threatens to become increasingly bitter and divisive. As family therapists we belong right in the middle of these debates transforming them from good versus evil, to the complex relational issues they truly are. Whether the debate is about gay clergy, same-sex marriage, or second parent adoption, the question is consistent: How will we as a culture acknowledge the lives and contribution of queer people?

Queer lives have been routinely ignored, ridiculed, and rejected outright. This happens in overt acts such as the proposed Constitutional amendment to ban same-sex marriage and it happens in less obtrusive ways as well. I (RGH) am reminded of a newspaper article about a local women's hockey team. Friends of mine had lovingly started and run this team for a number of years devoting many hours at night and weekends, for months at a time, to practice, fundraise, and travel to and from games. The majority of these women, save two, were openly queer. When the article came out it focused entirely on two heterosexual women (who were not even founding members of the team) noting in great detail the one woman's boyfriend watching in the stands and interviewing the other woman's husband and children. It said nothing, nothing, about the majority of same-sex partners and the lesbian community who routinely trekked across counties and even across states for tournaments. This team and these games were full of lesbians, but we had all been erased in this article as if we were never there.

What is the effect on people, couples, families, and society when the contributions of a group of human beings are consistently erased? The research clearly demonstrates serious ramifications for the health and well-being of queer youth and their families. Feelings of shame, guilt, and inferiority are routine for queer youth. The idea that their queerness makes them somehow valuable and gifted is mostly a foreign concept. Yet this is exactly what queer theory proposes: Queerness offers freedom, and complexity, and new ways of existing which, although once disowned, enhance life. This complicated sounding idea can be most simply understood be watching "Queer Eye for the Straight Guy." The premise of the show is that heterosexual men have learned to disown their attention to clothing, grooming, cooking, culture, and interior design. Perhaps they are hardwired for that, perhaps they were afraid to develop these feminine parts of themselves, or perhaps it simply was not expected of them to pay attention to these more feminine concepts. Whatever the case, the "fab five" (five openly gay men) are unafraid and full of concrete, practical advice about how to improve in these areas.

Part of the gift of queer theory is in learning to explore what has been dispossessed: The dispossessed has power. It has freedom and meaning. What we have been arguing in this book is that everyone loses when we disposses parts of ourselves and cease to be whole people. It is precisely because of the divisive nature of the debate that, as marriage and family therapists, we belong front and center, promoting healing and relationship building. We hope you will join us.

EDUCATIONAL RESOURCES

BOOKS

Istar-Lev, A. (2004). *Transgender emergence: Therapeutic guidelines for working with gender-variant people and their families.* Binghamton, NY: Haworth Press.

This book is an extensive overview of the history, theory, politics, clinical, practice, and research regarding transgender people. It includes discussions about language and practical advice for therapists, as well as a separate chapter on transgender youth.

Owens, R. E. (1998). *Queer kids: The challenges and promise for lesbian, gay, and bisexual youth.* New York: Haworth.

In a comfortable style, using kids' own voices, Owens describes what it is like to be a sexual minority adolescent. This is a great book for everyone—adolescent, family member, or therapist—and provides resources at the end of the book for all involved.

Ritter, K. Y., & Terndrup, A. I. (2002). *Handbook of affirmative psychotherapy with lesbians and gay men.* New York: Guilford Press.

This is a comprehensive text that addresses sociopolitical contexts, psychological theory, and clinical practice about sexual minority individuals. It provides a thorough review of the literature on the history, terminology, and research about this population.

Savin-Williams, R. C. (2001). *Mom, dad, I'm gay: How families negotiate coming out.* Washington, D. C.: American Psychological Association.

Relying on extensive data gained by interviewing sexual minority youth about the process of coming out, Savin-Williams provides helpful hints to families in the midst of this transition. Recognizing the different developmental trajectories for girls and boys and fathers and mothers, Savin-Williams details the differing relationships between dyads and also includes a chapter on negotiating healthy relationships among family members.

WEBSITES AND ORGANIZATIONS

PFLAG (Parents, Families, and Friends of Lesbians, Gays, Bisexual and Transgender). www.pflag.org, 1726 M Street NW, Suite 400, Washington, DC 20036

PFLAG is an organization, started in 1982, devoted to educating and supporting everyone involved in the life of a sexual minority individual. It is an excellent resource and has local chapters all over the United States.

Oasis Magazine. www.oasismag.com

This is a website devoted to the voices of sexual minority teens. There are members, forums, diaries, journals, and poetry sections. This is a great way for sexual minority adolescents to feel a sense of community.

MOVIES

A Question of Equality

This is a five-part video documentary series chronicling the gay and lesbian rights movement. It has an important message about today's queer youth, and discusses civil liberties and equal rights.

Boys Don't Cry

This is a disturbing but educational movie about a transgender female-to-male youth and the violent treatment she/he received in the hands of homophobic individuals. When addressing sexual minority issues, we often forget transgender individuals and their particular plight.

In and Out

A tongue-in-check movie in which a teacher is outed as gay before he has come into himself about his sexual identity. While the movie focuses on an adult, the principle character of the teacher goes through a process similar to what queer youth go through—i.e., they often feel as if the whole world is watching their own internal struggle with minority sexual identity.

My Life in Pink

This is a French movie with subtitles that follows a young boy who wants to be a girl. It is an excellent exploration, not only of the youth's struggles, but also of his family's and community's struggles.

REFERENCES

Armesto, J. C. (2001). Attributions and emotional reactions to the identity disclosure ("coming out") of a homosexual child. *Family Process, 40,* 145–161.

Beaty, L. A. (1999). Identity development of homosexual youth and parental and familial influences on the coming out process. *Adolescence, 34,* 597–601.

Beeler, J. & DiProva, V. (1999). Family adjustment following disclosure of homosexuality by a member: Themes discerned in narrative accounts. *Journal of Marital and Family Therapy, 25,* 443–459.

Ben-Ari, A. (1995). The discovery that an offspring is gay: Parents', gay men's and lesbians' perspectives. *Journal of Homosexuality, 30,* 89–112.

Benjamin, H. (2001). *Harry Benjamin standards of care* (6th ed). Minneapolis, MN: Harry Benjamin International Gender Dysphoria Association.

Bepko, C., & Johnson, T. (2000). Gay and lesbian couples in therapy: Perspectives for the contemporary family therapist. *Journal of Marital and Family Therapy, 26,* 409–419.

Bloom, S. (1997). *Creating sanctuary: Toward the evolution of sane societies.* New York: Routledge.

Bornstein, K. (1994). *Gender outlaw: On men, women and the rest of us.* New York: Routledge.

Boszormenyi-Nagy, I., & Spark, G. (1973). *Invisible loyalties: Reciprocity in intergenerational family therapy.* New York: Harper & Row.

Boxer, A. M., Cook, J. A., & Herdt, G. (1991). Double jeopardy: Identity transitions and parent-child relations. In K. Pillemer & K. McCartney (Eds.), *Parent-child relations throughout life* (pp. 59–92). Hillsdale, NJ: Erlbaum.

Breunlin, D. C. (1988). Oscillation theory and family development. In C. J. Falicov (Ed.), *Family transitions: Continuity and change over the life cycle* (pp. 133–154). New York: Guilford Press.

Butler, J. (1990). *Gender trouble: Feminism and the subversion of identity*. New York: Routledge.

Butler, J. (1993). *Bodies that matter: On the discursive limits of "sex."* New York: Routledge.

Carlson, H. M., & Steurer, J. (1985). Age, sex role categorization and psychological health in American homosexual and heterosexual men and women. *Journal of Social Psychology, 125,* 203–211.

Cass, V. C. (1979). Homosexual identity formation: A theoretical model. *Journal of Homosexuality, 4,* 219–235.

Clark, W. M., & Serovich, J. M. (1997). Twenty years and still in the dark? Content analysis of articles pertaining to gay, lesbian, and bisexual issues in marriage and family therapy journals. *Journal of Marital and Family Therapy, 23,* 239–253.

Coleman, E. (1982). Developmental stages of the coming out process. *Journal of Homosexuality, 7,* 31–43.

Collins, L., & Zimmerman, N. (1983). Homosexual and bisexual issues. In J. Woody & R. Woody (Eds.), *Sexual issues in family therapy* (pp. 82–100). Rockville, MD: Aspen Systems Corp.

Compton, S. (1998). *Contextual therapy and relational ethics: A dynamic ethical perspective*. Unpublished dissertation. Syracuse University, Syracuse, NY.

Dank, B. M. (1971). Coming out in the gay world. *Psychiatry, 34,* 180–197.

D'Augelli, A. R. (1995). Victimization of lesbian, gay, and bisexual youth in community settings. *Journal of Community Psychology, 23,* 34–56.

D'Augelli, A., & Hershberger, S. (1993). Lesbian, gay and bisexual youth in community settings: Personal challenges and mental health problems. *American Journal of Community Psychology, 21*, 421–448.

D'Augelli, A., Hershberger, S., & Pilkington, N. (1989). Lesbian, gay, and bisexual youth and their families: Disclosure of sexual orientation and its consequences. *American Journal of Orthopsychiatry, 68*, 361–371.

Deisher, R. W. (1991). Risk factors for attempted suicide in gay and bisexual youth. *Pediatrics, 87*, 869–875.

Devine, J. L. (1984). A systemic inspection of affectional preference orientation and the family of origin. *Journal of Social Work and Human Sexuality, 2*, 9–17.

Diamond, L. M. (1998). The development of sexual orientation among adolescent and young adult women. *Developmental Psychology, 34*, 1085–1095.

Doherty, W. J., & Simmons, D. S. (1996). Clinical practice patterns of marriage and family therapists: A national survey of therapists and their clients. *Journal of Marital and Family Therapy, 22*, 9–25.

Dube, E. M. (2000). The role of sexual behavior in the identification process of gay and bisexual males. *Journal of Sex Research, 37*, 123–132.

Dube, E. M., & Savin-Williams, R.C. (1999). Sexual identity development among ethnic sexual-minority male youths. *Developmental Psychology, 35*, 1389–1399.

Eliason, M. J. (1996). Identity formation for lesbian, bisexual, and gay persons: Beyond a "minoritizing" view. *Journal of Homosexuality 30*, 31–58.

Elizur, Y., & Mintzer, A. (2001). A framework for the formation of gay male identity: Processes associated with adult attachment style and support from family and friends. *Archives of Sexual Behavior 30*, 143–167.

Elizur, Y., & Ziv, M. (2001). Family support and acceptance, gay male identity formation, and psychological adjustment: A path model. *Family Process, 40,* 125–144.

Erikson, E. (1963). *Childhood and society.* New York: Norton.

Fausto-Sterling, A. (2000). *Sexing the body: Gender politics and the construction of sexuality.* New York: Basic.

Feinberg, L. (1993). *Stone butch blues.* Ithaca, NY: Firebrand.

Feinberg, L. (1998). *Transliberation: Beyond pink or blue.* New York: Beacon.

Friedman, T. (2004, May 30). Tilting the playing field. *The New York Times,* p. 9.

Green, R. (1987). *The "sissy boy syndrome" and the development of homosexuality.* New Haven, CT: Yale University Press.

Green, R. J. (1996). Why ask, why tell? Teaching and learning about lesbians and gays in family therapy. *Family Process, 35,* 389–400.

Green, R. J. (2000). "Lesbians, gay men, and their parents": A critique of LaSala and the prevailing clinical wisdom. *Family Process, 39,* 257–266.

Green, R. J., & Mitchell, V. (2002). Gay and lesbian couples in therapy: Homophobia, relational ambiguity, and social support. In A. S. Gurman & N. S. Jacobson (Eds.), *Handbook of couple therapy* (3rd ed. pp. 546–568). New York: Guilford Press.

Green, S., & Bobele, M. (1994). Family therapists response to AIDS: An examination of attitudes, knowledge, and contact. *Journal of Marriage and Family Therapy, 20,* 349–367.

Greenan, D. E., & Tunnell, G. (2002). *Couple therapy with gay men.* New York: Guilford Press.

Hammersmith, S. K. (1987). A sociological approach to counseling homosexual clients and their families. *Journal of Homosexuality, 14,* 173–190.

Hammersmith, S. K., & Weinberg, M. S. (1973). Homosexual identity: Commitment, adjustment, and significant others. *Sociometry, 36,* 56–79.

Hardy, K. V., & Laszloffy, T. A. (2002). Enraged to death: A multi-contextual approach to LGBT teen suicide. *In the Family, 7*(4), 8–13.

Harvey, R. G. (2002). Witnessing: The process of hope. *Journal of Systemic Therapies 21*(3), 93–103.

Helminiak, D. A. (1989). Self-esteem, sexual self acceptance and spirituality. *Journal of Sex Education and Therapy, 15,* 200–210.

Henderson, M. G. (1998). Disclosure of sexual orientation: Comments from a parental perspective. *American Journal of Orthopsychiatry, 68,* 372–375.

Herdt, G. (Ed.). (1989). *Homosexuality and adolescence*. New York: Haworth.

Herman, J. L. (1992). *Trauma and recovery*. New York: Basic.

Heron, A. (Ed.). (1994). *Two teenagers in twenty*. Los Angeles: Alyson Publications.

Hetrick, E. S., & Martin, A. D. (1987). Developmental issues and their resolution for gay and lesbian adolescents. *Journal of Homosexuality, 14,* 25–43.

hooks, b. (1994). *Teaching to transgress: Education as the practice of freedom*. New York: Routledge.

Istar-Lev, A. (2004). *Transgender emergence: Therapeutic guidelines for working with gender-variant people and their families*. Binghamton, NY: Haworth.

Jacobs, A. (2004, June 27). For young gays on the street, survival comes before pride; few beds for growing class of homeless. *The New York Times,* pp. 23, 29.

Johnson, B. (1998). Coming out healthy: What helps. *In the Family, 4,* 6–11.

Kegan, R. (1982). *The evolving self: Problems and process in human development*. Cambridge, MA: Harvard University Press.

Klein, F. (1990). The need to view sexual orientation as a multivariable dynamic process: A theoretical perspective. In D. P. McWhirter, S. A. Sanders, & J. M. Reinisch (Eds.),

Homosexuality/hetersexuality: Concepts of sexual orientation (pp. 277–282). New York: Oxford University Press.

Krestan, J. (1988). Lesbian daughters and lesbian mothers: The crisis of disclosure from a family systems perspective. *Journal of Psychotherapy and the Family, 3,* 113–130.

Laird, J. (1993). Lesbian and gay families. In F. Walsh (Ed.), *Normal family processes* (pp. 282–328). New York: Guilford Press.

Laird, J., & Green, R. J. (1996). *Lesbians and gays in couples and families: A handbook for therapists.* San Francisco: Jossey-Bass.

LaSala, M. (2000). Lesbians, gay men and their parents: Family therapy for the coming out crisis. *Family Process, 39,* 67–81.

Long, J., & Serovich, J. M. (2003). Incorporating sexual orientation into MFT training programs: Infusion and inclusion. *Journal of Marital and Family Therapy, 29,* 59–68.

Markowitz, L. (1999). Dangerous practice: Inside the conversion therapy controversy. *In the Family, 5,* 10–13.

Markowitz, L. (2001). Thinking outside the symptom: A conversation with Betty Carter. *In the Family, 7,* 12–19.

Martin, A. D., & Hetrick, E. S. (1988). The stigmatization of the gay and lesbian adolescent. *Journal of Homosexuality, 15,* 163–183.

Mattison, A. M., & McWhirter, D. P. (1995). Lesbians, gay men, and their families: Some therapeutic issues. *The Psychiatric Clinics of North America, 18,* 123–137.

Napier, A., & Whitaker, C. (1978). *The family crucible.* New York: Harper & Row.

Newman, B. S., & Muzzonigro, P. G. (1993). The effects of traditional family values on the coming out process of gay male adolescents. *Adolescence, 28,* 213–226.

Owens, R. (1998). *Queer kids: The challenges and promise for lesbian, gay, and bisexual youth.* New York: Haworth.

Pearlman, S. (1992). Heterosexual mothers/lesbian daughters: Parallels and similarities. *Journal of Feminist Family Therapy*, 4, 1–21.

Radkowsky, M., & Siegel, L. J. (1997). The gay adolescent: Stressors, adaptations, and psychosocial interventions. *Clinical Psychology Review*, 17, 191–216.

Remafedi, G. (1987). Adolescent homosexuality: Psychosocial and medical implications. *Pediatrics*, 79, 331–337.

Remafedi, G., Farrow, J. A., & Deisher, R. W. (1991). Risk factors for attempted suicide in gay and bisexual youth. *Pediatrics*, 87, 869–879.

Ritter, K., & Terndrup, A. (2002). *Handbook of affirmative psychotherapy with lesbians and gay men*. New York: Guilford Press.

Robinson, B. E., Walters, L. H., & Skeen, P. (1989). Response of parents to learning that their child is homosexual and concern over AIDS: A national study. *Journal of Homosexuality*, 18, 59–80.

Roesler, T., & Deisher, R. W. (1972). Youthful male homosexuality: Homosexual experience and the process of developing homosexual identity in males aged 16 to 22 years. *Journal of the American Medical Association*, 219, 1018–1023.

Rosario, M., Rotheram-Borus, M. J., & Reid, H. (1996). Gay-related stress and its correlates among gay and bisexual male adolescents of predominantly black and hispanic background. *Journal of Community Psychology*, 24, 136–159.

Rosenblatt, J. (1994). *The smell of burning ants*. [video cassette]. Harriman, NY: Transit Media.

Rotheram-Borus, M. J., Hunter, J., & Rosario, M. (1994). Suicidal behavior and gay-related stress among gay and bisexual male adolescents. *Journal of Adolescent Research*, 9, 498–508.

Rottnek, M. (Ed.). (1999). *Sissies and tomboys: Gender noncomformity and homosexual childhoods*. New York: New York University Press.

Saltzburg, S. (1996). Family therapy and the disclosure of adolescent homosexuality. *Journal of Family Psychotherapy, 7,* 1–18.

Sanders, G. L., & Kroll, I. T. (2000). Generating stories of resilience: Helping gay and lesbian youth and their families. *Journal of Marital and Family Therapy, 26,* 433–442.

Satir, V. (1988). *The New Peoplemaking.* Palo Alto, CA: Science and Behavior Books.

Satir, V., Banmen, J., Gerver, J., & Gomori, M. (1991). *The Satir Model.* Palo Alto, CA: Science and Behavior Books.

Savin-Williams, R. C. (1989a). Parental influences on the self-esteem of gay and lesbian youths: A reflected appraisals model. *Journal of Homosexuality, 17,* 93–109.

Savin-Williams, R. C. (1989b). Coming out to parents and self-esteem among gay and lesbian youth. *Journal of Homosexuality, 18,* 1–35.

Savin-Williams, R. C. (1990). *Gay and lesbian youth: Expressions of identity.* New York: Hemisphere.

Savin-Williams, R. C. (1994). Verbal and physical abuse as stressors in the lives of lesbian, gay male and bisexual youths: Associations with school problems, running away, substance abuse, prostitution, and suicide. *Journal of Consulting and Clinical Psychology, 62,* 261–169.

Savin-Williams, R. (1998). *". . . And then I became gay."* New York: Routledge.

Savin-Williams, R. C. (2001). *Mom, dad, I'm gay.* Washington, DC: American Psychological Association.

Schnarch, D. (1991). *Constructing the sexual crucible: An integration of sexual and marital therapy.* New York: Norton.

Sedgwick, E. K. (1993). How to bring your kids up gay. In M. Warner (Ed.), *Fear of a queer planet: Queer politics and social theory* (pp. 69–81). Minneapolis: University of Minnesota Press.

Spargo, T. (1999). *Foucault and queer theory.* New York: Totem Books.

Stone Fish, L. (2000). Hierarchical relationship development: Parents and children. *Journal of Marital and Family Therapy*, *26*, 501–510.

Strommen, E. F. (1989). "You're a what?": Family member reactions to the disclosure of homosexuality. *Journal of Homosexuality*, *18*, 37–58.

Swann, S., & Herbert, S. (1999). Ethical issues in the mental health treatment of gender dysphoric adolescents. *Journal of Gay & Lesbian Social Services, 10,* 19–34.

Switzer, D. K., & Switzer, S. S. (1980). *Parents of the homosexual.* Louisville, KY: Westminster/John Knox.

Tremble, B., Schneider, M., & Appathurai, C. (1989*)*. Growing up gay or lesbian in a multicultural context. *Journal of Homosexuality, 15,* 79–91.

Troiden, R. R. (1979). Becoming homosexual: A model of gay identity acquisition. *Psychiatry, 42,* 362–373.

Troiden, R. R. (1989). The formation of homosexual identities. *Journal of Homosexuality, 17,* 43–73.

Turek, C. (1998). Stages parents go through when a child comes out. *In the Family, 4,* 16.

Wachtel, E. (1994). *Treating troubled children and their families.* New York: Guilford Press.

Waldner, L. K., & Magruder, B. (1999). Coming out to parents: Perceptions of family relations, perceived resources, and identity expression as predictors of identity disclosure for gay and lesbian adolescents. *Journal of Homosexuality, 37,* 83–100.

Weingarten, K. (2000). Witnessing, wonder, and hope. *Family Process, 39,* 389–402.

Weingarten, K. (2003). *Common shock: Witnessing violence every day: How we are harmed, how we can heal.* New York: Dutton

Weston, K. (1991). *Families we chose: Lesbians, gays, kinship.* New York: Columbia University Press.

INDEX

therapeutic, provided by parents, 157–58
of tolerance, for trying on labels, 122–23
culpability, risking, by witnessing, 115–16
culture
acknowledging contributions of queer people in, 226
mandates of
about gender, shame from conflict with, 96–98
about sexuality and gender, countering, 94
about sexuality and gender, heterosexual models, 217–18
negative messages about queer people in, 27
ignoring the contributions of queer youth, example, 226–27

deficit model, of queerness, 30
definitions, used by the therapists, 3–5
dehumanization of loss, as an aggravating factor for queer youth, 58
denigration
of children in the family, 110–11
by the therapist, example, 116
depression, of a family member, 9

DeProva, V., research on family after disclosure by sexual minority youth, 67–68
devaluation, as an aggravating factor for queer youth, 58
developmental psychopathology, training for treating children with, 82
developmental tasks
disclosing to family members, 67–68
in shame, 97
transitions, 134
developmental trajectory
differential, 56
for the family, 138–40
derailed, 150–52
reinvolvement in, 163–66
on track, 142–50
for queer youth, 51
the gift of sexual minority status in, 205
on track, as the purpose of therapy for some youth, 171
Diamond, L. M., on stages of development of queer youth, 55–56
dichotomies
defining roles, moving past, 31–32
in gender description, 95
differences
asserting in queer theory, 15
change from discussion of, 217

DATE DUE

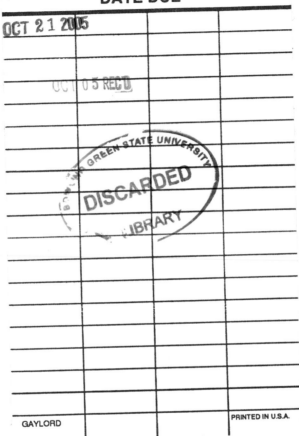